S0-ABU-307

Multicultural Holidays

Share Our Celebrations

Written by Julia Jasmine

Illustrated by Sue Fullam and Theresa M. Wright

Teacher Created Materials, Inc.
6421 Industry Way
Westminster, CA 92683
www.teachercreated.com

©1994 Teacher Created Materials, Inc.
Reprinted, 1999

Made in U.S.A.

ISBN-1-55734-615-1

The classroom teacher may reproduce copies of materials in this book for classroom use only. The reproduction of any part for an entire school or school system is strictly prohibited. No part of this publication may be transmitted, stored, or recorded in any form without written permission from the publisher.

Table Of Contents

Table of Contents *(cont.)*

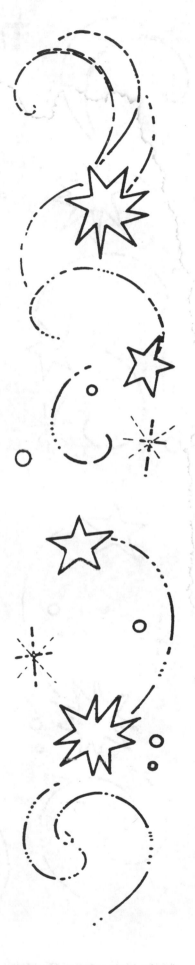

Table of Contents *(cont.)*

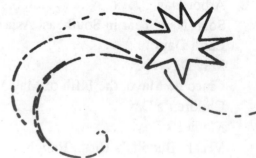

Introduction

In many countries throughout the world, one holiday follows quickly on the heels of another. This is especially true of countries with a rich cultural diversity. Individuals from all over the world bring their holidays, holy days, and celebrations with them. Some of these holidays stay the same and some change because they are being celebrated in a new place, but either way they remain important to the people who celebrate them.

It is fun to know from where the old, established holidays came, and it is interesting to learn about the new ones that are becoming part of the cultural mix. Understanding what people are celebrating and why is helpful to the big job of getting along with people from diverse cultures and backgrounds.

The emphasis on cultural pluralism has always been an important theme of life in multicultural societies. It is symbolized in the United States by the Statue of Liberty raising her torch to the world in New York Harbor. In the United States and other countries throughout the world, people come together to form what has commonly been called a "melting pot." However, the "melting pot" idea has become less and less acceptable as we approach the 21st century. The new way of looking at any cultural mix in a society is as a "salad bowl." (The ingredients still mix but they retain their individual characteristics.) People new to a country want to preserve their cultural and ethnic roots. People who have been there for a long time may want to rediscover theirs. As educators, we need to modify our approach, and the way in which we do this is becoming more important on a daily basis as tensions rise and tempers flare and respect for one another's beliefs and attitudes becomes a legal and political necessity as well as a moral or ethical choice.

So, how—in the face of all of these needs and requirements—do we make this respect for ethnic and cultural diversity happen? Is it possible to make it pleasant? Can we still have fun?

An easy way to approach these issues is to concentrate on holidays, both new and old, familiar and unfamiliar. This has always seemed to be a natural and pleasant method, and with a little more awareness and sensitivity, can be adapted to new and changing conditions. The recognition of cultural diversity through the celebration of holidays is particularly appropriate in school environments since more holidays are observed in school than anywhere else. So, if you teach in a classroom composed of many ethnic groups, celebrate the holidays that will make each child feel welcome and validated. If you teach in a classroom in which all the students belong to the same ethnic group, introduce them to the real, multicultural world through holiday celebrations that are unfamiliar to them. Additionally, give all of the children both the history and the ethnic background that accompanies even the most familiar holidays. You will enrich their lives as well as your own.

Kinds of Holidays

There are basically four different kinds of holidays: religious, political, heroic, and cultural. Holidays can start out in one of these categories and switch to another as times and conditions change.

Holidays that began solely as religious, political, or heroic in one country have sometimes moved elsewhere with the people who celebrate them and have become traditional holidays enjoyed by all. Saint Patrick's Day is one example of this kind of holiday. Cinco de Mayo is another.

Some holidays that citizens of one country are used to celebrating as traditional are becoming more culturally "true" as people place greater importance on recognizing their own ethnic roots, particularly in such places as the United States where virtually everyone has an ancestry outside of the country. The recognition of Halloween as the Eve of All Saint's Day and Mardi Gras as the Carnival before the season of Lent are examples of this.

Many holidays that began as religious holidays and are still celebrated in great part as religious holidays, have also moved over into the traditional classification. Such religious holidays include Easter, Passover, Christmas, and Hanukkah. (Interestingly, the word "holiday" itself started out as "holy day"!)

Political holidays are celebrated throughout the world. In Canada there is Canada Day, in Mexico there is Cinco de Mayo, and in France there is Bastille Day. Also, the birthdays of famous people are often celebrated as heroic holidays. In France, the birthday of Jean Baptiste Colbert is honored and in South America it is Simon Bolivar. These days are set aside for honor and remembrance.

There are many other ways of classifying holidays. For example, Sunday in many countries is a holiday recognized by common law. It is based on the religious idea of the sabbath as a day of rest after six days of work, and commemorates the biblical day that God rested after creation.

Holidays depend on and are influenced by the calendar. (See pages 260-262.) The dates on which many holidays are celebrated are the result of correlating the solar calendar with the lunar calendar. Easter, for example, falls on the first Sunday after the first full moon after the vernal equinox. Passover and other Jewish holidays are celebrated at different times each year in accordance with the Jewish calendar. They, however, stay within the same general season. In contrast to this, the Muslim calendar, which consists of a 354-day lunar year, results in holidays that move right around the year. They have no connection whatsoever to the seasons and the same holidays that occur in summer at one time will eventually occur in the middle of winter. For that reason, Muslim holidays are grouped together in this book in a special section beginning on page 263.

The ways people celebrate personal holidays, such as birthdays and graduations, are as different as the people themselves. And if people can't find enough reasons to celebrate, they will invent some new ones. Personal holidays and ideas for culminating holiday activities are presented beginning on page 279.

Teaching Strategies

Teaching about the positive implications of cultural diversity can be difficult. Differences are often perceived as threatening and changes as stressful. But holidays are already understood, by children and adults alike, as times for fun and celebration. Using a holiday to bridge the gulf between one culture and another helps to bring us together.

Informed Parents Are Helpful Parents

Coping with the differences and changes they see all around them is very difficult for parents. If without warning, they notice that these differences and changes have crept into the schools and are influencing the curriculum that is being taught to their own children, they are likely to react loudly and negatively. It is much better to face this issue head-on with information, with advance notice, with positive appeals for cooperation, and with invitations to share in the fun. A note (or newsletter) in time, saves nine. (See pages 9-10 for suggestions.)

Planning for Exceptions

Have an alternative plan in mind for meeting the needs of those students who are not allowed to celebrate holidays. You could substitute an art and literature experience related to the culture on which the holiday celebration is based. Or you could allow the students who cannot celebrate to present an activity to a class of younger students. If you are ready and prepared with substitute activities and a non-judgmental attitude, the students in question will be happier and the parents will feel that their right to hold different beliefs has been acknowledged. In addition, if you act out of a belief that it is all right to be different, if you are absolutely matter-of-fact about the student who cannot celebrate holidays, the other students will learn that different is okay. This will make it easier to accept the inevitable occurrence of something different, and noticeable, about themselves.

Coping With Religious Holidays

It seems that the only time religious holidays are a problem is when they are not given equal time and equal recognition, especially by the language that is used around them. For example, Christmas vacation was a problem for many non-religious and ethnic groups until schools began to call it "Winter Vacation," showing menorahs along with trees and singing Hanukkah songs as well as Christmas carols at the "Winter Holiday Program." Now that people seem a little more comfortable with the Christian and Jewish holidays, schools and the teachers in them would be well advised to begin recognizing the holidays of other religions and cultures.

Cultural diversity, of course, encompasses religious beliefs. What could be a better time than childhood to learn that the only appropriate response to unfamiliar beliefs is "How interesting!" Children can be helped to know that their beliefs are not being questioned, nor are they questioning the beliefs of others. They are just learning interesting information about other cultures. And information about differences often replaces fear of differences.

Teaching Strategies *(cont.)*

Consult Your Resident Experts

You probably have children representing various ethnic backgrounds in your classroom. If not, you can look for an ethnic representative in your school or community. (If no other option is available, appoint someone to be an expert.) These ethnic representatives are your resident experts. Ask them questions. Expect them to know. Give them the responsibility of finding out. They should not just inform; they should also interpret information for the class. Let their families know that they will be asking questions, not only for the purpose of informing the class but also to increase their own awareness of their culture and heritage. There will be huge self-esteem and peer-respect benefits from this process.

Consult Your Maps and Globes

Most classrooms have one or more rolled-up maps above the chalkboard and a globe over in the corner. Pull down the map, and as long as it doesn't take up too much writing space on the chalk board, leave it down. (If it is really in the way, show the kids how to put it up and down safely and give them permission to use it.) Put the globe in the middle of a table where it will be used, too.

Maps and globes put cultural differences into the context of geography. It is very satisfying to know where you are in the world, and if you came from somewhere else, where that country is. It is also fun to know from where your parents and grandparents came. If your maps and globes are out of date (which tends to happen overnight), use that circumstance as the basis for a history lesson. Happily, students don't know enough about how the world used to look to worry about the changes in names and borders. Just try to keep up-to-date yourself, so you can answer questions. Your resident expert (see above) can also keep current on what is happening in his or her area of expertise.

Have Fun

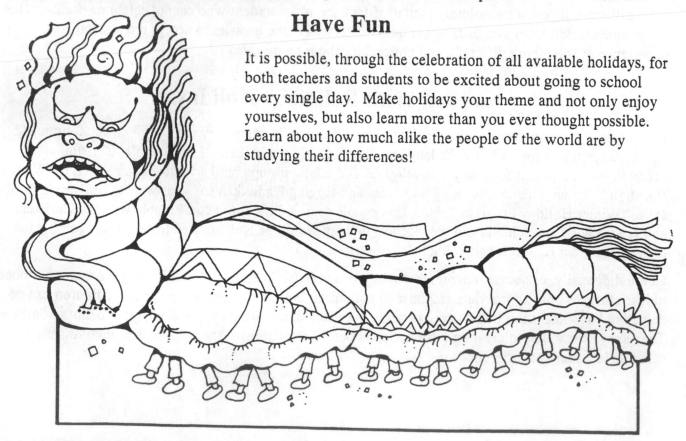

It is possible, through the celebration of all available holidays, for both teachers and students to be excited about going to school every single day. Make holidays your theme and not only enjoy yourselves, but also learn more than you ever thought possible. Learn about how much alike the people of the world are by studying their differences!

Teaching Strategies *(cont.)*

Information Letter

This information letter is adapted from the introduction to this book. Make any changes you want, or run it off as is, and send it home with the students in your class.

Dear Parents,

Throughout the world, we celebrate our way around the year with one holiday following on the heels of another. This is, of course, because people come to some countries from all over the world, bringing their holidays, holy days, and celebrations with them. Some of these holidays stay the same and some change because they are being celebrated in a new place, but either way, they remain important to the people who celebrate them.

It is fun to know from where the old, established holidays came, and it is interesting to learn about the new ones that are becoming part of our cultural mix. Understanding what people are celebrating and why is helpful to the big job of getting along with one another from diverse cultures and backgrounds.

The emphasis on cultural pluralism has always been an important theme of life in multicultural societies. It is symbolized in the United States by the Statue of Liberty raising her torch to the world in New York Harbor. In the United States and many other countries, people come together to form what has commonly been called a "melting pot." However, the "melting pot" idea has become less and less acceptable as we approach the 21st century. The new way of looking at any cultural mix in a society is as a "salad bowl." (The ingredients still mix but they retain their individual characteristics.) People new to a country want to preserve their cultural and ethnic roots. People who have been there for a long time may want to rediscover theirs.

An easy way to approach these issues is to concentrate on holidays, both new and old, familiar and unfamiliar. This has always seemed to be a natural and pleasant method. The recognition of cultural diversity through the celebration of holidays is particularly appropriate in the school environment, since more holidays are observed in school than anywhere else.

We are going to celebrate the holidays that will make each of the students feel welcome and validated. We will introduce them to holiday celebrations that are unfamiliar to them. And we will give them the ethnic background that accompanies even the most familiar of our holidays. We are going to be celebrating a lot of holidays and we plan to ask you for help. We hope you will want to celebrate, too!

Sincerely yours,

Teaching Strategies *(cont.)*

Request and Invitation

Send home requests for donations and help. Also send invitations to attend. Use these forms as they are or adapt them to fit your particular needs.

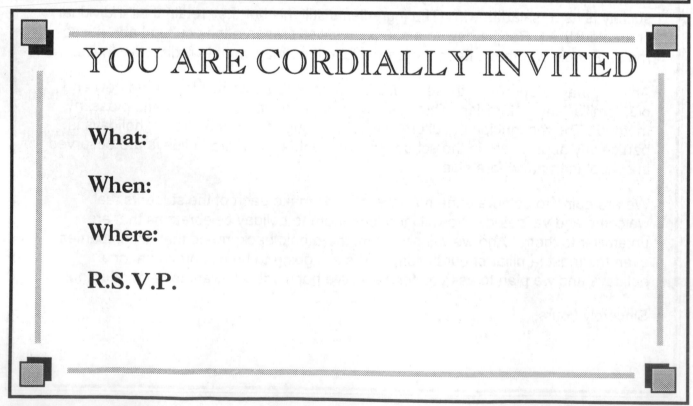

Dear Parents,
The next holiday we plan to celebrate is

_____

We understand it is celebrated in

_____

If you can help with the celebration of this holiday, please let us know.

Thank you,

_____

Happy Holiday!
Happy Holiday!
Happy Holiday!
Happy Holiday!
Happy Holiday!
Happy holiday!

YOU ARE CORDIALLY INVITED

What:

When:

Where:

R.S.V.P.

Making It Work in Your Classroom

All of the holidays in this book can be taught (or celebrated) in a variety of ways. Some of them are more serious than others and lend themselves to research projects, reports, or even puzzles, while others seem to demand parades and parties. Here are some ideas to help make any holiday celebration work in your classroom.

Research Projects And Reports

A research project that is intended to turn into a report—either written or oral—should be of interest to the person or people doing it. If it offers the opportunity to work with a partner or in a group, it may encourage social skills as well as learning. (See Student-to-Student Learning, pages 12-13.) If the assignment is flexible, it allows students to demonstrate initiative and originality while building self-esteem and a sense of accomplishment. (See Contracts, page 14.)

Puzzles

You can make puzzles to reinforce any area of the curriculum. Think of a group of related words that you want your students to know, lay them out on graph paper, fill in with other letters, and you have a wordsearch! Vary this by giving kids the words and having them make wordsearches or by simply giving them the topic and letting them go from there. They love to make really hard wordsearches to stump each other.

Cards

Cards are appropriate for any holiday, whether it is solemn or just plain silly. A card is just as nice to give and receive for April Fool's Day as it is for the Vietnamese Autumn Moon Festival. And cards can be the result of using any art medium. Students love to write their own messages on cards. Poetry and prose are both acceptable, as is a simple "Congratulations" or "Love and Best Wishes." The activities for any holiday in this book can be augmented easily by adding the creation of a greeting card.

Parades

A parade is more appropriate for some holidays than for others. A parade would certainly fit in with the celebration of Mardi Gras, Las Posadas, and Saint Patrick's Day. This kind of parade could be for the purpose of showing costumes and art work to other classrooms. A parade that might be called a "march" could be put on to show the meaning of Labor Day or International Women's Day. A whole-school parade might be appropriate for Halloween. If everyone wears a costume, it is fun to serpentine around the playground, ending up in a huge circle. The teachers can stand in the middle and judge the costumes. Or let the kids who didn't wear costumes be judges. Free homework passes are wonderful prizes!

Parties

Parties are marvelous culminating activities for thematic units based on holidays. They are both enjoyable and natural for a holiday theme. You can give any kind of party you want: one that the students plan and bring from home, one that parents give, one that you give to honor the parents, or one that reinforces a learning experience. Remember that a cookie or two and a cup of punch can turn a completely ordinary afternoon of report presentations into a party that the rest of the school will envy. It doesn't have to be fancy to be a party.

Student-to-Student Learning

There are several kinds of student-to-student learning. Peer tutoring and cross-age tutoring can be thought of as helping modes. Partner learning and group learning are cooperative modes.

Peer Tutoring and Cross-Age Tutoring

In both peer tutoring and cross-age tutoring, the teacher directs the learning process, setting up the lesson content and evaluating the progress. The students are not equals in the process, and when the student being helped has been remediated, the process stops.

Cross-Age Tutoring Another Class

In a different kind of cross-age tutoring, one or more students are asked to present a prepared lesson to another class, usually in a lower grade. These lessons may be the result of an individual contract, or they may be prepared by the class as a group project. (Clear this with flexible teachers in lower grade levels before you start.) Samples of appropriate lessons for students to present are:

1. **Story Time**—Student practices reading a book with expression and then presents a story time in a primary classroom. Many teachers really appreciate this around a holiday.

2. **Music Time**—One or more students teach a song to a group of younger students.

3. **Art Project**—Student gathers together the materials for a simple art project and teaches it to a group of younger students. It helps to practice first on a group of his or her own classmates.

4. **Seat Work**—Student prepares several sets of appropriate holiday seat work for a primary class. There might be a follow-the-dots page, a finish-the-picture page, and a page with a simple story and a few comprehension questions to go with it.

5. **A Holiday Center**—One or more students work to put together a Holiday Center for a primary classroom. It might contain seat work as described above, a simple self-explanatory art project with all necessary materials, an assortment of related books, and ideas for story writing. It should include a poster or stand-up sign identifying the purpose of the center.

Student-to-Student Learning *(cont.)*

Partner Learning and Group Learning

Partner learning and group learning differ from the other types of student-to-student learning because the teacher acts as a facilitator. The students plan their own progress toward a goal and evaluate their own improvement and possible success. Although the students in each group are likely to vary in abilities, they work together as equals. The working-together process is part of the learning.

Every holiday in this book can be adapted to the partner learning and/or group learning.

Partner Learning

For partner learning try this:

1. Students sitting next to each other (or across from each other) become partners.

2. Students take turns reading directions and then talk over every step of the project as they go along, reaching agreement before proceeding.

3. Students discuss their success in terms of cooperation as well as in terms of the finished project.

Group Learning

For a very informal approach to cooperative group learning, especially with students who are experienced with group work, try this:

1. Students divide into their regular groups, or they form new groups through some random method such as numbering off.

2. Students identify and assign tasks for the project.

3. Teacher stays available and circulates to give needed help or make suggestions.

4. Each group presents its finished work to the class as a whole.

5. Students discuss what they would do differently if they were to do the project again.

Contracts

All holidays and seasons of the year can be approached through the use of contracts. Contracts are particularly rewarding because they empower students. The necessity for doing independent research and for making use of time-management skills helps students to feel in control of their own learning process.

Contracts Are Flexible

Contracts between teacher and student can be as formal or as informal as you want them to be. Contracts can cover a long time span. They can cover many areas of the curriculum, offering an opportunity for literature-based experiences in language arts including oral language, an area that is sometimes overlooked in the busy school day.

The same contract can be used with a few modifications for many different grade levels. The products will be different, of course, depending on the maturity of the students, but the prompts can be much the same. (You may want to omit some requirements and simplify the language to make a contract more appropriate for primary students.) You can spend a great deal of time planning and writing a contract, or you can invent one, more or less, on the spur of the moment. Students who are familiar with this kind of assignment enjoy brainstorming for the activities to be included.

Contracts Provide Enrichment

The best contracts are open-ended, providing for a basic set of requirements but allowing a great deal of choice and scope for the student who discovers an area of new or extended interest. You may wish to invent a grading system for your contracts so that students who do excellent work within the basic limits of the contract will still receive excellent grades even though some students go far beyond the requirements. Grading on a curve, even if this is an inadvertent response to one student's superior product, may create the kind of peer pressure that inhibits excellence! Some kind of extra credit may solve this problem for you and for the students while still encouraging the high achievers to explore and experiment.

Sample Contracts

Sample contracts are provided at the beginning of each major section of this book: fall, winter, spring, and summer. They may be modified for use at different grade levels, to outline different goals, and to cover different holidays. All the sample contracts allow for great cultural diversity, creating an opportunity for you to encourage your students to share their own experiences and traditions in comfortable and meaningful ways.

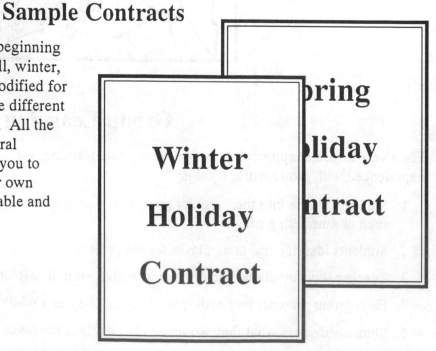

Winter Holiday Contract

Fall Holidays

September

Birthstone: Sapphire

Flower: Aster

September was originally the seventh month of the Roman calendar. The name comes from *septem*, which is the Latin word for the number seven.

October

Birthstone: Opal

Flower: Marigold

October was the eighth month of the Roman calendar. The name comes from *octo* which is the Latin word for the number eight.

November

Birthstone: Topaz

Flower: Chrysanthemum

November was the ninth month of the Roman calendar. The name comes from *novum* which is the Latin word for the number nine.

The word "fall" was first used in America by the early settlers. They got the name from Native Americans who described the season as the time when the leaves fall.

Fall (or autumn) arrives officially in the northern hemisphere on or around September 22. That is the time when the hours of daylight and darkness are equal. Known as equinoxes, they occur once each spring and fall when the sun is directly over the equator. The days will then get shorter and shorter until the winter solstice. (When fall arrives in the northern hemisphere, by the way, spring begins in the southern hemisphere and vice versa).

September, October, and November are usually considered the fall months, even though fall does not really start until the fall equinox around September 22. The early weeks of September are sometimes called Indian Summer.

This book about holidays around the year begins with fall because that is the start of the traditional school year. However, you will find, as you read about the holidays in this book, that many cultures actually celebrate the start of the New Year in fall. It feels like a new beginning.

Fall is also associated with the harvest and with abundance and prosperity. The Horn of Plenty is often used as the symbol of the fall season.

This is an upper grade contract to be used in connection with the fall holidays. You can run it off and distribute it your students. Use the part of this page below the line as a cover and the two following pages as an instructional packet and sign-up slip to keep track of student presentations.

Fall Holiday Contract

      16   ©1994 *Teacher Created Materials, Inc.*

Fall Holiday Contract *(cont.)*

1. Choose the fall holiday in which you are most interested. If you (or your family) are from another country, please consider sharing your own customs and traditions with the class.

2. Research your fall holiday. You may use all kinds of reference books and encyclopedias. You may also consult primary sources - people with first-hand, personal knowledge. Interview your parents, older relatives, and family friends. Just be sure to write down where you got your information.

3. Your report will be due during the two-week period from _____ to _____. Make an appointment so your presentation can be scheduled. Try not to wait until the last minute.

4. Here is what to do for your report/presentation:

   a. Write an information paper to be turned in. Here are some things to include (though you may think of many more):
      - What is the name of your holiday?
      - What is the theme of your holiday?
      - When is it celebrated?
      - Where is it celebrated? In public? At home?
      - Is it celebrated differently in different countries?
      - Have the customs of your holiday become well-known or are they practiced only by a special group of people?
      - Does your holiday have a religious significance?
      - What are the symbols of your holiday?
      - Are there costumes? Parades? Dances? Special foods?
      - Is your holiday for everyone? Just for children? Just for adults?

   b. Include a bibliography. Don't forget to list any primary sources.

   c. Do at least _____ of the following:
      - Plan, draw, and paint a mural representing the symbols of your holiday. Use a long sheet of butcher paper that can be displayed on the classroom wall. Your teacher may want you to do this activity in a cooperative group. If many students choose this activity, you might want to get permission to display the murals in your school's cafeteria or auditorium.

Fall Holiday Contract *(cont.)*

- Cut out articles and pictures about your holiday from newspapers and magazines. Mount them on stiff poster board to make a display center to be used by your classmates. Attach supports to the back of your poster boards so they will stand up. Finish off the center with some books and one or more kinds of activity sheets, such as wordsearches or crossword puzzles. Remember to make answer keys.

- Prepare an art activity and get permission to teach it to a primary class. Have all of your materials and supplies ready ahead of time. Keep a sample for your own presentation.

- Write and illustrate a simple picture storybook. Share it with a kindergarten or first grade class.

- Make simple puppets from paper bags or socks. Use them to tell the story of your holiday.

- Write a song for your holiday. Teach it to the class.

- Make a wordsearch using the names of the fruits and vegetables that are associated with fall. Have enough copies for everyone and don't forget an answer key for the teacher.

- Create your own activity. Check with the teacher before preparing it.

d. Be prepared to make an oral presentation to describe and display the activities you have completed for your holiday contract. Plan to read your information paper aloud to the class.

e. Optional: Bring the class a food treat representing your holiday. Distribute it at the end of your presentation.

If you schedule your presentation early enough, you may invite your parents to come and be part of the audience. (If you wait until the last minute, we will not be able to guarantee a definite time.)

Fill out the form below, clip it off, and return it to the teacher.

Name _____

The holiday I have chosen is _____ .

I would like to schedule my presentation on _____ .

This is a primary grade contract to be used in connection with the fall holidays. You can run it off and distribute it your students. Use the part of this page below the line as a cover and the two following pages as an instructional packet and sign-up slip to keep track of student presentations.

Fall Holiday Contract

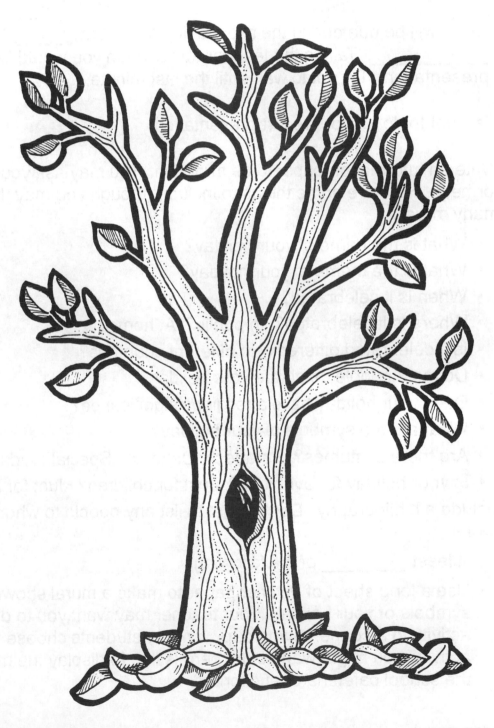

Fall Holiday Contract *(cont.)*

1. Choose the fall holiday in which you are most interested.

2. Find out about your fall holiday. You may use all kinds of reference books and encyclopedias. You may also ask people who have first-hand, personal knowledge. Talk to your parents, older relatives, and family friends. Just be sure to write down where you got your information.

3. Your report will be due during the two-week period from _____ to _____. Talk to the teacher about when you would like to make your presentation. Try not to wait until the last minute.

4. Here is what to do for your report/presentation:

   a. Write an information paper to be turned in. You may ask your parents for help. Here are some things to include (though you may think of many more):

   - What is the name of your holiday?
   - What is the theme of your holiday?
   - When is it celebrated?
   - Where is it celebrated? In public? At home?
   - Is it celebrated differently in different countries?
   - Do most people celebrate your holiday?
   - Does your holiday have a religious significance?
   - What are the symbols of your holiday?
   - Are there costumes? Parades? Dances? Special foods?
   - Is your holiday for everyone? Just for children? Just for adults?

   b. Include a bibliography. Don't forget to list any people to whom you spoke.

   c. Do at least _____ of the following:

   - Use a long sheet of butcher paper to make a mural showing the symbols of your holiday. Your teacher may want you to do this activity in a cooperative group. If many students choose this activity, you might want to get permission to display the murals in the school cafeteria or auditorium.

20

©*1994 Teacher Created Materials, Inc.*

Fall Holiday Contract *(cont.)*

- Cut out articles and pictures about your holiday from newspapers and magazines. Use them to make a fall holiday bulletin board in your classroom. Ask the teacher to set aside part of the wall space for this activity. Work with other students to make an attractive display.

- Write a story or poem about your holiday.

- Make simple puppets from paper bags or socks. Use them to tell the story of your holiday.

- Make up a song for your holiday. Sing it for the class.

- Write the name of your holiday vertically (up and down) on a piece of paper. Use each letter as part of one or more words that tell about your holiday. Here is an example describing the season "autumn":

  LEAVESFALL
  PUMPKINS
  FOOTBALL
  INDIANSUMMER
  STORMY
  WINDY

Decorate the paper around the edges.

d. Be prepared to make an oral presentation to describe and display the activities you have completed for your holiday contract. Plan to read your information paper aloud to the class.

e. Optional: Bring the class a food treat representing your holiday. Distribute it at the end of your presentation.

If you schedule your presentation early enough, you may invite your parents to come and be part of the audience. (If you wait until the last minute, we will not be able to guarantee a definite time.)

Fill out the form below, clip it off, and return it to the teacher.

- -

Name_____

The holiday I have chosen is _____ .

I would like to schedule my presentation on _____ .

Parent signature _____

Labor Day

The first Monday in September

The three-day Labor Day weekend has come to mean both the beginning of fall and the end of summer. It is the last long weekend before the "traditional" school year begins in the United States. In many places it is very often the last weekend before the shorter, chillier days of fall arrive. Because it often occurs before school starts, the real meaning of the holiday is not usually taught in connection with its celebration. Students in the upper elementary grades learn about the labor movement when they study history or social studies, usually in association with the Industrial Revolution and people's reactions to the harsh working conditions that accompanied it. These conditions were especially bad in the textile mills and in places where clothing was manufactured. They particularly affected women and children. Today, however, Labor Day has become more a day of rest and recreation than a day associated with political action and protest.

Labor Day as a celebration of the worker is actually a result of the labor movement and the growth of labor unions. In many countries of the world, the people who began the labor movement formed a separate political party. This did not happen in the United States where labor unions worked through the established two-party system and pressed for their demands with strikes. In 1882, workers put on the first Labor Day parade as the Knights of Labor marched in New York City. Oregon was the first state to officially recognize Labor Day in 1887, and President Grover Cleveland signed a bill making it a legal holiday in 1894. Labour Day, as Canadians call it, became a national holiday in Canada that same year. Many other countries also celebrate a day to honor workers.

Making It Work

Review the history of the Labor Day holiday as a kick-off for a unit on careers. Use the activity on the following page to prompt review and research or to serve as an introductory activity.

Organize a parade with picket signs and costumes (chef's hats, hard hats, aprons, overalls, uniforms, etc.).

Discuss strikes, their meaning, and their historical bond with unions. Also discuss resolutions of recent strikes. (There are almost always strikes taking place nationally). Have students stage a mock "strike" for some desired benefit: less homework, longer recesses, etc.

Invite parents and other members of the community to come in and explain their jobs to the class.

Take students through the process of becoming a teacher: length of time in college, types of classes, practice-teaching, state tests and requirements, the necessity for on-going education.

Ask students to research the average salaries/wages for different types of work. Have them work in groups to organize and graph this information in a meaningful and interesting way for display in the classroom or to share with other classes.

Name_____

Labor Day Puzzle

Use your social studies book or an encyclopedia to help you fill in the blanks in the statements below. Then find the answers in the wordsearch.

```
Q  W  E  R  T  Y  U  I  O  P  A  S  C  D  F  G  H  J  K  L  N
G  R  O  V  E  R  C  L  E  V  E  L  A  N  D  M  Q  W  E  R  E
R  T  R  Y  U  E  I  O  P  A  S  D  N  F  P  G  H  J  K  L  W
Z  X  E  C  V  V  B  N  M  Q  W  P  A  R  A  D  E  E  R  T  Y
U  I  G  O  P  O  A  S  D  F  G  H  D  F  R  G  H  J  K  L  O
A  S  O  D  F  L  A  B  O  R  G  H  A  J  T  J  K  L  Z  X  R
C  V  N  B  N  U  M  Q  W  E  R  T  Y  U  Y  U  S  Y  U  I  K
Z  X  C  V  B  T  B  N  M  Q  W  E  R  T  Y  U  T  I  O  P  C
A  S  D  K  N  I  G  H  T  S  O  F  L  A  B  O  R  F  G  H  I
J  K  L  Z  X  O  C  V  B  B  N  M  Q  W  E  P  I  C  K  E  T
A  S  D  C  O  N  D  I  T  I  O  N  S  F  G  H  K  J  K  L  Y
Z  X  C  V  B  N  M  Q  W  E  R  T  Y  U  I  O  E  A  S  D  F
Q  W  E  R  T  Y  U  I  O  P  A  S  D  F  G  H  S  D  F  G  H
```

1. _____ made Labor Day a legal holiday in 1894.

2. _____ was the first state to recognize Labor Day.

3. Working conditions were harsh during the Industrial _____.

4. The first Labor Day Parade was put on by the _____.

5. In many countries of the world, labor formed its own _____.

6. Labor unions used _____ to obtain their goals.

7. One of these goals was the improvement of _____ for women.

8. Labor Day is called Labour Day in _____.

9. Both workers and the work they do can be called _____.

10. Labor Day is traditionally celebrated with a _____.

11. People who are on strike carry _____ signs.

12. The first Labor Day Parade was in _____.

Grandparents' Day

2nd Sunday in September

Grandparents' Day is a fairly new holiday. Where did it come from and why? Have you begun to celebrate it in your family?

Honoring older members of the family is customary in many eastern religions and forms a part of most holidays in Japan, Korea, and many other Asian countries. However, it has not been that common elsewhere. Are customs changing?

For a long time in the western world, people tended to live far away from their families because of their commitment to a career or their desire to move around and see the country. This trend seems to be reversing itself lately as young men and women move back in with parents to get a second start, and parents move in with adult children either to give help or to get it.

Also, older people may be getting more respect because there are so many more in that age group than there used to be. Older people are beginning to appear in commercials because advertisers realize that they have money to spend. Their needs and desires are addressed by surveys and polls. They are simply more visible than they once were and certainly very different. Does your grandmother have white hair and sit by the fire and knit? Or does she wear pants and recycle her aluminum cans?

Making It Work

Use various art activities that are appropriate for recognizing Grandparents' Day as sponge activities for the start of the school year.

- Make cards from folded construction paper. Decorate the front. Write a message inside.

- Make coupon books with coupons for free jobs. You can get ideas from pages 210-211, but be sure to make up coupons that your grandparents will enjoy.

Invite older members of the community to come in and help students in your class. They can hear kids read, help to edit stories, and generally act as honorary grandparents.

Have students write essays telling why grandparents are important in the world and to them in particular. Have them copy and mount these essays and give them to their grandparents as gifts. (See page 25.)

Name_____

Why Grandparents Are Important

Read the Writing Situation and the Directions for Writing. Then write your piece on the lines provided.

Writing Situation

A friend of yours has just learned that his/her grandparents are coming from far away to visit for the first time. Your friend has never met them, is not looking forward to it, and wants you to explain why grandparents are so important.

Directions for Writing

Write an essay describing the importance of grandparents, either to the world or to you in particular. Organize your ideas in a way that will convince your friend that they are important. Use the kind of grammar, punctuation, and spelling you would want your grandparents to see!

_____

_____

_____

_____

_____

_____

_____

_____

_____

_____

_____

_____

Scoring Rubric

Use this rubric to score your students on the writing activity, page 25. (You may also use it for the other writing activities included in this book.)

Score 3: High Pass

Student . . .

- responds to prompts.
- demonstrates noticeable evidence of organizational skills (e.g., strong opening and conclusion).
- demonstrates mastery of conventions (grammar, usage, mechanics, spelling).
- expresses interesting ideas; uses lively language.

Score 2: Pass

Student . . .

- responds to prompt.
- demonstrate adequate evidence of organizational skills (e.g., opening and conclusion).
- demonstrates use of conventions that do not inhibit reader's understanding.
- demonstrates understanding of language through use of appropriate vocabulary.

Score 1: Needs Revision

Student . . .

- may not respond to prompt.
- demonstrates little or no ability to organize material.
- does not use conventions correctly; reader's understanding is inhibited.
- uses inappropriate vocabulary.

Score 0: No Response

Mexican Independence Day

September 15 and 16

Independence Day celebrations in Mexico begin just before midnight on September 15th and continue all day on the 16th. This holiday commemorates the day in 1810 when a Catholic priest, Miguel Hidalgo Costilla, proclaimed Mexico's independence in the town of Dolores, Mexico, and began an 11-year war of rebellion against Spain. Mexican Independence Day is a national holiday in Mexico. People gather in the town plazas to hear their mayors give the Grito De Dolores (Cry of Dolores). Bands play, bells ring, fireworks explode, and everyone cries out, "Viva, Mexico!"

People celebrate in the United States, too, usually on the weekends around September 15-16. The festivals often occur in parks and recreation centers and include all kinds of Mexican (and American) foods, music, and carnival rides and games. Although these festivals are more common in the southwestern part of the United States, they can and do occur anywhere in the country.

Some of these festivals are large and elaborate. For example, during the weekend of September 18-20, 1992, a festival called Las Fiestas Patrias took place in Santa Ana, California. It included a parade, a carnival, Mexican and American food, craft booths, and cultural activities. The event was televised by Televisa, the largest television programming network in the world. World-renowned performers participated. It is estimated that between 250,000 and 300,000 people attended this one event. Also in the same city on September 16th, there were four Independence Day parties for elementary and junior high school children with food, music, and carnival rides. In addition, a famous Folklorico group was giving free performances at local libraries.

Making It Work

Watch the newspaper (or assign this duty to some students) for the announcement of local Mexican Independence Day celebrations. The parties given especially for students would make wonderful field trip destinations, particularly if—as in Santa Ana, California—admission is free.

Have students find out what is meant by the Grito de Dolores.

Decorate your classroom, invite some musicians, and have a party. Students can decide on the menu and sign up to bring a particular food or drink (after consulting with someone at home).

Name_____

The Mexican Flag

Research the Mexican flag and draw it below. Also, answer these questions.

1. How many sections does it have? _____

2. What are the colors? _____

3. For what do the colors stand? _____

4. What is the design on the flag? _____

5. When was this flag adopted? _____

Citizenship Day

September 17

Citizenship Day is an American holiday that has changed its name several times. It was originally called "Constitution Day," because the United States Constitution was signed on September 17, 1787. Then its name was changed to "I Am an American Day." Finally, it was renamed "Citizenship Day" because it is a day on which naturalization ceremonies are held. Naturalization ceremonies are the last step in the process by which people from other countries can become "naturalized" citizens of the United States.

People who were not born in the United States can become naturalized citizens by going through a series of steps. The last step is the part that is celebrated on Citizenship Day. It is at that time that people go to court and swear an oath of allegiance. They are then declared citizens of the United States. Pictures in newspapers can often be found of groups of people waving flags and smiling at the end of one of these ceremonies.

There are also other ways to become a citizen of the United States. A person who marries a United States citizen becomes a citizen. A person who becomes the child of a United States citizen becomes a citizen, too. Serving in the U.S. military during wartime, or being a seaman on a U.S. vessel, will also make a person a citizen.

It is important for people who were born in the United States to know how hard it is for others to become citizens. The people who are becoming citizens also sometimes have very mixed feelings. They may have left their own countries because of war or persecution and may know they will never go back, but they are often very sad about this. They miss their birth countries and wish that things could be different.

Making It Work

Ask students to research the requirements for becoming a naturalized citizen of the United States. For your information these requirements are:

- File a petition to become a citizen.

- Live in the U.S. continuously for five years.

- Have a good moral character.

- Speak, read, and write simple English.

- Have knowledge about the history and government of the U.S.

- Pass a test on these subjects.

- Go to court and swear an oath of allegiance.

Survey your students: Are any of them citizens of another country? Have any of their parents or other relatives become naturalized citizens? Did the students attend the ceremony? Are any members of their families studying (or planning to start to study) to become citizens?

Good Citizens

Read the captions of the boxes on pages 30-32. Find or draw an appropriate picture for each box.

A Good Citizen Obeys the Laws

A Good Citizen Votes

Name_____

Good Citizens *(cont.)*

A Good Citizen Protects His/Her Own Rights

A Good Citizen Protects the Rights of Others

Name_____

Good Citizens *(cont.)*

A Good Citizen Respects the Rights of Others

A Good Citizen Is Ready to Help

Native American Powwow

4th Friday in September

There is a campaign in the United States to make the fourth Friday in September Native American Day. A few states have already proclaimed this is an "official day" in response to pressure from various groups. It is listed as a holiday in many sources. However, the Bureau of Indian Affairs, which is part of the Department of the Interior of the United States Government, does not recognize this day. They recognize "American Indian Heritage Day" (or Week or Month) as the President or the Congress may choose to declare in any given year. They do not have information ahead of time about when it will be or whether it will be a day, a week, or a month.

Nevertheless, since people are becoming more aware of this day and since the Powwows held by Native Americans can occur all year round, this is a good time to recognize these ceremonies.

Powwows are like family reunions on a grand scale. They are times when tribes come together, gathering related families from far and near for times of dancing, singing, feasting, and storytelling. People wear traditional costumes. Ancient customs and rituals are passed down from elderly people to young ones. Powwows are times set aside for Native Americans to celebrate their heritage.

Making It Work

Write or call for information about Native Americans:

Bureau of Indian Affairs
Washington, D.C.
(202) 208-3100

Tribal Services
Washington, D.C.
(202) 208-3710

Invite a group of Native American dancers to give a performance for your class (or your school). A division of the Boy Scouts of America—the Order of the Arrow—specializes in authentic Native American dances.

Decorate cylindrical oatmeal boxes with Native American designs, beads, and feathers. Use them for drums or for decorations.

String bells to make wrist and ankle bands. Small bells can be purchased at hobby shops.

The items listed below represent the major divisions of Native American tribes. Directions for making replicas of some of them follow on the next pages. If you are interested in others, you can read about them in encyclopedias and other reference books.

- **Northeastern:** birchbark canoes, moccasins
- **Plains:** tepees, arrowheads
- **Northwestern:** totem poles, longhouses
- **Southwestern:** Kachina dolls, adobe bricks

Moccasins

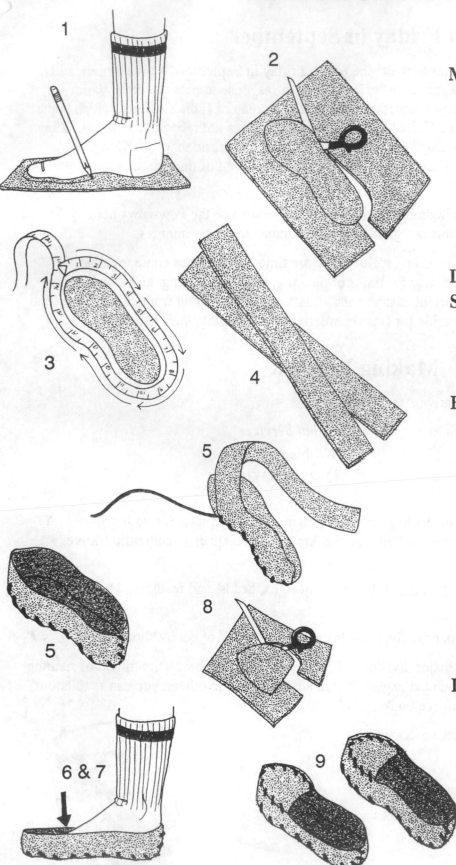

Materials:

- brown felt
- leather thongs *(strips for lacing)*
- scissors
- paper
- fabric chalk or pencil

Directions:

Soles:

- Draw around each foot.
- Cut each from brown felt.

Band:

- Measure outside of sole all the way around.
- Cut 2 strips of felt 2 inches wide and as long as the outside perimeter of the sole.
- Lace band to sole with leather thongs. Either punch small holes or use a very strong needle.

Instep:

- Try on sole and band.
- Use paper to make a pattern of the instep piece.
- Trace pattern on felt.
- Cut 2 and lace to band as shown.

Totem Pole

Materials:
- cardboard tube
- clay
- tempera paints
- paintbrush
- paper (colors optional)
- pencil
- glue
- crayons or markers (optional)

Directions:
- Use a cardboard tube weighted on the bottom with a lump of clay.

- Paint with tempera.

- Represent your family's characteristics with animals.

- Draw or trace the animals you choose and glue them on the tube.

- You can duplicate these animals on the back or make three different animals.

Name_____

About the Tipi

The Tipi (tepee) was not just a simple tent. It was a well-constructed home built to stand up to the harsh weather of the Great Plains. It had to be warm in winter to protect from the cold and snow, and cool in the summer to keep people comfortable in the scorching heat. It had to be easily moved from place to place so its people could follow the buffalo herds.

The name tipi comes from two words: "ti" means to dwell, "pi" means used for. The tipi is constructed of a frame of wood poles arranged in a cone shape. This is covered by buffalo hides. The cone shape is very sturdy and can stand up to the very strong prairie winds. Also, there are no pockets to catch water, so it can withstand severe rainstorms as well.

The number of poles for a tipi vary. The average number is about fifteen. These poles are about 20 feet (6 m) long and weigh 15 to 20 pounds (6.75 kg-9 kg).

Pitching the Tipi Experiment

Experiment 1: Take fifteen straws and tie them together so they stand up in a cone shape. Describe what happens.

_____

_____

Experiment 2: Now take three (or four) straws and tie them together so they stand up in a cone shape. Describe what happens.

_____

_____

Which way was easier? _____ Why do you think it was easier?

_____

_____

Now you can see why a three (or four) pole frame was used by the Plains tribes. Then the other poles were attached. It was not the men of the tribe, but the women, who were in charge of constructing, transporting, and erecting the tipi. The snugness and comfort of the tipi reflected the woman's ability as a housekeeper. A well-made tipi was a source of great pride to a woman.

Tipi Pattern

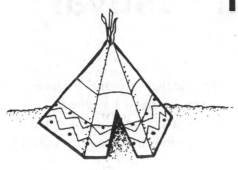

Materials:
- brown construction paper
- crayons or markers
- scissors
- glue
- pencil

Directions:
- Copy pattern on brown construction paper.
- Draw Native American designs and symbols.
- Fold along dotted lines.
- Glue Tab A to Tab B on the inside of tipi.
- Cut a flap for the door. Add sticks from nature for the poles.

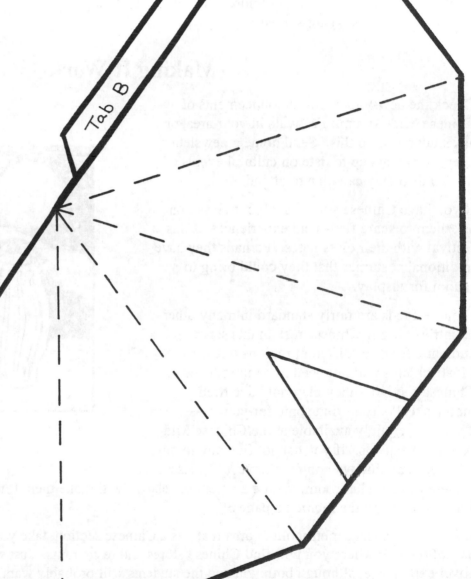

Tab B

Tab A

Chinese Mid-Autumn Festival

September/October

The Chinese Mid-Autumn Festival is a thanksgiving celebration. It is held at the time of the harvest moon on the fifteenth day of the eighth lunar month. This is the time when the crops have been harvested and the farmers can rest from their labors. The two most important symbols of this day are paper lanterns, made in a variety of different shapes, and moon cakes, big round filled cookies baked in the shape of (what else!) the moon.

Chinese people living outside of China adapt this festival to their circumstances. They often use community facilities such as recreation centers to bring large groups of people together for this celebration. Adults as well as children take part in lantern parades, and traditional foods (such as the symbolic mooncakes) are served.

Making It Work

Check the newspapers for announcements of Chinese Mid-Autumn Festivals in your area, or ask students to do this. Send home a newsletter keeping parents up to date on cultural events of this kind so they can plan to attend.

If you have Chinese students in your classroom, ask them to share first-hand experiences of this festival with their classmates. Perhaps they have traditional costumes that they could bring to school for display.

Chinese foods are fairly standard in many other countries. Many Chinese restaurants serve authentic foods of different regions in China. Most students will not need to be introduced to Chinese food, but they may not have tried mooncakes! Try to find some for your class. They are certainly available at the Chinese Mid-Autumn Festivals. If you cannot find any to buy, and if you are lucky enough to have a Chinese student in your classroom, maybe a parent or relative will make them for your class. If not, they can be approximated by the recipe on page 39.

If you are in a large metropolitan area that has a Chinese section, take your students on a field trip to the part of the city where you will find Chinese stores and restaurants. Just window shopping will be a novel experience, although both you and the students will probably want to buy some sweets or keepsakes. When you return to school, have the students write and illustrate their impressions of the places they saw. Bind the results into a book for use in your classroom library.

Make a Thanksgiving bulletin board in your classroom that combines all of the different thanksgiving celebrations. See page 79 for a list of ways to say "thanks" in many different languages.

Mooncakes

This is not a traditional Chinese recipe. It is a simple way to use ordinary ingredients to make a cookie that is enough like a Chinese mooncake to be used as a substitute.

Ingredients:

- 3 ½ cups (850 mL) flour
- 1 teaspoon (5 mL) salt
- 1 cup (250 mL) shortening
- ²/₃ cup (170 mL) sugar
- 2 eggs
- 1 teaspoon (5mL) vanilla extract
- jam for filling

Directions:

Sift the flour and salt together. Set aside. Cream shortening and sugar together until light and fluffy. Add whole eggs, one at a time, beating well after each addition. Add the vanilla. Work in the flour. Roll to a thickness of about ⅛ inch (.3cm) on a floured board. Cut into rounds. (You can use the open end of a glass that has been dipped into flour.)

Lay half of the rounds on ungreased cookie sheets. Top each round with a teaspoonful (5 mL) of jam. Lay the rest of the cookie rounds on top of the jam filling. Seal the edges together with the tines of a fork and prick the tops (see illustration). Bake at 350° F (180° C) for about 10 minutes. Cool on wire racks.

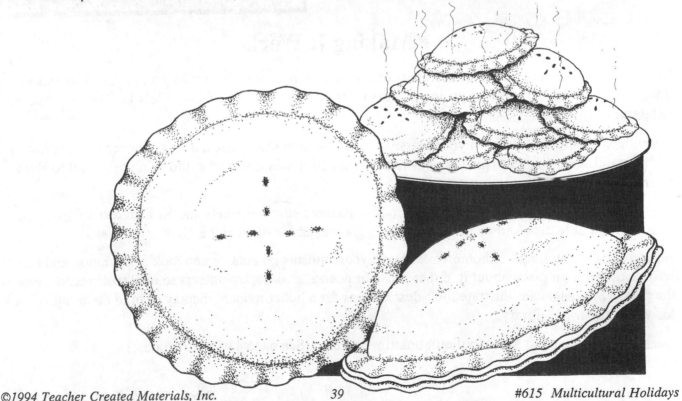

Chu-Sok, the Korean Harvest Moon Festival

September/October

Chu-Sok, or Choo-Suk, is the Korean Harvest Moon Festival. It is celebrated on the fifteenth day of the eighth lunar month when the brightest moon of the year shines. It is the equivalent of the American Thanksgiving and the second most important holiday of the year in Korea. Only the Lunar New Year is more important.

In Korea, people celebrate Chu-Sok with their family and have community feasts, complete with games, dances, new clothes, and visits to the graves of their ancestors. They also take time to really look at and enjoy the moon. They enjoy reading and writing poetry about the moon, which is a favorite topic of Korean poetry.

Outside of Korea, the holiday celebration is adapted to the new country. Groups of Koreans use community center facilities as festival sites. The food, however, is kept as authentic as possible, and so is the dancing. Korean-American dancers make dramatic use of fans, clicking them open and shut as they dance. They wear traditional costumes to perform the age-old folk dances, bringing back memories of their homeland to the audience.

Making It Work

Check the newspapers for announcements of Harvest Moon Festivals in your area, or ask students to do this. Send home a newsletter keeping parents up-to-date on cultural events of this kind so they can plan to attend.

If you have Korean students in your classroom, ask them to share first-hand experiences of this festival with their classmates. Perhaps they have traditional costumes that they could bring to school to show their classmates.

Treat your class to a selection of Korean foods. Explore ethnic markets and Korean restaurants. The pickled vegetable dish known as "kimchi" is a good example of an authentic Korean dish.

Assign "moonwatching" as homework. Have your students go outside and look at the moon and then write a descriptive piece about it, either prose or poetry. Ask for volunteers to read their pieces aloud to the class. Students can illustrate their descriptions for a bulletin board display or bind them into a book for your classroom library.

Decorate your Harvest Moon bulletin board with fans. (See page 41 for directions.)

Making a Fan

In order to make a fan that resembles the fans used by Korean dancers, you will need:

- a large sheet of decorative paper

  You can decorate the paper yourself with colored designs, pictures, or an all-over effect achieved by fingerpainting or applying a wash.

- feathers or paper from which to make "feathers"

  Crepe paper or tissue paper will work for this.

- scissors, glue, glitter, pencil, etc.

If you painted the large sheet of paper, allow it to dry. Then accordion-pleat it into a fan. Hold one end of the pleated paper together and staple firmly.

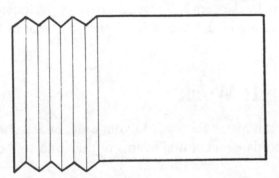 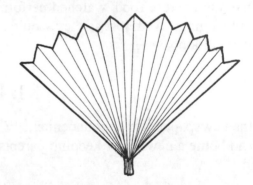

Use either real feathers or feathers cut from crepe or tissue paper to trim the edge of the fan. Decorate finished fan with glitter if you wish.

 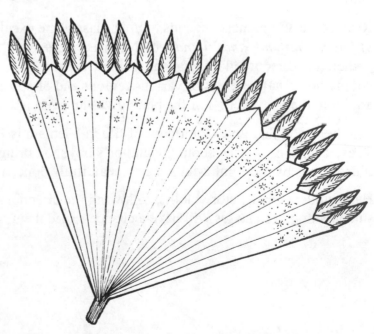

Tet Trung Thu, the Vietnamese Autumn Moon Festival

September/October

Tet Trung Thu, the Autumn Moon Festival, is a favorite with Vietnamese children. In fact, it is sometimes called Children's Day. It comes at the time of the harvest moon on the fifteenth day of the eighth lunar month and is a festival of thanksgiving for the crops that have been harvested.

In Vietnam, Tet Trung Thu is celebrated with feasting and dancing. There are lion dances and dragon dances. Children make paper lanterns and march in lantern parades. They eat mooncakes and listen to the legends of Hang Nga, the moon fairy.

Outside Vietnam, Tet Trung Thu is a time for the Vietnamese people to make their children happy with a day that will be remembered all year long. It is a time to preserve and pass on their culture and their language. It is a time to remember their roots. In 1990, around 15,000 people attended the Tet Trung Thu Festival put on at Golden West College in Huntington Beach, California. There, they ate traditional Vietnamese food, watched performances by dancers and martial arts groups, listened to music and singing. And, just as they would have in Vietnam, the children listened to stories about Hang Nga and ate mooncakes.

Making It Work

Check the newspapers for announcements of Autumn Moon Festivals in your area, or ask students to do this. Send home a newsletter keeping parents up-to-date on cultural events of this kind so they can plan to attend.

If you have Vietnamese students in your classroom, ask them to share first-hand experiences of this festival with their classmates. Perhaps they have traditional costumes that they could bring to school to show.

Read some Vietnamese legends to your class. One excellent book is *Folk Tales of the Hmong: Peoples of Laos, Thailand, and Vietnam* by Norma J. Livo and Dia Cha. The traditional tales in this book were gathered and recorded by Dia Cha from primary sources. There are many beautiful color plates of people in the native dress of various regions and of *pa ndau*, the traditional Hmong "story cloths." In addition, the first section of the book gives an overview of the history and culture of the people.

Another book that gives the flavor of life in Vietnam is *The Land I Lost* by Quang Nhuong Huynh. These charming stories about the author's boyhood bring the country to life for the reader. The illustrations by Vo-Dinh Mai are also beautifully done.

Have students make story cloths, following the directions on page 43. Display the story cloths where students in other classes will have a chance to see them.

Making a Story Cloth

Story cloths made by the Hmong people of Southeast Asia are very much like the craft called applique, a type of needlework done elsewhere in which pieces of material are cut, arranged, and sewn together to make a picture. A unique feature of the Hmong story cloth is the addition of writing to explain and add to the picture.

Looking at pictures of Hmong story cloths will give you some ideas. There are beautiful examples of this art in *Folk Stories of the Hmong: Peoples of Laos, Thailand, and Vietnam* by Norma J. Livo and Dia Cha. You will notice that the colors used are extremely vivid, so try to choose fabrics in bright colors.

Materials:
- drawing paper
- pencils, markers
- scissors
- scraps of fabric
- fabric square
- fabric glue
- needles, thread (optional)
- fabric paint (optional)

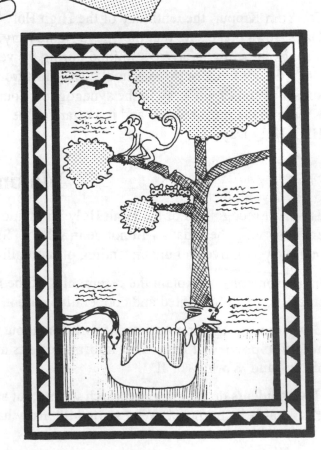

Directions:

1. Draw a picture of an incident from a book you have read or from your own life.

2. Cut out the main shapes from these pictures and use them as patterns to cut matching shapes from material.

3. Glue (or sew) these cut-out fabric shapes to your fabric square to recreate your picture. Add other fabric shapes as needed to complete the picture.

4. Use fabric paint or markers to add words and decorative touches to your story cloth.

Jewish High Holy Days: Rosh Hashana to Yom Kippur

September or October

The first ten days of the Jewish month of Tishri are the High Holy Days of the Jewish religion. The first of these days is called Rosh Hashana. This is the Jewish New Year. The last of the ten days is called Yom Kippur or the Day of Atonement. These are very solemn days in the Jewish religion. During this time Jews are to remember the things they might have done wrong during the past year and think of ways to make up for them. They also consider ways in which they can help to make the world a better place.

On Rosh Hashana people greet each other with the words "May you be inscribed in the Book of Life for a happy year!" A ram's horn (shofar) is blown in the synagogue to call people to prayer. In spite of all the solemnity, there is a festive New Year's family dinner. Many of the special foods have traditional meanings. The fruit is dipped in honey to symbolize a year full of sweetness. The eggbread (challah) is baked in a circle to represent the year's cycle.

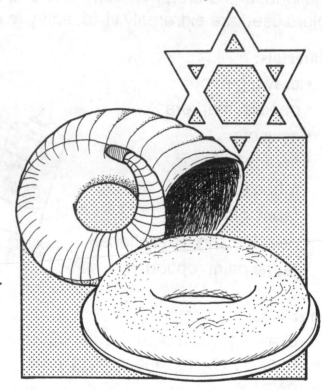

On Yom Kippur, the tenth day of the High Holy Days, Jews make sure that they have righted any wrongs they might have committed during the year. They do not work or go to school. They fast from sunset to sunset and pray in the synagogue. Yom Kippur is the most solemn and important of the High Holy Days.

Making It Work

Try to fit recognition of the High Holy Days into your schedule in advance because any students who are observing these days will not be in school. Students who know what is happening ahead of time are more appreciative and understanding of unfamiliar customs.

Invite someone to explain the ceremonies of the High Holy Days to your class. One of your own students, or an interested and cooperative parent, may be the best choice for this.

Give students age-appropriate information about the Holocaust. You might consider showing a film, but try to preview it first. This information fits in with a social studies curriculum that includes modern history and World War II.

Have students do their own research to find out about the recently opened Holocaust museum. Where is it? What is its purpose? Who started it? How have visitors reacted to it?

Jewish High Holy Days Word Meanings

Write a definition for each of the following words or phrases. Then find them in the wordsearch on the next page.

1. Rosh Hashana _____

2. Sabbath _____

3. Jews _____

4. New Year _____

5. Synagogue _____

6. Torah _____

7. Star of David _____

8. Holocaust _____

9. Book of Life _____

10. Challah _____

11. Shofar _____

12. Yom Kippur _____

13. Scroll _____

14. High Holy Days _____

15. Atonement _____

16. Hebrew _____

17. Fast _____

18. Rabbi _____

Jewish High Holy Days Wordsearch

Find the words on page 45 in the wordsearch below.

```
Q W E R T Y U H I G H H O L Y D A Y S
R O S H H A S H A N A S I O P A S S B
Y J E W S D H F G H T Y J K L Z T X O
O C V S C R O L L B O N E W Y E A R O
M N S M Q W F A S T N A E R T Y R U K
K I A O P A A S D F E G G H J K O L O
I Z B X T O R A H C M O V B N M F Q F
P W B E R T Y U E I E G O P A S D D L
P F A G H J K L B Z N U X C V B A N I
U M T Q W E R T R T T E Y U I O V P F
R C H A L L A H E A S D R A B B I F E
G H J K L Z X C W V B N M Q W E D F G
H O L O C A U S T H J K L Z X C V B N
```

Sukkot, the Jewish Harvest Festival

September or October

Sukkot is the Jewish harvest festival. It begins five days after Yom Kippur and it lasts for nine days. This happy festival has three other names. It is also called the Festival of Ingathering, the Feast of Booths or Tabernacles, and the Season of Our Rejoicing. The nine days include a variety of different customs and traditions. Some of the days have been given special names to recall special times in Jewish history.

Sukkot is called the Feast of Booths or Tabernacles because of the special custom of building a small, temporary hut or booth, the *sukkah*, outdoors. Jewish people who have gardens build their sukkah at home. People who live in the city or in apartments may share one built at a school or synagogue. This custom commemorates the time when the Israelites wandered in the desert with no permanent place to live. The little booths are decorated with autumn leaves, pumpkins, and wheat stalks, and people eat outdoors in them as often as they can during Sukkot. If the weather is nice, people may even sleep outdoors in the sukkah just as the Israelites did.

Making It Work

The reason for calling Sukkot the Feast of Booths or Tabernacles is given above. Ask students to do some research to find out the reasons behind the other two names: the Feast of Ingathering and the Season of Our Rejoicing.

Have students find the special names given to different days during Sukkot, the reasons for the names, and the ceremonies performed on those days.

Ask students who have had experience with the holiday to share with the class.

- Did they have their experiences here or in another country?

- Did they or someone else in the family build a sukkah?

- How was it decorated?

- Did the family eat there?

- What special foods are served during this season?

A very good reference book is *Shake a Palm Branch: The Story and Meaning of Sukkot* by Miriam Chaikin. It contains information on the history of the holiday. Ms. Chaikin has written a whole series of books on Jewish holidays, *The Jewish Holidays Series*, published by Ticknor and Fields.

Leaf Rubbings

Leaf rubbings make beautiful autumn decorations. They have the added advantage of not drying up and crumbling the way real autumn leaves do. Plan to make several because each one will be unique.

To make a leaf rubbing, follow the directions below.

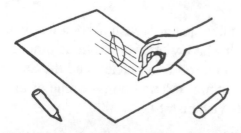

Materials:

- drawing paper: white works the best
- crayons: old ones without wrappers
- a variety of leaves and other plant materials such as weeds and dried grasses

Directions:

1. Lay down a sheet of paper and arrange your leaves and other plant materials on it. Experiment with moving them around until you find an arrangement you like.

2. Carefully place another sheet of paper on top of your leaf arrangement.

3. Hold on to the papers so they don't slip, and, using the side of a crayon, rub it across the top paper until the shapes of the leaves start to show. Continue to rub until you get the effect you want.

4. You can vary the effect by changing crayons to a different color and by moving the arrangement around then repeating the coloring process.

Note: Autumn colors such as brown, orange, yellow, and red make effective rubbings. Mount your finished product on a sheet of construction paper in a color that sets the rubbing off to its best advantage.

Oktoberfest

October

Oktoberfest comes from Germany. In Germany it is a major holiday, continuing for more than a week and consisting of parades as well as huge fairs with carnival rides, shows, bands, and dancing. People drink beer and eat foods such as sausage and sauerkraut.

Outside of Germany, Oktoberfest has moved into the mainstream, especially in places where there are many people with a German background. It is a happy holiday that focuses on eating, drinking, and dancing. People may dress in traditional costumes: *dirndl* dresses for the women and *lederhosen* for the men. Parties are held in restaurants, and there may be festivals in parks and recreational facilities. The traditional dance is the *polka*, a lively dance that people enjoy both watching and performing.

Making It Work

Ask students to find the answers to these questions:

- When was the first Oktoberfest held in Germany?
- What was the reason?
- Which German city holds the biggest and most famous Oktoberfest?

Get someone to come to class and teach the students the polka. Play recordings of polka music.

Read some of Grimm's fairy tales to the class. Have students choose one to perform. ("Snow White" and "Hansel and Gretel" are both popular Grimm's fairy tales.) They can do this in the form of a reader's theater or actually write a script and create their own play, make scenery, and wear costumes. Invite parents to your production or present it for another class.

If you invite parents to see your play, plan to make it a real Oktoberfest by serving traditional refreshments. You could serve frankfurters and sauerkraut, pretzels, and root beer. Have each student make an invitation for his/her own parents or for a member of another class, depending on whom you decide to invite. (See page 50.)

Parent Requests for Oktoberfest

Send home a request for help and donations, or send an invitation to attend (or maybe send both!).

Dear parents,

Would you like to help with our Oktoberfest?

We need

_____

_____

_____

_____

Please let us know if you will be able to help. The party will take place on

_____ .

Thank you,

_____

You are cordially invited to our

OKTOBERFEST

When:

Where:

Please R.S.V.P.

Columbus Day

October 12

1992 marked the 500-year anniversary of Christopher Columbus' discovery of the New World. In the United States, October 12th is called Columbus Day. In Canada and Latin America it is called Dia de la Raza. Dia de la Raza means, literally, "day of the race." It is a day set aside to celebrate the ways in which the Spanish people (race) have influenced the world.

Many people are concerned that students do not know that other explorers came to North America before Columbus, and, of course, they should know this. However, these earlier explorations do nothing to diminish the fact that when Columbus landed in the Bahamas and went back to report his discoveries, he opened the North and South American continents to further exploration and eventual settlement.

Making It Work

Have students do research on these topics:

- What did most people believe about the shape of the earth in Columbus' time?
- What was the main purpose of Columbus' voyage? What did he hope to find?
- Who financed Columbus' first voyage? How?
- Where did Columbus think he had landed when he reached the Bahamas?
- Why did he name the native people "Indians"?

The Spanish people have had a great effect on the New World. (Note: While it is true that Columbus was Italian, it was Spain that supported and financed his explorations.) Have students find evidence of the great Spanish effect on the New World by observing modern North America, particularly in the United States. They can consider these areas:

- common expressions that have become part of the English language
- lifestyle of the Old West in America/the cowboy
- well-known people
- laws
- names of people, places, and things
- food
- clothing
- music
- art

Name_____

Hispanic Heritage

Use an encyclopedia or other reference books to find information for a brief biographical sketch of each of the following famous people of Hispanic heritage. Then use their names to make your own wordsearch puzzle (see page 55). Add other names as desired. When you complete your puzzle, make copies for your classmates to try.

Cesar Chavez _____

_____

_____

_____

Porfirio Diaz_____

_____

_____

_____

Miguel Hidalgo_____

_____

_____

_____

Benito Juarez _____

_____

_____

_____

Hispanic Heritage *(cont.)*

Jose Maria Morelos _____

_____

_____

_____

_____

Alvera Obregon _____

_____

_____

_____

_____

Jose Orozco _____

_____

_____

_____

_____

Diego Rivera _____

_____

_____

_____

_____

Name_____

Hispanic Heritage *(cont.)*

Antonio Santa Ana_____

_____

_____

_____

_____

Pancho Villa _____

_____

_____

_____

_____

Emiliano Zapata _____

_____

_____

_____

_____

Ignacio Zaragosa_____

_____

_____

_____

_____

Name_____

Hispanic Heritage Wordsearch

Use this graph paper to make a wordsearch puzzle using the names on the preceding pages. Be sure to make an answer key.

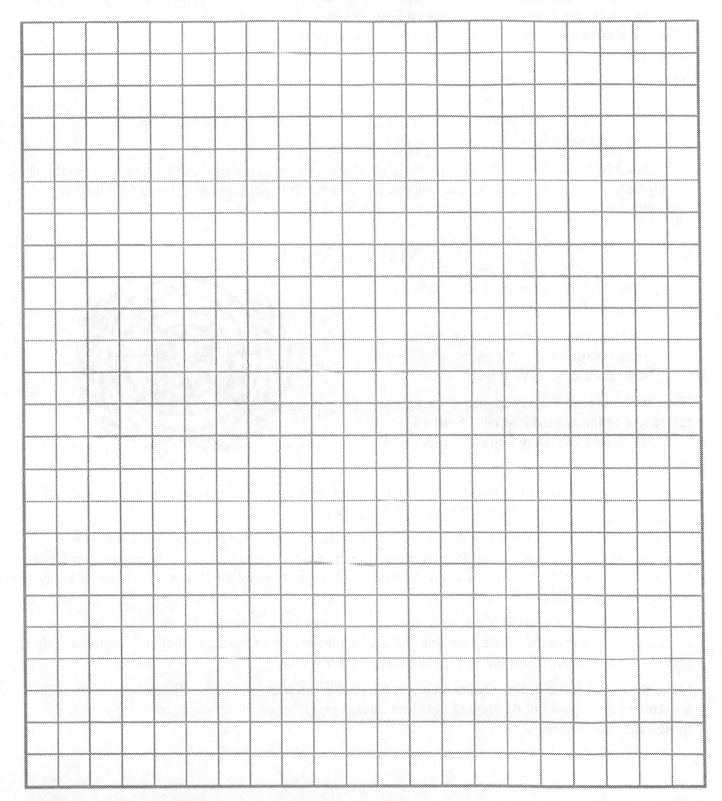

United Nations Day

October 24

The United Nations was founded on October 24, 1945. It was begun as an international peacekeeping organization. Its first meetings were in San Francisco and delegates came there from all over the world at the end of World War II to begin this exciting new project. Its headquarters are now in New York City, and almost every nation in the world sends its representatives there to meet and discuss world developments.

Although there have been many wars since the United Nations was founded, there has not been another World War. This was a great fear in the era of nuclear weapons and Super Powers, such as the United States and the former Soviet Union. Surely, just having a meeting place where people could talk instead of fight has helped to prevent a major war.

The United Nations also reminds us of the rights of the oppressed, the rights of women, and the rights of children. It is an organization that makes it possible for us to get into countries to feed the hungry and help the sick.

Make It Work

Write to the United Nations for information about programs that affect children.

> **UN Department of Public Information**
> United Nations
> New York City, NY 10017

Have students read the newspapers looking for references to the United Nations. Start a United Nations/Current Events bulletin board or scrap book.

If someone in your class has taken a tour of the United Nations building in New York City, ask that person to share a first-person impression of the experience.

Assign each student the names of several of the countries in the United Nations. Have them use construction paper to make small flags representing the flags of those countries. Decorate your United Nations bulletin board with the flags, or display a map surrounded by the flags with a piece of yarn leading from each flag to its country.

For advanced students, stage a debate concerning a current topic of worldwide concern. Divide the students into groups representing nations with differing point-of-view. Have them research the topic so they can defend the various nations' positions in a class debate.

Make the paper doll cut-outs shown on pages 57-59. Research and discuss traditional costumes. Ask students to draw paper dolls dressed in the traditional costumes of additional countries, particularly those of their ancestry.

Paper Doll Cut-Outs

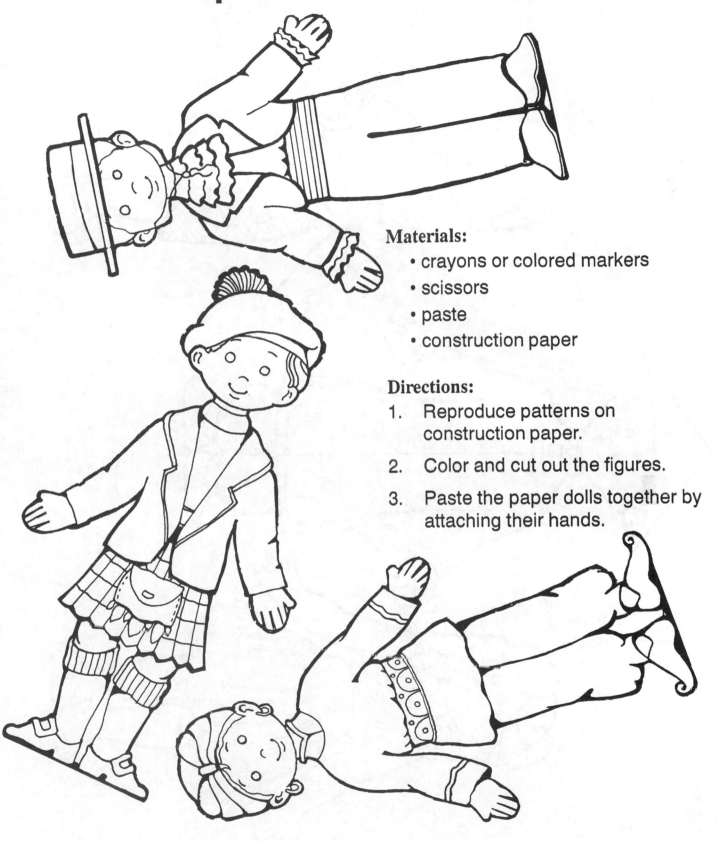

Materials:

- crayons or colored markers
- scissors
- paste
- construction paper

Directions:

1. Reproduce patterns on construction paper.

2. Color and cut out the figures.

3. Paste the paper dolls together by attaching their hands.

Paper Doll Cut-Outs (cont.)

58

©1994 Teacher Created Materials, Inc.

Paper Doll Cut-Outs *(cont.)*

Halloween

October 31

Many of the customs that are celebrated on Halloween come to us from the ancient past. October 31st was the New Year's Eve of the Celts who lived in Britain and northern Europe around 2,000 years ago. On that night they would gather with their priests, called Druids. Together they would honor their most important god, the Lord of the Dead. They feasted and told stories of their ancestors. The Celts believed that the spirits of those who had died during the year were wandering around on that night, cold and lonely, while they themselves were warm and sheltered. For this reason they took lanterns when they went outside. They also believed that the spirits were hungry and apt to play tricks, so they left offerings of food and drink on their doorsteps for them. The Celts who had to go outside on that scary night put on disguises so that the spirits would not recognize them. In order to feel safe, they tried to make themselves look like the spirits they thought were restlessly wandering around.

When church leaders were trying to convert the Celts in the early days of Christianity, they simply added their religious ideas to the beliefs and ceremonies the Celts already had. They made November 1st and 2nd All Saint's Day and All Soul's Day, both of which recognized the spirits of the dead. October 31st then became the Eve of All Saint's (or All Hallow's) Day, which was eventually shortened to Halloween.

All of the Halloween customs of the Celts moved elsewhere with the people who came from Britain and northern Europe. Although the customs have been modified over the years, they have stayed basically the same: lanterns, gifts of food, and scary disguises.

Making It Work

How did witches and black cats come to be associated with Halloween? Have students write a story that explains this in an imaginative way.

Ask students to research answers to these questions:

- Who was the original Jack-O-Lantern?
- How did he get his name?
- Why does he still wander about?
- Where did people first begin to trick-or-treat?
- Who brought this custom to the United States?
- In which modern country is Halloween a national holiday?

Have students use some or all of the patterns on pages 61-66 to create bulletin boards or other decorations for Halloween.

Halloween Patterns

Halloween Patterns *(cont.)*

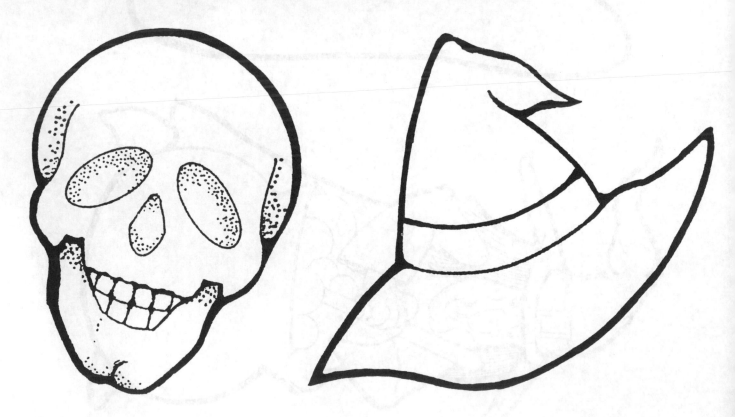

Halloween Patterns *(cont.)*

Halloween Patterns (cont.)

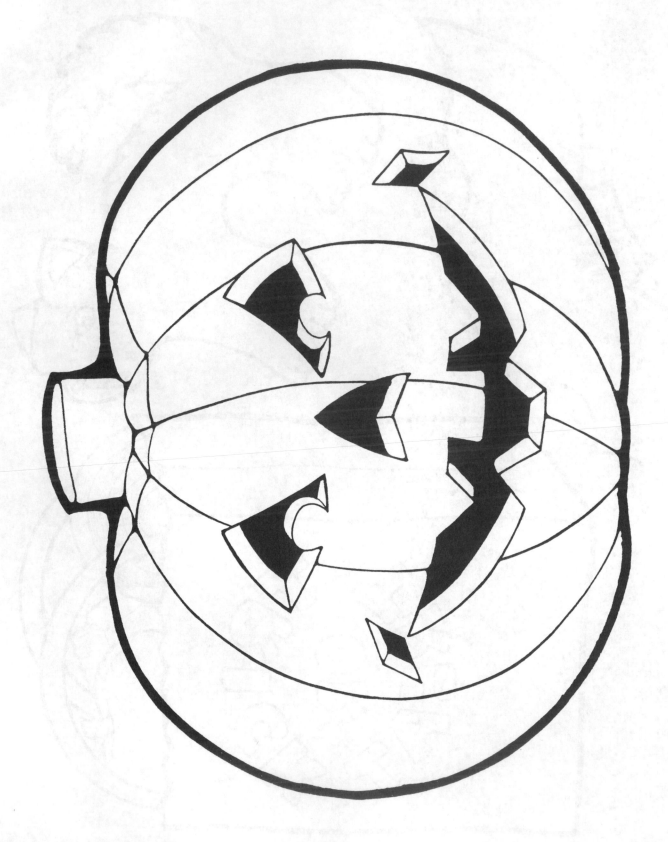

©1994 Teacher Created Materials, Inc.

Halloween Patterns (cont.)

Halloween Patterns (cont.)

All Saints' Day and All Souls' Day

November 1 and 2

All Saints' Day and All Souls' Day are days on which many Christians honor the saints—the people who lived such good lives that they went straight to heaven—and offer prayers for the rest—the people who might need a little help in getting to heaven. These days originated in an effort to Christianize the early Celts whose festival honoring the Lord of the Dead fell on October 31st. (See Halloween, page 60.)

All Saints' Day is a special day in many Christian churches. It is a day set aside to honor all the saints, but especially those who do not have an exclusive day of their own. It may have been started to honor all of the unknown martyrs who died for their faith in the early centuries of Christianity. In Catholic churches, it is a day when people must attend mass. In Protestant churches, it is often observed on the Sunday following November 1st.

All Souls' Day is a day on which all Catholics, and some Protestants, pray for the souls of the dead whether or not they are believed to be saints. They pray for them to be happy with God in the afterlife.

Praying for and honoring the dead is not just something that Christians do. People of many religions all over the world have been doing this for thousands of years. Almost all religions still have a ceremony of this kind today.

Making It Work

Ask students to find out if the churches they attend have a ceremony having to do with All Saints' Day or All Souls' Day. What takes place during the ceremony? Have they ever attended this ceremony?

Have students research the ways in which ancient people tried to help those who died. For example, in what ways did the ancient Egyptians prepare the dead for the afterlife? What did they do to make sure those who had died would be comfortable, safe, and happy? How do we know what they did? (If possible, take students on a field trip to a museum that has an Egyptian mummy in its collection.)

People of Asia are very devoted to the well-being of their departed ancestors. What religions found in Asia have ceremonies of this kind?

Find any other instances when the early Christian church converted people by incorporating existing pagan beliefs into the new religion they were preaching.

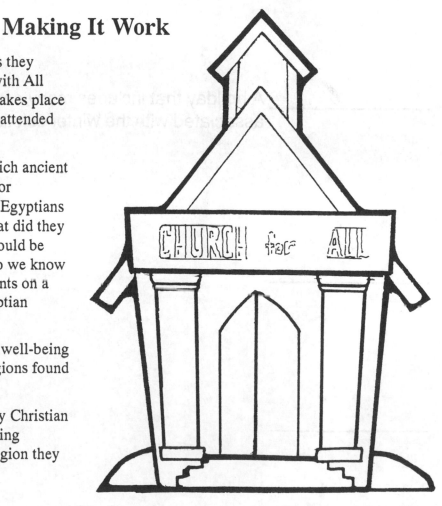

What Do We Call It Now?

Read each clue and write in the name of the modern holiday. Then think up some clues of your own and try to stump your classmates.

_____ A holiday associated with the ancient Celt's festival honoring the Lord of the Dead.

_____ A holiday associated with the ceremony for Eostre, the Saxon goddess of the dawn, who was worshiped each spring.

_____ A holiday that includes many ceremonies and customs once associated with the winter solstice.

_____

_____

Los Dias de Los Muertos, the Days of the Dead

October 31, and November 1 and 2

Los Dias de Los Muertos are really a two-day and sometimes three-day ritual. This holiday is the Hispanic version of Halloween, All Saints' Day, and All Souls' Day rolled into one. It is festive, intended to honor dear departed ones. People go to cemeteries and have picnics among the graves of the people they love. They do this because they believe that the souls of the dead return once a year at this time for a visit.

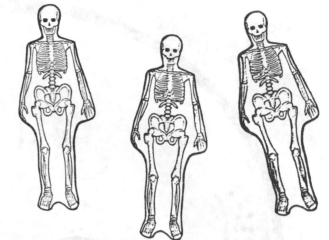

In Mexico, this festival dates from pre-Columbian times. It is a mixture of Christianity and ancient ritual and is celebrated most colorfully in the state of Michoacan. People in Michoacan, and in many other parts of Mexico, spend the 31st of October getting ready for the festival. The next day they go to the cemetery and spend all day and all night with dead relatives and friends. Food stalls sell candy skulls made of decorated sugar and special bread decorated with skulls and coffins made of icing. (This food is offered to the spirits as well as eaten by the picnickers.) Flowers, particularly yellow marigolds, are for sale to decorate the graves. People also decorate special altars in their homes with these flowers. There, a best-loved relative might be honored with the display of a photograph and some favorite possessions.

In the United States, people from Mexico, especially those from Michoacan, are transplanting and adapting the celebration of Los Dias De Los Muertos. In the U.S. it may take place on a weekend-day near the date and consist of a public ceremony at a cemetery, with an altar banked with marigolds, a formal procession, and a sermon by a priest. But the reason for attending is the same elsewhere as in Michoacan —the desire to honor and be near the spirits of loved ones.

Making It Work

Ask students to share the ways in which they celebrate Los Dias de Los Muertos in their own families. If you have students from Mexico in your class, ask them to describe ceremonies they may have attended there as well as ceremonies they may have attended in your country.

Investigate Hispanic markets and buy candy skulls or decorated loaves of sweet bread for your class to experience.

Read about similar celebrations that take place in other countries. For example, try France, Sicily, Spain, Portugal, and the Philippines.

Cut-paper decorations are a feature of this holiday in Mexico. You can make cut-paper (*papel picado*) skulls out of tissue paper to use as decorations in your classroom. (See page 70.)

Los Dias de Los Muertos, the Days of the Dead *(cont.)*

Materials:

- pattern, this page
- tissue or construction paper square, larger than pattern
- pencil
- scissors

Directions:

- Cut out the pattern and trace it on tissue paper square. Cut traced pattern from tissue paper. Unfold for display or mounting.

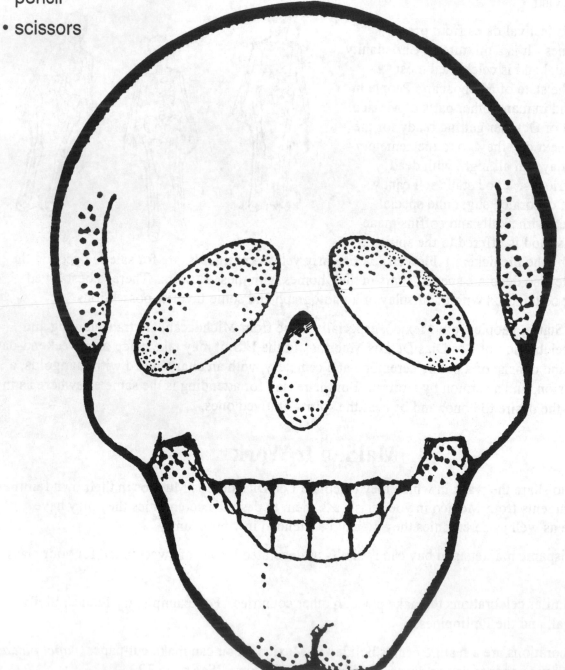

Divali, the Hindu New Year

October or November

Divali (sometimes spelled Diwali) is the Hindu New Year. Its celebration lasts for five days and is the most popular festival of the year. The word "divali" means a garland or row of lights, and small lamps called dipa lights line roads and rooftops, fences and windowsills, to greet Lakshmi, the goddess of good fortune. (Hindus worship many gods and goddesses, but they believe that each one is an incarnation or form that expresses a characteristic of the one God.)

People clean their homes—they may even whitewash them—to prepare for Lakshmi's coming. They make beautiful floor paintings with rice flour, much as Native Americans make sand paintings. People who run businesses clean and decorate their stores and shops and fill them with dipa lights. Everyone believes that Lakshmi will not bring her blessings of wealth and prosperity to any place that is dark. Some people may even put lighted dipas in rivers to see if they will float to the other side before sinking, a sure sign of coming prosperity.

Since Divali is the start of a new year, in addition to cleaning their houses and businesses, people pay their old debts and dress in their finest clothes. If they own jewelry, they will be sure to wear it.

In the United States, Hindus celebrate Divali in their homes and temples. They clean the temples as well as their homes and have a feast with lights and entertainment.

Making It Work

If you have a student from India in your class, ask him or her to share the customs surrounding Divali. How have these customs been adapted to life in your country?

- Are traditional foods eaten? What are some examples of these foods?
- Is it hard to get the right ingredients or is everything they need available here?
- Do they have real dipa lights? (If so, would it be possible to bring one to show the class?)
- Are dipa lights used in homes and temples? How about in businesses?
- Do people wear their best clothes and jewelry to the temples? At home?
- Do people pay their old debts?

Hindu Floor Painting

Hindu floor paintings, which are done using rice flour for "paint," are not at all permanent. (Neither are the sand paintings done by Native Americans.) Here is an idea for approximating this type of design in a medium that will not blow away easily.

Materials:

- a piece of heavy paper, cardboard, tagboard, etc.
- an assortment of grains and small beans in as many colors as possible.
- glue that will be colorless when dry (tacky glue is best)

Directions:

1. Look through books on India until you find a design that appeals to you. This may be on a rug, a wall hanging, or a fabric. Sketch the general idea of the design you have chosen on the paper.

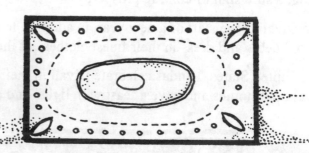

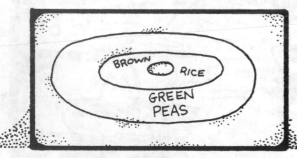

2. Plan your use of color. In light pencil, write words on the pattern itself to remind you of your color choices.

3. Apply glue to small areas of the design and cover with the grains or beans. Press down. Continue to next area.

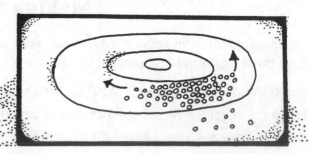

4. Allow to dry thoroughly. Move carefully.

Veterans Day/Remembrance Day

November 11

Veterans Day in the United States and Remembrance Day in Canada and England were originally called Armistice Day. Armistice Day was the day on which the armistice agreement between the Allies and the Central Powers was signed, ending World War I at 11 o'clock on November 11, 1918. This was the eleventh hour of the eleventh day of the eleventh month. At the time, many people thought there would never be another war.

After World War II, England and Canada changed the name of Armistice Day to Remembrance Day. The United States changed the name to Veterans Day to honor those who have served in the armed forces during all of its wars. Veterans Day is different from and much more inclusive than Memorial Day (May 30th) which honors those who died in the service of their country.

On Veterans Day there are parades and speeches. People visit war memorials and place wreaths there.

Making It Work

Review the meaning of the word "veteran" and the names of the various armed services with the students. Have them ask at home if anyone in their family is a veteran.

What benefits does the United States provide for veterans? If students were able to find a veteran at home, have them ask about benefits they may have received.

Contact a recruiting office of one or more of the armed services and ask them to send a speaker to your classroom to talk to the students about the modern armed services and the importance of a good education for those who might want to enlist when they are older. Also, ask the speaker to explain veterans' benefits to the class.

People in the U.S. speak of fighting in wars as defending the American flag. Discuss the design of the American flag. Why are there thirteen stripes? Why are the stripes on the top and bottom of the flag red and not white? What do the stars represent? Why was each color chosen? What does it mean when the flag is flown upside down?

The artists who draw the pictures for postage stamps work on a much larger scale, of course, than the size of a stamp. Use the frame on page 74 to design a postage stamp in honor of Veterans Day.

Designing a Stamp

Design a postage stamp in honor of Veterans Day/Remembrance Day in the frame below.

74   ©1994 Teacher Created Materials, Inc.

Thanksgiving

Fourth Thursday in November

Thanksgiving in the United States is celebrated on the fourth Thursday in November. It is often thought of as a particularly American holiday because of the story of the Pilgrims and the Indians. You will find, however, as you go through this book that most cultures, religions, and/or countries have some kind of a holiday that involves giving thanks. Many of them are associated with harvest time. Some of them are still celebrated as separate holidays. Some of them provide background for the United States' Thanksgiving.

In ancient times the Hebrews had a feast at which they gave thanks to God for their harvest. It was called Sukkot and Jews still celebrate it today. (See pages 47-48.)

The ancient Greeks had a harvest festival in honor of Demeter, the goddess of the harvest. They brought gifts of honey, fruit, and grain to her shrines.

The Romans honored Ceres, the goddess who protected their crops. They called the festival the Cerelia, and that is where the word "cereal" is derived.

For hundreds of years the Chinese have celebrated a festival of the harvest moon. This brightest moon of the year shines on the fifteenth day of the eighth month of the Chinese lunar calendar. The festival is called the Mid-Autumn Festival. (See pages 38-39.) The Vietnamese call this festival Tet Trung Thu. (See pages 42-43.) Koreans celebrate it as Chu-Sok. (See pages 40-41.)

People in southern India celebrate at least two harvest festivals, Onam in the fall and Pongal in mid-winter. Onam is a harvest festival associated with the legendary King Mahabalia. Pongol is the celebration of the rice harvest, the biggest festival of the year. (See pages 123-124.)

In England, the thanksgiving celebration was called Harvest Home. It took place when the last field was harvested and the crops were brought safely to the barns. Thanksgiving has also been celebrated in Canada for a long time. It was probably begun many years before the Pilgrims landed in America.

So when the Pilgrims did land in their new home on December 21, 1620, they already knew about ceremonies of thanksgiving. They had, of course, come from England and were familiar with the custom of giving thanks after the harvest. So, one year later, after a year of terrible hardship and frighteningly little success, Governor William Bradford proclaimed the first day of Thanksgiving in the Plymouth Colony. This was the feast day that many think of when we hear "the first Thanksgiving." It was the one shared with the Indians, who had helped the Pilgrims and introduced them to the native foods and strange farming practices of the New World.

Thanksgiving (cont.)

For many years, Thanksgiving was primarily a New England holiday. It was celebrated on different days in different states. A woman named Sara Josepha Hale was the first to suggest that it should be celebrated nationwide. She campaigned for twenty years and finally brought the idea to the attention of President Abraham Lincoln. In 1864, Lincoln issued a proclamation declaring the last Thursday in November to be Thanksgiving Day.

Thanksgiving has changed its date several times since Lincoln's era. But its message each year is the same. We give thanks, each in our own way, for all the good things we have. When times are good, everybody celebrates. During hard times, it is customary for the more fortunate to help those who do not have as much.

Making It Work

Have students use reference materials to find the answers to these questions:

- What were the foods that were new to the Pilgrims in the New World?
- Was it easy for the Pilgrims to make this adjustment in their eating habits? Why or why not?
- What was the name of the Indian tribe that helped the Pilgrims?
- What three main crops did the Indians give to the Pilgrims?
- What secrets of agriculture did the Indians share with the Pilgrims?
- What was the name of the colony in Virginia that was settled before the Pilgrims landed in Plymouth? What year was it settled?
- What else did Sara Josepha Hale accomplish in her lifetime?
- What famous song did she write?
- At what age did she die?

Ask students to share this information:

- Describe how Thanksgiving is celebrated at your home?
- Do you celebrate more than one Thanksgiving?
- What foods does your family eat for the Thanksgiving feast?

Giving Thanks

My name is _____

The date is _____

These are the people who are important in my life:

1. _____ because _____

   _____

2. _____ because _____

   _____

3. _____ because _____

   _____

This year I am most thankful for _____

_____

_____

When I think of Thanksgiving, I think about _____

_____

_____

My best Thanksgiving memory is _____

_____

_____

Organize a Food Drive

Organize a food drive for the needy as your Thanksgiving gift to the world.

1. Ask your teacher to help you:
   • clear your project with the principal.
   • communicate with your parents about your project.
   • find an appropriate group to accept your gift.
   • arrange to have the food picked up and delivered where it is supposed to go.

2. Make signs to let people know about your project. Be sure to include:
   • what kind of food you are collecting (cans, jars, and other non-perishable items).
   • where people can bring the food.
   • who will receive the food.

3. Follow through in these ways:
   • be there to receive the donations and thank people.
   • package the donations so nothing gets broken.
   • have things ready to be picked up.

4. Personalize your project by:
   • making greeting cards to go with the food.
   • adding some gifts other than food, such as mittens and scarfs for adults and stuffed animals for children.
   • tying big bows on the boxes.

Thanks Around the World

Here are many ways to say thank you in different languages. See how many you can use in making a greeting card for your family.

Arabic:	*shoukran*	Serbo-Croatian:	*hvala*
Czech:	*děkuji*	Spanish:	*gracias*
Danish:	*tak*	Swahili:	*asante*
Dutch:	*dank*	Swedish:	*tack*
Esperanto:	*dankon*	Turkish:	*tesekkür*
Estonian:	*dekui*	Yiddish:	*dank*
Finnish:	*kiitos*		
French:	*merci*		
German:	*danke*		
Greek:	*efcharistó*		
Hebrew:	*todah*		
Hungarian:	*köszönöm*		
Indonesian:	*terima kasih*		
Italian:	*grazie*		
Japanese:	*arigato*		
Latvian:	*paldies*		
Lithuanian:	*tänan*		
Norwegian:	*takk*		
Polish:	*dziekuje*		
Portuguese:	*obrigado*		
Rumanian:	*multumiri*		
Russian:	*spasíbo*		

Plymouth Puzzle

Find these words associated with the Pilgrims and their life in the Plymouth Colony in the wordsearch below.

blessing	preacher	dugouts	farmer
corn	tinsmith	shopkeeper	potter
blacksmith	religion	explorers	supply
settlement	Plymouth	fishing	harbor
succotash	colonies	Indians	winter
kettle	Pilgrims	freedom	wampum
cobbler	teacher	miller	furs
supplies	printer	trading	feast

```
J  J  D  W  Y  J  T  I  N  S  M  I  T  H  O  U  I  H  K  P
F  S  L  V  P  L  Y  M  O  U  T  H  N  Z  Q  Z  C  A  V  D
Q  R  R  Z  I  N  T  E  A  C  H  E  R  E  A  X  F  N  Z  M
Z  C  E  N  F  S  Q  H  Q  C  Y  K  F  M  J  Q  F  H  O  Y
P  O  S  T  E  U  M  X  W  O  F  Y  E  X  D  Q  U  W  X  T
I  B  U  R  P  P  J  S  E  T  A  A  A  Y  N  K  Q  C  O  W
L  B  P  A  K  P  E  V  C  A  R  S  S  N  O  E  N  A  E  R
G  L  P  D  B  L  A  C  K  S  M  I  T  H  I  T  G  I  G  D
R  E  L  I  G  I  O  N  R  H  E  P  R  G  U  T  A  O  Y  X
I  R  Y  N  M  E  X  P  L  O  R  E  R  S  O  L  P  G  M  R
M  X  S  G  G  S  B  O  W  P  R  E  A  C  H  E  R  R  Y  A
S  X  Q  V  F  J  E  Z  S  K  W  Q  F  I  S  H  I  N  G  J
X  G  I  N  D  I  A  N  S  E  T  T  L  E  M  E  N  T  I  Q
W  A  M  P  U  M  C  B  L  E  S  S  I  N  G  D  T  M  N  F
E  M  V  B  G  I  B  E  W  P  N  W  W  I  N  T  E  R  C  U
E  K  V  C  O  L  O  N  I  E  S  R  I  Y  H  A  R  B  O  R
K  V  E  G  U  L  B  L  F  R  E  E  D  O  M  E  C  Z  R  S
R  P  O  T  T  E  R  T  T  H  K  H  C  Z  L  F  N  N  N  M
E  J  P  Q  S  R  Y  Y  C  W  E  Q  P  M  E  J  E  K  X  O
```

Winter Holidays

December

Birthstone: Turquoise

Flower: Narcissus

December was the tenth month of the Roman calendar. Its name comes from *decem* which is the Latin word for the number ten.

January

Birthstone: Garnet

Flower: Carnation

January was named for the Roman god Janus who has been pictured with two faces, one looking to the future and one to the past.

February

Birthstone: Amethyst

Flower: Violet

February was added to the Roman calendar about 700 B.C. It originally had 29 days, but the Emperor Augustus Caesar took one of its days to make August, his month, longer. Its name comes from a Latin word, *februare*, meaning "to purify."

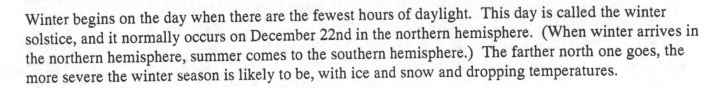

Winter begins on the day when there are the fewest hours of daylight. This day is called the winter solstice, and it normally occurs on December 22nd in the northern hemisphere. (When winter arrives in the northern hemisphere, summer comes to the southern hemisphere.) The farther north one goes, the more severe the winter season is likely to be, with ice and snow and dropping temperatures.

Winter is a dark time, too, with slowly shortening days. This may be why so many of these holidays are celebrated with fire and light. Candles are often a big part of winter celebrations. Before the invention of electric lights, Christmas trees were decorated with burning candles. (Someone always had to watch for fires!) Hanukkah is often called the Festival of Lights because it is celebrated by lighting special candles.

Food also plays a big part in winter celebrations. Many traditions include foods that are not made at any other time of the year. Just think of Christmas cookies and special Hanukkah foods such as *latkes*.

Most winter holidays feature gift-giving. People give presents to others they love. These gift-giving occasions often center around children.

This is an upper grade contract to be used in connection with the winter holidays. You can run it off and distribute it to your students. Use the part of this page below the line as a cover and the two following pages as an instructional packet and sign-up slip to keep track of student presentations.

Winter Holiday Contract

Winter Holiday Contract *(cont.)*

1. Choose the winter holiday in which you are most interested. If you (or your family) are from a country other than where you live now, please consider sharing your own customs and traditions with the class.

2. Research your winter holiday. You may use all kinds of reference books and encyclopedias. You may also consult primary sources— people with first-hand, personal knowledge. Interview your parents, older relatives, and family friends. Just be sure to write down where you got your information.

3. Your report will be due during the last two weeks before winter vacation. Make an appointment so your presentation can be scheduled. Try not to wait until the last minute.

4. Here is what to do for your report/presentation:

   a. Write an information paper to be turned in. Here are some things to include (though you may think of many more):

   - What is the name of your holiday?
   - Where is it celebrated?
   - When is it celebrated?
   - What are the customs associated with it?
   - Are there special ceremonies? Feasts? Foods? Parades?
   - Are there special costumes?
   - Are gifts exchanged?
   - Is there a gift-giver (like Santa Claus)?
   - What Is the gift-giver called?
   - What stories are told about the gift-giver?
   - Is the holiday different for children and adults?
   - Does your holiday have a religious significance?

   b. Include a bibliography. Don't forget to list any primary sources.

Winter Holiday Contract *(cont.)*

c. Do at least _____ of the following:

   - Create a holiday wordsearch or crossword puzzle. Make enough copies for the class. Include an answer key for the teacher.

   - Create a center for a primary class with books, pictures, worksheets, and activities. Present the center to the primary class of your choice two weeks before vacation. (Remember to get permission from the teacher of the class.)

   - Make an ornament or a door or table decoration representing your holiday. Display it in class.

   - Prepare and teach a holiday art project. This may be done in your class or you may arrange to do it for another teacher. Make an appointment for the time you will need.

   - Write and illustrate a poem or a story to go with your holiday.

   - Find a book about your holiday and practice reading it aloud with expression. Present a story time to a primary class. Remember to arrange this with the teacher of the class.

   - Create your own activity. Check with the teacher first.

d. Be prepared to make an oral presentation to describe and display the activities you have completed for your holiday contract. Plan to read your information paper aloud to the class.

e. **Optional:** Bring the class a food treat representing your holiday. Distribute it at the end of your presentation.

If you schedule your presentation early enough, you may invite your parents to come and be part of the audience. (If you wait until the last minute, we will not be able to guarantee a definite time.)

Fill out the form below, clip it off, and return it to the teacher.

- -

Name_____

The holiday I have chosen is _____ .

I would like to schedule my presentation on _____ .

This is a primary grade contract to be used in connection with the winter holidays. You can run it off and distribute it to your students. Use the part of this page below the line as a cover and the two following pages as an instructional packet and sign-up slip to keep track of student presentation.

Winter Holiday Contract

Winter Holiday Contract *(cont.)*

1. Choose the winter holiday in which you are most interested.

2. Find out about your winter holiday. You may use all kinds of reference books and encyclopedias. You may also ask people who have first-hand, personal knowledge. Talk to your parents, older relatives, and family friends. Just be sure to write down where you got your information.

3. Your report will be due during the last two weeks before winter vacation. Talk to the teacher about when you would like to give your report. Try not to wait until the last minute.

4. Here is what to do for your report/presentation:

   a. Write an information paper to be turned in. You may ask your parents for help. Here are some things you may want to include (though you may think of many more):

      - What is the name of your holiday?
      - Where is it celebrated?
      - When is it celebrated?
      - What are the customs associated with it?
      - Are there special ceremonies? Feasts? Foods? Parades?
      - Are there special costumes?
      - Are gifts exchanged?
      - Is there a gift-giver (like Santa Claus)?
      - What is the gift-giver called?
      - What stories are told about the gift-giver?
      - Is the holiday different for children and adults?
      - Does your holiday have a religious significance?

   b. Include a bibliography. Don't forget to list any people you talked to.

©*1994 Teacher Created Materials, Inc.*

Winter Holiday Contract *(cont.)*

c.   Do at least _____ of the following:

- Create a holiday word search or crossword puzzle. Make enough copies for the class. Include an answer key for the teacher.
- Make an ornament or a door or table decoration representing your holiday. Display it in class.
- Draw a picture to go with your report.
- Write a poem or a song to go with your holiday.
- Find a book about your holiday and practice reading it aloud with expression. Present a story time to a lower class. Remember to ask the teacher to arrange this with the teacher of the other class.

d.   Be prepared to make an oral presentation to describe and display the activities you have completed for your holiday contract. Plan to read your information paper aloud to the class.

e.   **Optional:** Bring the class a food treat representing your holiday. Distribute it at the end of your presentation.

If you schedule your presentation early enough, you may invite your parents to come and be part of the audience. (If you wait until the last minute, we will not be able to guarantee a definite time.)

Fill out the form below, clip it off, and return it to the teacher.

- -

Name _____

The holiday I have chosen is _____ .

I would like to schedule my presentation on _____ .

Parent signature _____

Advent, the Coming of Jesus Christ

Begins the Fourth Sunday Before Christmas

Advent means "coming" and it is the name given to the four weeks before Christmas. It was once a period of penitence and fasting in the Christian religion, much like Lent, the period of time leading to Easter. Now, however, it is viewed as a time of happy anticipation, and its observation is more widespread because Christmas has become a traditional as well as a religious holiday.

Some churches and families use Advent wreaths to mark the time as it passes. An Advent wreath is a special candleholder. It contains four candles surrounded by a wreath of evergreen or holly. One candle is lit on the fourth Sunday before Christmas. Two candles are lit on the next Sunday, and so on. The Advent wreath makes a lovely table centerpiece during the four weeks before Christmas.

Many families give children Advent calendars to help them with the anticipation that builds before Christmas. An Advent calendar has 24 little windows or doors to be opened, one each day, from the first of December until the 24th, Christmas Eve. Behind each door is a picture, an ornament, a piece of candy, or a Bible verse.

Making It Work

Have students share Advent customs that are practiced in their own families. Do they sing special songs? Prepare and eat special foods? Bake special cookies? Light candles in an Advent wreath? Receive Advent calendars?

Buy an Advent calendar for your classroom. Open one door or window each morning. The calendars containing miniature ornaments are nice for classroom use because the ornaments can be placed on the classroom tree or added to the general seasonal decorations and then kept from year to year. Play catch-up on Mondays and finish the calendar before school is dismissed for vacation.

Have students make Advent calendars to take home. Draw and color an appropriate scene, cut flaps in 24 places, and back each opening with the picture of a symbol associated with the season. Collect and save old Christmas cards and December issues of magazines to use for this purpose.

Make Advent wreaths to give parents for early presents. They should be ready to take home the Friday before the first Sunday of Advent. (See page 89.)

Making an Advent Wreath

Your advent wreath can be as fancy or as simple as you would like it to be. You'll need a base for your wreath, four candles, four candleholders, and some greenery. You can add other decorations such as ribbons and glitter if you wish.

Base:
The base of your wreath is a hollow circle. It can be cut out of heavy cardboard or it can be made of styrofoam.

Candleholders:
Candleholders can be made of clay or papier-mâché. Or they can simply be nails inserted through the wreath base onto which the candles are placed. (If you decide to use clay or papier-mâché, make sure that your candles will fit inside of them.)

Candles:
Buy four candles at the store. Remember that you will want to let them burn for awhile on four different Sundays. Fat candles last longer than skinny ones. The candles may be any color, but the traditional wreath has three purple candles and one pink candle. The purple ones represent penitence and are lit on the first, second, and fourth Sundays. The pink candle represents hope and is lit on the third Sunday of Advent.

Greenery:
The greenery for your wreath can be real or artificial. If you choose to use pieces of real evergreen, you will probably need to replace them once or twice during the month to keep your wreath looking fresh and pretty.

Hanukkah or Chanukah, the Jewish Festival of Lights

Sometime in December

The Jewish festival of Hanukkah, or Chanukah, is also called the Festival of Lights. It lasts for eight days and usually occurs in December, although in some years it may start in November. It commemorates not only the triumph of the Maccabees over the great army of the Syrian king, Antiochus IV, in 165 B.C., but also the universal message that all people have the right to be free.

After the Jews had won their battle, they went to their temple and found that the Syrians had brought in statues of their own gods. The eternal light had been allowed to go out. The Jews rekindled the light, but they had only enough oil to keep it burning for one day, and it would take eight days for a messenger to get more oil. The miracle of Hanukkah is that the oil kept burning for eight days, long enough for the messenger to return with more. Jews use a candleholder called the *menorah* to symbolize this miracle. It holds nine candles. One, the *shamus*, is used to light the others. They stand for the eight days that the oil kept burning.

Hanukkah is celebrated by lighting the candles of the menorah, playing games of chance with a spinning top called a *dreidel*, and eating special holiday foods such as potato pancakes called *latkes*. Children often receive a gift on each night of Hanukkah in addition to Hanukkah *gelt* (money). This gelt sometimes consists of chocolate wrapped in gold foil to look like money.

Making It Work

Invite a parent of one of your students to give a Hanukkah party in your classroom. This can be very simple or very festive, but it should include at least one traditional food, some gelt, and a chance to play the dreidel game.

If no parent is willing or able to give a party for you, you can easily give one yourself with the help of a Jewish delicatessen. Gelt can be purchased everywhere in its little net bags. A student in your class will probably know how to play the dreidel game, but if not, directions can be found on page 91.

Buy inexpensive plastic dreidels for your students or have each student make his or her own. (See page 91.)

Beautiful Hanukkah cards can be made easily. Fold blue paper into a card shape. Lay the cut-out shape of a candle on the front of the card. Lightly sponge thin white tempera paint over the entire front. Carefully lift away the candle. Allow to dry and write a message inside. (See page 92.)

The Dreidel Game

Making a Dreidel:

1. Cut out the dreidel along the solid lines.

2. Fold along the dotted lines and glue or tape together so you have a box shape.

3. Make two small holes where the circles are on the top and bottom and push a short pencil through. Spin the dreidel by twirling the pencil.

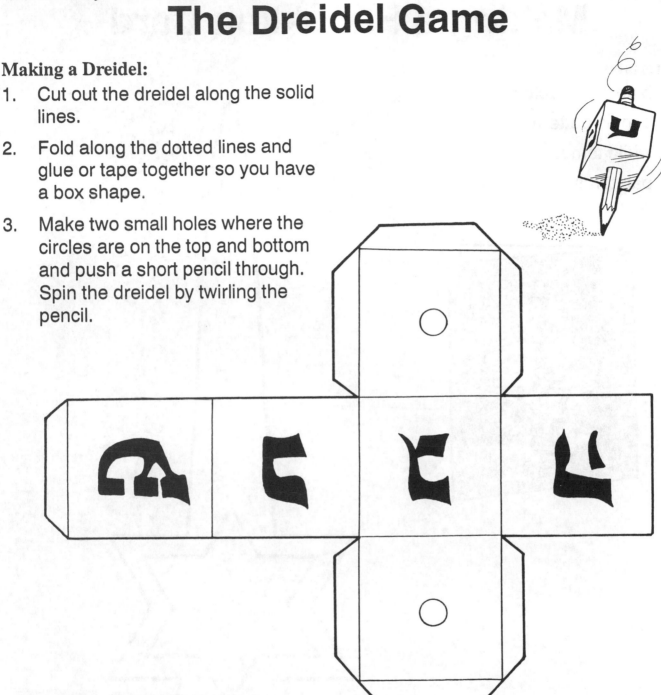

Playing the Dreidel Game:

The dreidel is a four-sided top. Each side has a Hebrew letter on it: *nun*, *gimmel*, *hay*, and *shin*. These four letters stand for the Hebrew words that mean "a great miracle happened there." The players sit in a circle. Each player receives an equal number of tokens (buttons, nuts, gelt) and puts five from his or her pile into the center. Everyone takes turns spinning the dreidel. The letter on top when the dreidel stops spinning tells what to do. *Nun:* Do nothing. *Gimmel:* Take the center pile. *Hay:* Take half the center pile. *Shin:* Give half of your pile. Players who lose all of their tokens are out. The last player with tokens is the winner.

Making a Hanukkah Card

Materials:
- blue construction paper
- candle pattern
- white tempera paint
- paintbrush or sponge

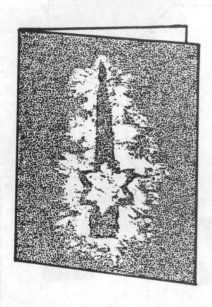

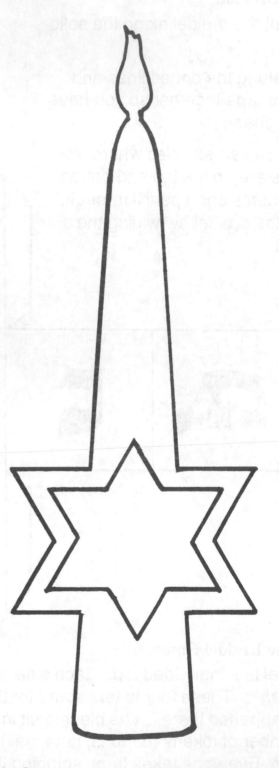

Directions:

Cut out the candle. Place it on the card. Sponge thin white tempera over and around the candle. Carefully remove the candle shape. Write a message inside the card.

Saint Nicholas Day

December 6

Saint Nicholas is the patron saint of children. He lived in Myra, in what is now Turkey, during the 4th century. He was a bishop and reputed to be very generous. Many stories are told about Saint Nicholas (see page 108). Children in parts of France, Germany, and Switzerland still receive their gifts on his day. Sint Nikolaas, or Sinterklaas, is a great favorite in the Netherlands. There, he travels by horse with his helper, Black Pete (Zwarte Piet). Dutch children set our their wooden shoes filled with hay and carrots for the horse on December 5th, the eve of Saint Nicholas Day. In the morning children who have been good find presents there. Children who have not been good find a birch switch!

Children in the United States may still remember Saint Nicholas on his day by putting out hay for his horse (or reindeer). Some families begin the regular Christmas season with this holiday by reading Christmas stories and beginning to decorate their homes. Some people begin baking Christmas cookies on this day. There are many ways of recognizing and celebrating Saint Nicholas Day.

Making It Work

Read Clement C. Moore's "The Night Before Christmas" to your students. Discuss the effect of this poem on the way Santa Claus is perceived. Ask students to do some research to find out why and for whom this poem was written.

Introduce the concept of "oral history" to your class. Have students each interview and record (either through audio or video) an older relative or friend about customs they remember from their own childhood about Santa Claus or Saint Nicholas. (Make sure they get permission for taping and also for sharing the tapes with the class.) The class can brainstorm an interview script before beginning this project. It is also a good idea to role-play this process with a partner. Have partners trade off, each taking the role of the interviewer and the person being interviewed.

Play interview tapes in the classroom. Discuss the differences and similarities in people's experiences. Compare/contrast these experiences as they may relate to ethnic backgrounds.

Display pictures of the traditional Saint Nicholas and the modern Santa Claus. Have students write a paper comparing and contrasting the two concepts.

Saint Nicholas Awards

Use these "Saint Nick Awards" during the month of December.

aka Santa Claus

(who has been keeping a list and checking it twice)

recognizes the **SUPER GOOD BEHAVIOR** of

_____

_____   _____

Signature of Nick's helper   Date

aka Santa Claus

(who has been keeping a list and checking it twice)

recognizes the **SUPER ACADEMIC ACHIEVEMENT** of

_____

_____   _____

Signature of Nick's helper   Date

Bodhi Day or Buddha's Enlightenment

December 8

Japanese Buddhists of the Mahayana sect celebrate Buddha's enlightenment on December 8th. Most other Buddhists celebrate it, together with Buddha's birth and death, in May on the feast of Vesak.

Buddha is said to have sat in meditation under a Bo or Bodhi tree. He sat there for 49 days, attempting to solve the puzzle of life, until he reached enlightenment or complete understanding. He then taught people by his word and his example for the rest of his life. His teachings are known as Buddhism, one of the major religions of the world.

Making It Work

If you have one or more students in your classroom who celebrate Buddha's enlightenment on December 8th, ask them to share their first-hand information with their classmates. If you do not have this kind of input, ask student volunteers to call local Buddhist churches and ask for information:

- How is Buddha's enlightenment celebrated here?
- How does the celebration here differ from the celebration of the same event in Japan?
- How does the celebration of Buddha's enlightenment differ from the celebration held on his birthday, April 8th?
- How do Buddhists seek their own enlightenment? What is involved in becoming enlightened?
- Do Buddhists have a holy book such as the Christian Bible or Muslim Koran? What is it called? What kinds of things does it contain?

Have students research the answers to these questions:

- How many people in the world are Buddhists?
- In which countries of the world is Buddhism the main religion?

Name_____

Ikebana, the Art of Flower Arranging

The Japanese take pride in the art of flower arrangement. They have definite rules for their arrangements and they spend a lot of time learning the art. It follows three basic principles: the tallest flower, or section of flowers, symbolizes Heaven, the middle section symbolize Earth, and the root symbolizes mankind. The entire arrangement is said to represent the harmony of people with nature. Therefore, flower arranging is the perfect activity in honor of Buddha's enlightenment, for the teachings of Buddha deal principally with the concepts of harmony, order, and unity.

Find a book in your school or public library describing the Japanese art of flower arrangement. Write its title and author here: _____

_____

After reading the book, write some important rules for making flower arrangements:

1. _____

_____

2. _____

_____

3. _____

_____

4. _____

_____

5. _____

_____

Now, make an arrangement of your own using what you have learned. You may use flowers from your own garden or weeds and dried grasses and seed pods found in parks and vacant lots.

Bring your arrangement to school and share it with your class. Explain how it matches the rules of Japanese flower arrangement.

St. Lucia Day

December 13

Luciadagen, the Swedish feast of St. Lucia, honors Santa Lucia of Sicily, a girl who is said to have given away her dowry to feed the poor, or to have been martyred in 304 A.D. because of her faith, depending on the research source one consults. No one knows how she came to be so important in Sweden, but her feast day used to fall on the date of the winter solstice and her name means "light," so it is said that she comes to take the darkness away. Her feast day certainly reminds the people of Sweden that the long, dark nights of winter will soon grow shorter.

To celebrate this day, the oldest girl in each family plays the part of St. Lucia. Wearing a long white dress with a red silk sash around the waist and a crown of lighted candles, she brings coffee and saffron buns to her parents early on the morning of December 13th. Her sisters, who are also dressed in white, follow in a procession, carrying lighted candles. Her brothers, who are called "star boys," wear white cone-shaped hats decorated with stars and long white shirts.

In Sweden, the feast of St. Lucia is celebrated not only in homes but also in schools, churches, and offices. Whole communities have a Lucia procession. Outside of Sweden, Swedish families continue the Lucia tradition. In many areas, they also put on Christmas Fairs where Swedish crafts and foods are sold. They may have a "Queen of Light" with a court of Lucia princesses and star boys.

Making It Work

Saffron is the most expensive spice in the world. Have students find out what it is and where it originates.

Have students find out as much as they can about:

- Jul Tomten
- Julbrock
- Dalarna Horses
- St. Knut's Day

Take your class on a field trip to a Swedish Christmas Fair. You and the students may get great ideas for gifts to make presents for the other winter holidays — if not this year, then next year.

Swedish Christmas cookies are world famous. Ask student volunteers to look through cookbooks for some of these recipes. Perhaps some students will want to get together and make cookies for the class.

Have students make St. Lucia crowns and Star Boy hats. (See pages 98-100.)

St. Lucia Day Pattern

Use this pattern to create St. Lucia crowns for the girls in the class.

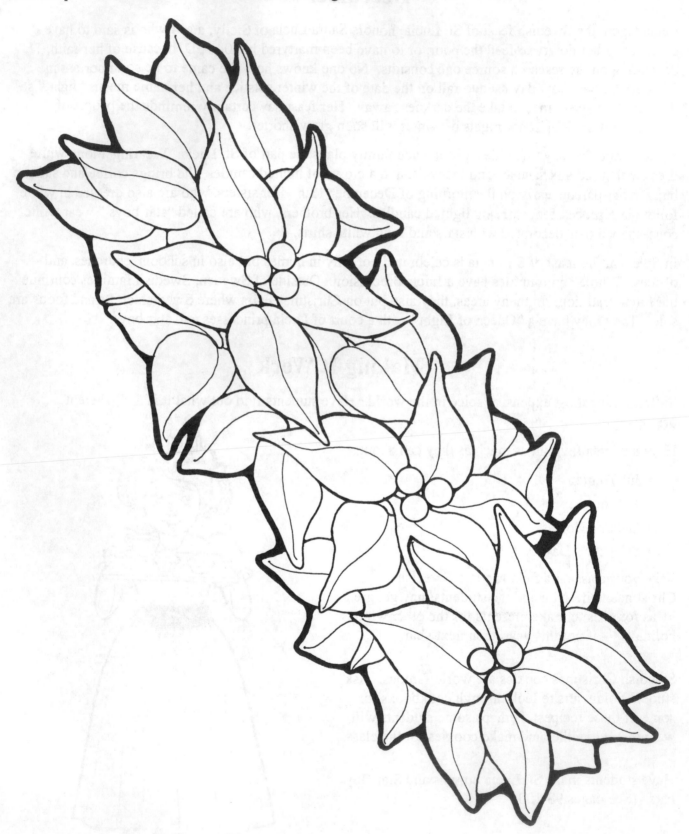

St. Lucia Day Pattern *(cont.)*

Use this pattern to create St. Lucia crowns for the girls in the class.

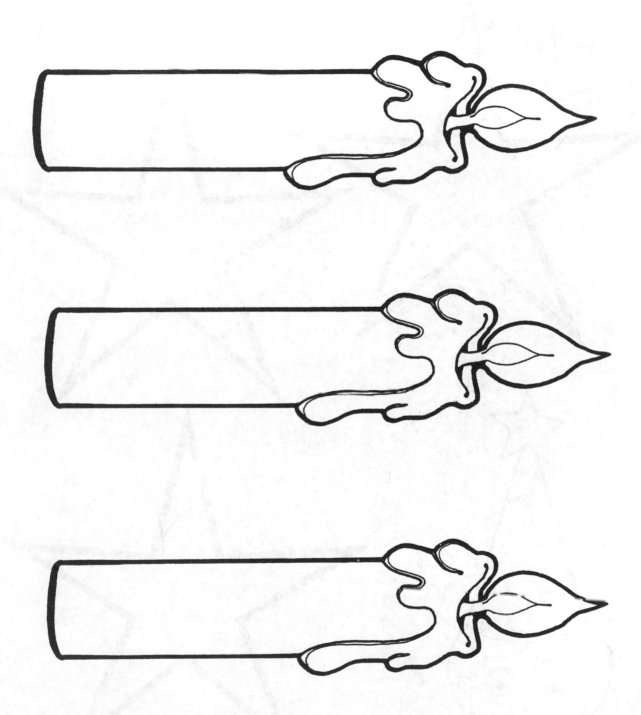

St. Lucia Day Pattern *(cont.)*

Roll a sheet of white construction paper into a cone-shape with an opening to fit the head. Use this pattern to cut stars from gold foil, and then use them to decorate Star Boy hats for the boys in the class.

Las Posadas, Mary and Joseph's Search for Shelter

December 16 through 24

Processions called Las Posadas are held on the nine nights before Christmas both in Mexico and in Hispanic communities elsewhere, particularly in the United States. Posada means a lodge or an inn, and these processions represent the Holy Family's search for lodging in Bethlehem long ago. People either dress as Mary and Joseph or carry nativity figures of them, as they go from house to house asking for a place to spend the night. Over and over they are told that there is no room for them. Each night, however, one home has been designated as the place where they are welcomed and a party follows. The last Posada is on Christmas Eve, and people often end the night by attending midnight mass.

Children play a big role in the Posadas, and in Mexico, children mean piñatas. Piñatas are hollow figures of animals or well-known storybook characters. They are filled with small toys, candies, and coins and hung on a rope that can be raised and lowered. The children take turns being blindfolded and trying to break the piñata with a long stick or bat as an adult raises and lowers it. When someone finally breaks the piñata, everyone scrambles for the treats.

Making It Work

Have a Posadas celebration at school. Invite several other classrooms to take part and have a procession that goes from room to room asking for lodging. End the procession in your own classroom, where you have left some students to act as the welcoming committee, and have a party complete with one or more piñatas.

Ask students to share their own experiences with Posadas. Where do they take place? What kind of food is served at the parties? Who is chosen to act the parts of Mary and Joseph? Have they ever had a Posadas party in their home?

Have students make piñatas to be used for your Posadas party or to take home for decorations. Students might want to make a piñata and fill it with small treats as a present for a younger brother or sister. A piñata also makes a dramatic gift container for an adult. (See directions for making a piñata on page 102.)

Making a Piñata

Start to make your piñata a week or more before your party to allow plenty of time for it to dry.

Materials:

- a large balloon
- newspaper
- flour and water paste (equal parts)
- glue
- poster paints
- other decorations like paper streamers and glitter
- string
- lots of wrapped candies, small toys, and coins

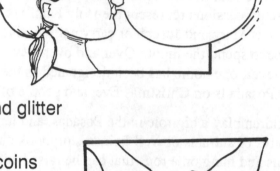

Directions:

1. Cover a work area with newspaper. You can use a table or the floor.

2. Blow up the balloon and tie it securely.

3. Tear newspaper into strips about 2 inches (5 cm) wide. Dip each strip in the paste, draw it between two of your fingers to wipe off excess paste, and smooth the strip around the balloon. Repeat until the whole balloon is covered with newspaper strips.

4. Let the papier-mâché covered balloon dry. Then repeat the whole process twice to make a strong piñata that will hold a lot of goodies.

5. When the papier-mâché is completely dry, pop the balloon inside with a pin. Cut a hole, about 5 inches (13 cm) in diameter, in the top of your piñata. Remove the balloon. Fasten string to either side of the hole to make a handle.

6. Paint and decorate your piñata. Fill with your choice of treats or use as a gift box.

The Winter Solstice

December 21 or 22

The winter solstice is the shortest day of the year in the northern hemisphere. It occurs exactly six months after the summer solstice, the longest day of the year. The farther north you go, the fewer hours of daylight you will have. If you go far enough north, there will be days when there is no sunlight at all. (This process is reversed in the southern hemisphere.)

The approaching winter solstice was once a frightening time for ancient people, especially those who lived in places like northern Europe. They did not have a scientific explanation for the shorter days and longer nights. They were afraid that the sun was losing its power, so they made up tales to explain what was happening and performed rituals to save the sun and restore its strength. They were certain that these rituals worked because — sure enough! — the sun then became stronger and stronger and the nights shorter and shorter. They eventually had to repeat this process, but it worked every time.

Making It Work

Have students write a story in the form of a myth or folktale explaining the reason for the shortening days and lengthening nights of winter. Illustrate, share, and display these stories in your classroom. (See page 104.)

Have students meet in cooperative groups to design their own appropriate rituals for making the days start to get long again. The entire class can come together and perform their rituals for one another. Discuss the rituals and their effect on the seasons. Did the rituals work? How do you know? (If you did not know that the earth is tipped on its axis as it rotates around the sun, would your answer be different?)

Plan a winter solstice party as a whole-group activity. Pretend that money is not a concern and brainstorm ideas. Where would the party be? Who would you invite? What food would you serve? Would you have entertainment? Games?

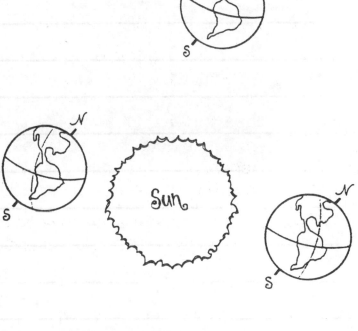

Name_____

Myth or Folktale

Read the Writing Situation and the Directions for Writing. Then write your piece on the lines provided.

Writing Situation

You are the official storyteller of a tribe of people living long ago in what is now northern Europe. Your people are very worried because the days are getting shorter and the nights are getting longer and longer. You must tell them a story that will explain these frightening events in terms they can understand.

Directions for Writing

Write your explanation for the situation described above. Make it an enjoyable and exciting story—something to be told at night around a campfire. Even though this will be a story that is meant to be told orally, organize your ideas so they will be clear to the reader. Use correct grammar, punctuation, and spelling.

_____

_____

_____

_____

_____

_____

_____

_____

_____

_____

_____

_____

_____

Name_____

Explaining the Winter Solstice *(cont.)*

The winter solstice is related to three other important days in the year: the summer solstice, the spring equinox, and the autumn equinox. While the winter solstice is the shortest day of the year and the summer solstice is the longest, both the spring and autumn equinoxes have days and nights that are exactly equal. They each have exactly twelve hours of daylight and darkness.

Use the space below to draw a diagram that explains this. You may consult an encyclopedia, your science book, or any other reference book you would like to use.

Christmas, the Birth of Jesus Christ

December 25

Christmas, the celebration of the birth of Jesus Christ, really begins with Christmas Eve on December 24th. Many families attend church, exchange presents, and enjoy their main family feast on the night before Christmas. It was on Christmas Eve that Mary and Joseph found refuge in a stable in Bethlehem, and it was on Christmas Eve that the angels were said to have appeared to shepherds tending their flocks outside Bethlehem to announce the birth of the Christ Child. It was also on Christmas Eve that the animals are said to have spoken. (Indeed, some people believe that they still talk at the stroke of midnight on that night!) And it is on Christmas Eve that Santa Claus delivers his gifts by a reindeer-powered sleigh around the world.

Although many families celebrate on Christmas Eve, many more save their main celebration for Christmas Day. Santa has come, the children get up, gifts are opened, people go to church, and the extended-family arrives. Some variation of this happens in homes all over the world.

Making It Work

Have students trace the development of Santa Claus as he is known today. Find out from where he came, how he dressed, what he was called, and how he became the Santa we know.

Have students research the other "gift givers" connected with Christmas. Some names to look up include Grandpa Koleda, Julemanden, Juletompte, Grandmother Babushka, Befana, Kristkind, Father Christmas, Le Pere Noel, and Papa Noel. Many of these good gift-givers travel with mean companions who threaten bad children. Find out their names, too.

Have students discover how Christmas is celebrated in countries of the southern hemisphere where the seasons are the reverse of the northern.

Read students a legend of the first Christmas tree. (You will find many versions. A nice one is "How the Fir Tree Became the Christmas Tree" by Hedwig Liebkind in *An American Christmas* edited by Peg Streep.) Then have students write legends of their own. Use these legends, which students can illustrate for a bulletin board display and later bind into a book to add to your classroom library.

Ask students to share the ways in which they celebrate Christmas and tell from what countries their customs come. Some people with several ethnic backgrounds have developed very rich celebrations by combining the customs of several countries.

For your classroom holiday party, ask each student to bring cookies reflecting his or her ethnic background. Have a cookie exchange, allowing each student to take home a selection of cookies from different cultures. Provide bags for the cookies.

French Door Hanger

The French way of saying Merry Christmas is "Joyeux Noel." If your heritage is French, this door hanging will reflect it.

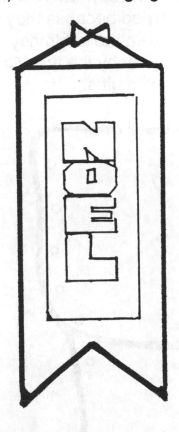

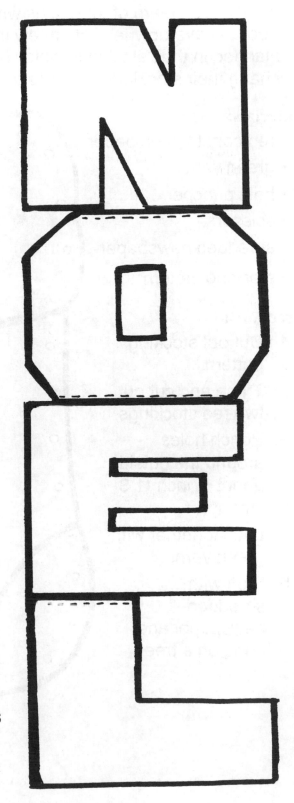

Materials:

- Noel pattern
- red and green construction paper
- string
- glue
- scissors

Directions:

1. Cut out the letter patterns.
2. Trace the letters on green paper and cut out.
3. Glue the letters on red paper strip (as illustrated) and decorate.
4. Glue string to the top.
5. Hang on a tree or door.

Stockings from Turkey

The custom of hanging stockings on Christmas Eve comes from a story about St. Nicholas who was then the bishop of Myra in what is now Turkey. St. Nicholas, so the story goes, heard of three girls who could not get married because they were too poor to have dowries. He threw three bags of gold down their chimney. The gold landed in their stockings which had been hung up to dry by the fire. Children now hang their stockings in hopes that they will be filled with gifts.

Materials:

- red construction paper
- green yarn
- hole puncher
- scissors
- shredded newspaper
- stocking pattern

Directions:

1. Cut out stocking pattern.
2. Trace and cut out two red stockings.
3. Punch holes around the outside about ½ inch (1.3 cm) apart.
4. Lace together with green yarn.
5. Stuff with shredded newspaper and hang on a tree.

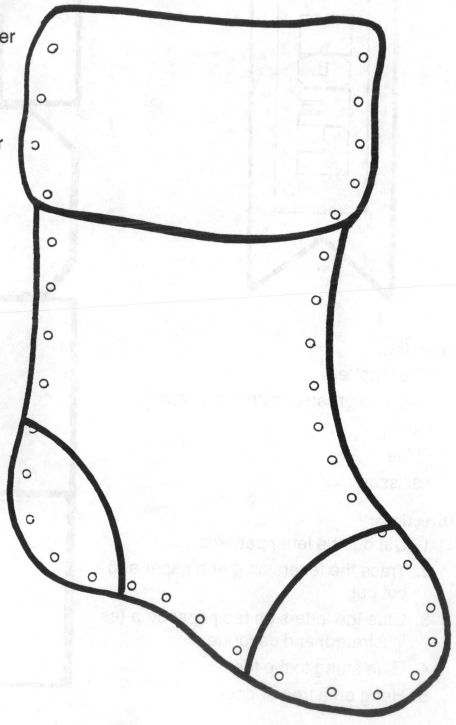

Christmas Trees from Germany

The Christmas tree began as a custom in Germany. There are many legends that tell from where the first tree came. See how many different legends you can find. Then, make the special Christmas trees below.

Materials:

- black construction paper
- green or red tissue paper
- scissors
- glue
- transparent tape

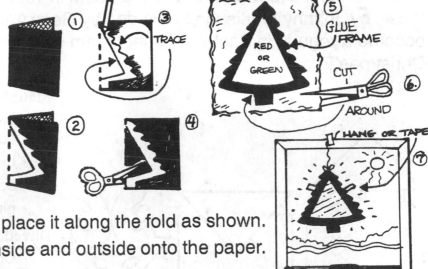

Directions:

1. Fold black paper in half.
2. Cut out tree pattern and place it along the fold as shown.
3. Trace the pattern both inside and outside onto the paper.
4. Cut out the tree "frame."
5. Glue the frame on top of red or green tissue.
6. Trim the tissue around the outer edges so that it doesn't go beyond the frame.
7. Hang on the windows using transparent tape. The light will shine through giving them a stained-glass effect.
8. You can repeat this process using other shapes as well, such as stars and snowmen.

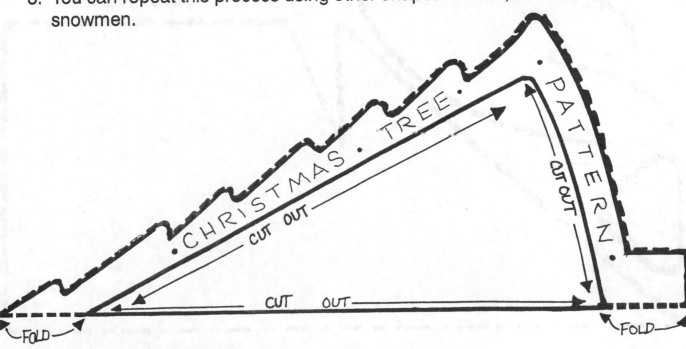

Rudolph: An American Christmas Character

Rudolph is one of the very few home-grown additions to Christmas found in the United States. He was invented in a poem in 1938 by a man named May, set to music by Johnny Marks, and recorded by Gene Autry in 1949. He has since become a regular in Santa's reindeer team which needs him to light the way on Christmas Eve.

Materials:

- brown (dark and light), red, and white construction paper
- black crayon or marker
- scissors
- glue

Directions:

Cut out all pattern pieces. Trace and cut out two white eyes; color pupils in each. Trace and cut out two dark brown antlers. Trace and cut out one red nose. Trace and cut out one light brown head and neck, placing the pattern along a fold; unfold. Fold the head down as illustrated. Glue on eyes, nose, and antlers. Roll neck back and glue as illustrated.

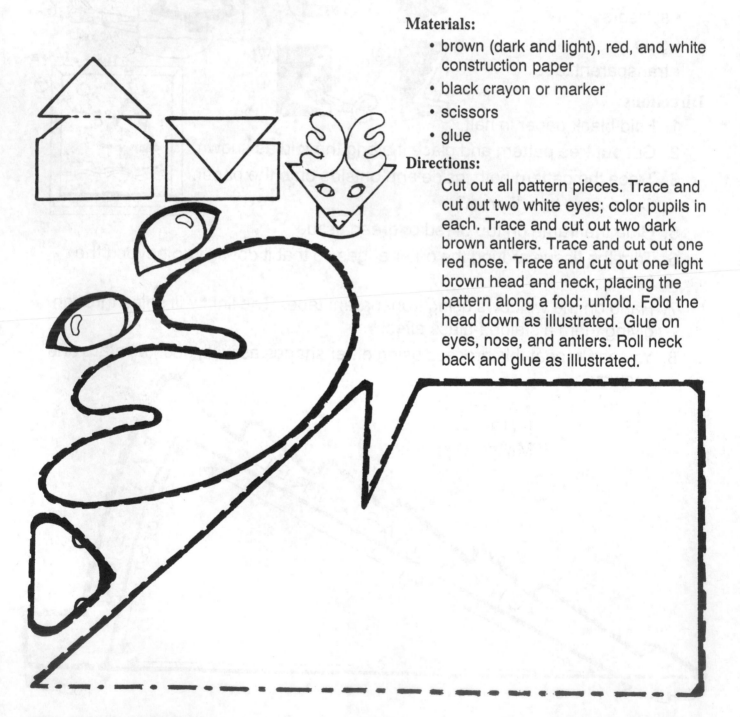

Peanut Butter Macaroons

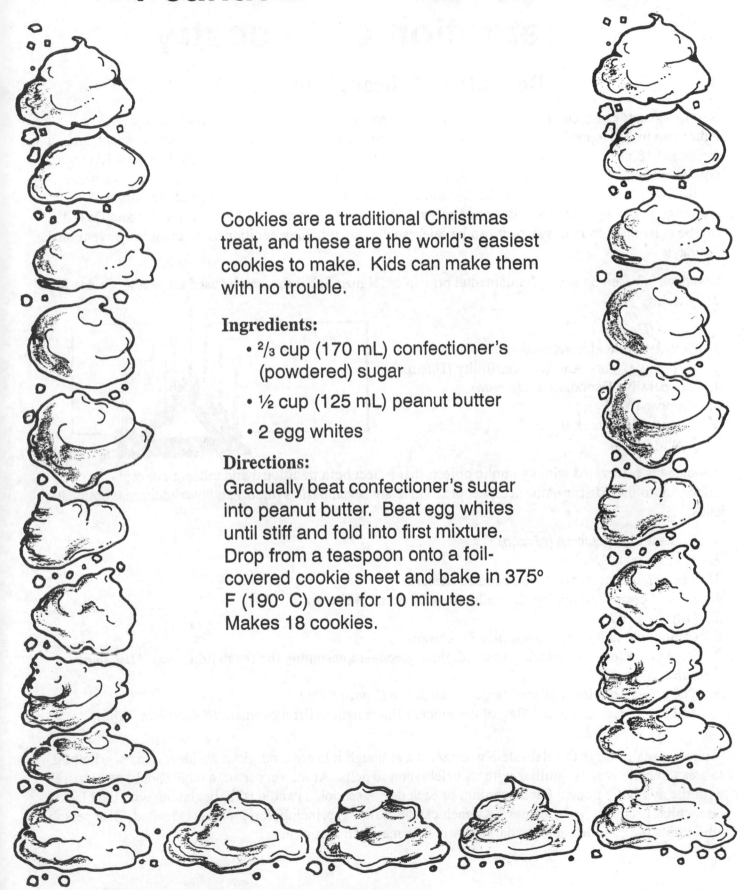

Cookies are a traditional Christmas treat, and these are the world's easiest cookies to make. Kids can make them with no trouble.

Ingredients:

- ²/₃ cup (170 mL) confectioner's (powdered) sugar
- ½ cup (125 mL) peanut butter
- 2 egg whites

Directions:

Gradually beat confectioner's sugar into peanut butter. Beat egg whites until stiff and fold into first mixture. Drop from a teaspoon onto a foil-covered cookie sheet and bake in 375° F (190° C) oven for 10 minutes. Makes 18 cookies.

Kwanzaa, the African-American Celebration of Ancestry

December 26 through January 1

Kwanzaa is an example of a cultural holiday. It is not religious, political, or heroic. It is uniquely American in its recognition of the cultural foundation common to Americans of African descent, and an estimated 18 million people observe the holiday each year. It was originated by Dr. Maulana Karenga, now chairman of the black studies department at California State University, Long Beach. The name itself, Kwanzaa, is taken from the Ki-Swahili language and means "the first fruits of the harvest." Although it was not purposely designed as a substitute for Christmas and New Year's Eve and Day, it can be celebrated in that way or it can be celebrated as an enriching addition to other more conventional holidays.

Kwanzaa is based on seven fundamental principles (Nguzo Saba) that can be used all year as guides for daily living.

1. Unity *(Umoja)*
2. Self-determination *(Kujichagulia)*
3. Collective Work And Responsibility *(Ujima)*
4. Cooperative Economics *(Ujamaa)*
5. Purpose *(Nia)*
6. Creativity *(Kuumba)*
7. Faith *(Imani)*

Kwanzaa is celebrated with symbolic objects that reflect both traditional and modern concepts important to the African-American people. There are seven basic symbols and two additional optional ones.

1. Fruits and vegetables *(Mazao)*
2. A place mat *(Mkeka)*
3. The candle holder for seven candles *(Kinara)*
4. Ears of corn symbolizing the children in the home *(Vibunzi)*
5. Gifts *(Zawadi)*
6. Communal unity cup *(Kikombe Cha Umoja)*
7. Seven candles—one black, three red, three green—representing the seven principles *(Mishumaa Saba)*
8. The seven principles printed large for all to see *(Nguzo Saba)*
9. The black, red, and green flag of the modern Black nationalist movement *(Bendera ya Taifa)*

There are many ways to celebrate Kwanzaa, and although it is not a religious holiday, it may be helpful to ask someone who is familiar with its celebration to help. At the very least, a table should be prepared with the symbolic items. Each evening, or each day in school, a candle is lit, beginning with the black one which is placed in the center. As each candle is lit, the principle it represents is recited. The person who lights the candle can tell what that principle means to him or her.

Kwanzaa, the African American Celebration of Ancestry *(cont.)*

A feast, the Kwanzaa Karumu, is held on the night of December 31st. People who plan to celebrate New Year's Eve hold the feast earlier in the evening. The table is decorated with the symbolic items, and the gifts, which should be educational and creative and given as a reward for merit, are exchanged. The feast itself usually consists of chicken, fish, rice, yams or sweet potatoes, and other vegetables. Everyone should make some contribution to the feast, bringing a cooked dish or something else that will add to the feast.

The place where the feast is held, whether it is in a school, a church, a community center, or at home, should be decorated. The decorations should be ethnic and reflect the use of the symbolic colors: black, red, and green. The entertainment, which can go on throughout the feast, should consist of African music, dances, stories, and chants. The celebrants are encouraged to wear ethnic clothing and hairstyles.

Making It Work

Create a Kwanzaa setting in the classroom. Ask students to bring symbolic items from home or create them from ordinary classroom materials.

Turn a piece of driftwood, or even scrap lumber that has been sanded and painted, into a candleholder by gluing on long tacks upside-down. Simply stick the tack points into the bottoms of the candles.

Make placemats from woven strips of paper. Each student can make one for his or her desk in preparation for a feast. Use black, red, and green construction paper.

Have students print the "seven principles" on poster board and illustrate them. Place these posters around the classroom.

Ask groups of students to research, plan, and rehearse African songs and/or dances and perform them for their own class and for other classes.

Plan a Kwanzaa Karamu (feast). Use all of the decorations and the entertainment your students have created. Assign different dishes to groups of students or individuals. (See page 115.) Create appropriate invitations and invite the students' parents or another class to join you for the celebration.

Allow students to create gifts for one another and/or for the guests. Since Kwanzaa strives to de-emphasize commercialism, the gifts should be made by the students and should reflect crafts that are relevant to the African heritage.

Prepare and learn one or more African games to play during your party or at free times during school. (See page 114.)

Kalah

The Arabs call this game Kalah. They brought it to Africa where it has many different names. In East Africa, it is called Mankala. In West Africa, it is called Owara. In South Africa, it is known as Ohora.

You can make this game out of an empty egg carton. Look at the diagram below. The end sections are the Kalahs. Each player's Kalah is on his or her right. These sections count as cups during the game.

Materials:

- empty egg carton
- dried beans
- scissors
- tape or glue

Directions:

1. Build the game board by separating the top and bottom of the egg carton. Cut the top section in half and affix each half to a side of the bottom section (see illustration).

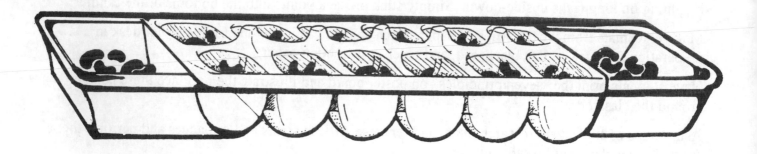

2. Play starts when the players put three beans into each of the cups on their own sides.

3. The first player begins by taking all of the beans out of one of his or her cups, and moving to the right, drops one bean into each of the next three cups. (Remember, the Kalah counts as a cup after play begins.)

4. If the first player is able to drop the third bean into his or her own Kalah, he/she gets another turn. If the last (third) bean does not end up in his/her own Kalah, it becomes the other player's turn.

5. Players continue to take turns trying to get as many beans as possible into his/her own Kalah, until all the cups on one player's side are empty.

6. The winner is the player with the most beans in his or her Kalah.

Sweet Potato Pie

The sweet potato is grown for its sweet, edible roots in the warm tropical areas of Africa and America. Sweet potatoes were grown in colonial Virginia as long ago as the early 1600's. George Washington Carver, the American scientist who experimented with uses for the peanut, also discovered many uses for the sweet potato. Sweet potato pie is often served in the United States, especially in the Deep South.

Ingredients:

- 3 eggs
- 1 cup (250 mL) brown sugar, firmly packed
- 1 teaspoon (5 mL) salt
- ½ teaspoon (3 mL) cinnamon
- ½ teaspoon (3 mL) nutmeg
- ½ teaspoon (3 mL) ginger
- ¼ teaspoon (1 mL) cloves
- 2 cups (500 mL) canned sweet potatoes, drained and mashed
- 1 cup (250 mL) evaporated milk or half and half
- 1 unbaked 9-inch (23 cm) pastry shell

Directions:

1. Beat the eggs with the sugar, salt, and spices in a large bowl. Stir in the sweet potatoes and milk and mix well. Pour the mixture into the unbaked pastry shell.

2. Bake in a preheated 350° F (180° C) oven for 1 hour and 15 minutes or until set.

3. Cool to room temperature. Serve plain or with ice cream or whipped cream.

4. Garnish with pecans, if desired.

New Year's Eve

December 31

Most of the western world celebrates New Year's Eve on December 31st according to the Gregorian solar calendar. Many people in Asia, who follow their own lunar calendar and celebrate their own New Year, also recognize the New Year of the solar calendar with an additional celebration.

Our New Year's Eve customs come from all over. People make noise like the Danes. They bang pots and pans together and sing "Auld Lang Syne" like the Scots. They drink a toast like the early Anglo-Saxons. And they refrain from doing things they don't want to do in the New Year like the Germans.

The custom of making New Year's resolutions goes back all the way to the ancient Romans. The month of January is named for the Roman god, Janus. Janus had two faces so he could look both ways at once. He was the god of doorways and beginnings and endings, a perfect symbol for an old year that was ending and a new one that was beginning. The ancient Romans honored Janus by making promises to him when they started the New Year. When we make resolutions, we make promises too, but now we make them to ourselves.

Almost everyone either stays up until midnight or tries to. At the stroke of midnight, people shout, "Happy New Year!" and hug each other. The telephone lines all over the United States are jammed as people call those they could not be with for the New Year.

Of course, not everyone has a party on New Year's Eve. Some people observe the New Year as a religious occasion. They attend church services and think about what they can do to be better during the next twelve months.

But somehow or another, whether they go to church or to a party, people recognize the chance for a new beginning.

Making It Work

Go over the customs associated with New Year's Eve when the students come back to school in January. Discuss customs that they may have in their own families.

Talk about resolutions. Brainstorm for help in generating ideas, but let each student decide on his or her own resolution(s). This can be a stressful experience for some students. All of them might find it less threatening to start their resolutions with words like "This year I plan to...." Many students will want to keep their resolutions private. If you use portfolios, they can put their written resolutions away in their portfolios and refer to them as they may wish.

My New Year's Resolution

Use the space below to write your resolution for the New Year.

Name _____ Date _____

This year I plan to _____

_____

_____

_____

_____

_____

_____

New Year's Day

January 1

January 1st is the first day of the year on the Gregorian calendar. The date of the New Year has moved around several times, but it settled at last on the day Julius Caesar had picked for it in about 40 B.C.

New Year's Day is a day of new beginnings. People indulge themselves in superstitions about lucky things to do and lucky foods to eat. For example, a food superstition that originated in America's Deep South is that it is lucky to eat black-eyed peas on New Year's Day. Some people go even farther and say that it is unlucky not to eat them. Other people believe that whatever you do on New Year's Day, you will do all year. These people are careful to do only things that make them happy.

The way in which New Year's Day is celebrated has changed since the middle of the twentieth century when television became a part of our lives. It used to be a day for visiting with friends and family. Now, it is often devoted to televised parades and sports, especially football in the United States. The Rose Bowl Parade in Pasadena, California has become almost synonymous with New Year's Day, as have the various Bowl Games played around the country. This can be a very festive way to spend the day except, of course, for people who really don't like parades or football games.

Making It Work

Have students write brief accounts of how they like to spend New Year's Eve and New Year's Day. Share these as a class and discuss. Do you do anything really different? Is this a family holiday in your home? Did you have any special things to eat?

Students might enjoy making New Year's cards for their families. Talk about the Roman god Janus and display an artist's idea of how he might have looked. There are all kinds of interesting interpretations of this "two-faced" god. Janus is a wonderful symbol to put on a New Year's card.

Run off copies of the calendar on page 119 and plan to give students fresh new ones each month. If you use a date book to plan your time, model the activity for them. They can three-hole-punch their monthly calendar and keep it in the front part of an often-used binder.

Keeping a Monthly Calendar

Enter very small numbers for the dates in January on this calendar and use the rest of each day's square to plan your time.

	Saturday	Friday	Thursday	Wednesday	Tuesday	Monday	Sunday

Twelfth Night and Epiphany, the Coming of the Magi

January 5 and 6

If you start counting from Christmas night, the "Twelfth Night" is the fifth of January. It is the Eve of the Epiphany, the holy day celebrating the arrival of the three Wise Men, also called the Three Kings or the Magi, who saw the star in the East and followed it to Bethlehem. Their names, according to Christian tradition, were Balthaser, Melchior, and Gasper. The gold, frankincense, and myrrh that they brought to give to the Christ Child are remembered as the first Christmas gifts. Because of this, children in many countries leave food for the Kings' camels on Twelfth Night and find gifts in the morning.

Children in Italy still sometimes receive gifts in the morning following the Twelfth Night. The legend surrounding this custom has it that when the Three Wise Men were going to Bethlehem they stopped to ask for directions. An old woman named Befana was too busy doing housework to stop and help them. When she finally finished, she tried to catch up with them, but they were too far ahead. She is still looking for them, and on her way she leaves gifts for children on the chance that one of them might be the Christ child.

In the United States, Twelfth Night and Epiphany are celebrated mostly by churches as part of the religious ritual surrounding Christmas. In some churches, the figures of the Wise Men are moved up close to the manger in the Christmas scene or creche in order to mark the occasion. In addition, there are also some families who have discovered ways to adapt many customs associated with Twelfth Night and/or Epiphany to create a happy ending to their Christmas season. One tradition is that all Christmas decorations must be taken down and put away at this time. This is, in effect, the opposite of a tree-trimming party. Another tradition gives the name Little Christmas to these days, and some people exchange small gifts to end the season. Still another tradition promises that the person who finds the coin (or the bean) that is baked into a special cake will have good luck all year.

Making It Work

Have students share their experiences with Twelfth Night and Epiphany. If they celebrate Christmas, do they or their families have a special way of bringing the season to an end?

Ask each student to draw the name of a "secret friend" in the class. Have students make and exchange greeting cards with their secret friends. The cards should express good wishes for the year ahead. (See page 121.)

Each student should choose a favorite custom from the winter holiday he or she celebrates and write a legend explaining how that custom originated. (See page 122.) A scoring rubric is provided on page 26.

Snowflake Card

Materials:
- white tissue paper
- scissors
- dark blue construction paper

Directions:

1. Fold a small sheet of white tissue paper in half and then in thirds.

2. Round the bottom edge with your scissors.

3. Cut fancy shapes in from the outside edges. Be careful not to cut all the way through to the opposite sides.

4. Unfold carefully to reveal a snowflake.

5. Fold dark blue construction paper into a card shape.

6. Carefully glue your snowflake on the front.

7. Write your message inside the card.

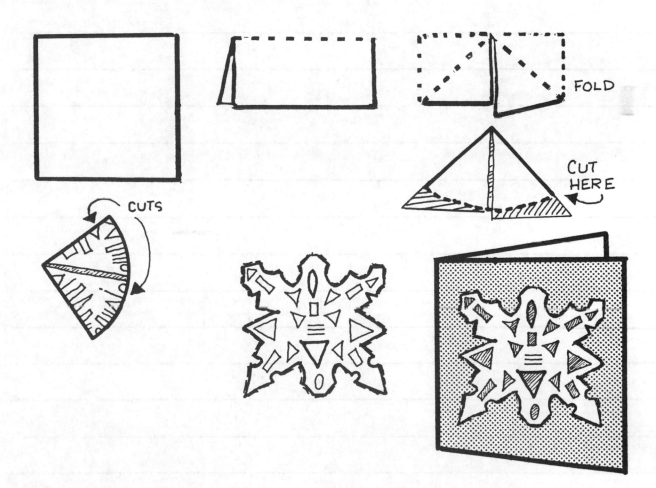

A Holiday Legend

Read the Writing Situation and the Directions for Writing. Then write your piece on the lines provided.

Writing Situation

A small child has asked you to explain how your favorite holiday custom came to be. You have always just taken this custom for granted, but now you want to think of a way to explain it that will make both you and the child happy.

Directions for Writing

Think of a way to explain how the custom came to be. Be careful not to spoil the custom for the child or for yourself with your explanation. Organize your ideas so they will be clear to the reader. Use correct grammar, punctuation, and spelling.

_____

_____

_____

_____

_____

_____

_____

_____

_____

_____

_____

_____

_____

Pongol, the Indian Rice Harvest Festival

January 14

Pongol is the great Rice Harvest Festival held in many parts of India. It lasts for three days and includes ceremonies of thanksgiving for the sun and rain that make the rice grow. The rice harvest is very important in India because rice is the main food crop of the area, as it is in most of Asia. Other important products are spices and tea. Half of the world's tea comes from India.

The local cattle are included in the Pongol festivities. They are bathed, painted, and garlanded with flowers. They are also fed a special mixture made from the newly harvested rice that has been cooked in milk. Cattle are considered sacred by most people in India. They are allowed to wander as they please and are treated with great respect.

Many people in India follow the Hindu religion or one of the other religions that have developed from it, such as Buddhism. An important part of these religions is respect for all life. This explains why many Hindus are vegetarians and why their cattle are treated with such respect.

People of Indian background who are now living elsewhere, adapt their celebrations in different ways. If they are members of the Hindu religion, they can experience their culture and share their rituals in temples. Others may invite friends and relatives to celebrations held in the home. There, they can at least serve the traditional foods that people miss when they are away from their homeland.

Making It Work

Show a video of India to your class. Preview it to make sure it shows the process of planting and harvesting rice.

Have students do research to find the answers to these and similar questions:

- Why are the rice fields flooded?
- From where does the water for flooding come?
- What is a monsoon?
- How are the rice seedlings planted?
- How is rice harvested?

The people of India wear distinctive traditional costumes. Find pictures of people dressed in these costumes.

Invite experts to come to your classroom and show the girls how to wrap a sari and the boys how to wrap a turban.

Indian Miniatures

After studying the customs and traditions
of Pongol, sketch small pictures
featuring them. (Use half of a page-size
sheet of paper.)

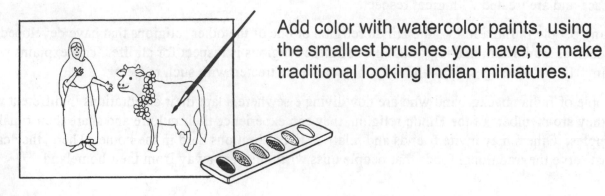

Add color with watercolor paints, using
the smallest brushes you have, to make
traditional looking Indian miniatures.

Allow your picture to dry, and then use
metallic crayons to design an elaborate
border for your picture.

Bind all pictures done by the class into
an album for display and later inclusion
in your classroom library.

Sol-Nal, the Korean New Year

Between January 21 and February 20, or January 1

Although many Koreans celebrate the New Year on January 1st, most have traditionally celebrated this important holiday according to the lunar calendar. Just recently, the Korean government made the Lunar New Year's Day celebration an official 3-day holiday and named it Sol-Nal.

People from Korea, like people from other Asian countries, make elaborate preparations for this holiday. They cook, clean, pay off debts, shop for gifts, and make traditional costumes (called han-bok) for themselves and their children. Most of the Korean New Year's celebration is centered in the home, preferably the home of the oldest member of an extended family. It involves ceremonies that honor both departed ancestors and family elders as well as a feast consisting of a variety of festive foods. On the second or third day, adults visit friends and family and also receive visitors. The children play games such as top-spinning and kite flying. Young girls enjoy a game called Korean seesawing. This involves bouncing on the ends of a long plank placed over a rolled straw mat, and it is rather dangerous. People of all ages play games with special decks of cards. Formerly, the celebration of the New Year lasted for many days, ending with the first full-moon festival, Tae-Bo-Rum.

Making It Work

Introduce the idea of making a family tree. (This fits right in with many units in the social studies curriculum.) Have students consult older family members to obtain brief biographical sketches of each person on the family tree. If this is not possible, they can try to get dates and maiden names. Pictures are wonderful additions. Ask students to make copies of the pictures for classroom display so you won't be responsible for family treasures that cannot be replaced. Have students design their own family tree presentation or use the one on the page that follows. If you have access to a machine that enlarges copies, you may want to make a bigger tree. Use completed family trees to create a bulletin board with a title such as "Our Ancestors."

Research/discuss the role of ancestors in the Buddhist tradition.

Have students do some research to find out what the traditional Korean costume (han-bok) looks like. If you have Korean students in your class, they may be able to bring examples. Students can draw small pictures of people in these costumes, color them with water colors, and mount them on the front of their own personally designed New Year's greeting cards.

Introduce students to old-fashioned top-spinning. Have a top-spinning contest.

Make (or buy) kites. Have a kite-flying contest. Invite other classes to join you. Give small prizes and serve refreshments.

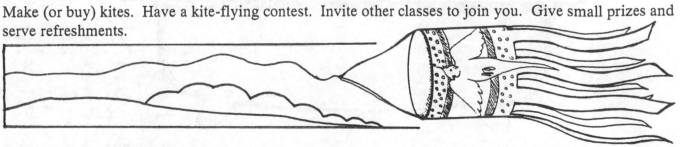

The Family Tree

Sun Nin, the Chinese New Year

Between January 21 and February 20

Chinese New Year is a movable holiday because it is celebrated according to dates on the ancient Chinese lunar calendar. It occurs sometime between January 21st and February 20th, and the celebration may last for a week. Each year is named after one of the twelve animals on the Chinese zodiac. It is said that a person born in a year dedicated to a particular animal will have that animal's characteristics.

Chinese families make great preparations for the new year. Everything must be very clean. Special foods are prepared. New clothes are purchased. Debts are paid. Everyone gets ready to start out fresh and new. Red and orange are the special colors used for decorations, and there are scrolls everywhere with good wishes written in Chinese characters: Good Health, Long Life, Luck, Prosperity, Happiness.

This day is also everyone's birthday party because Chinese people add a year to their age on this day no matter when they were born. Gifts are given. The children, who are encouraged to stay up as late as they can on New Year's Eve, receive gifts of money wrapped in red paper. At midnight firecrackers are lit to scare away the bad spirits.

On New Year's Day everyone is very careful to be good and polite because they believe that the way they act will affect the whole year to come. They visit friends and relatives and attend community celebrations. They may see the lion dance and the dragon parade, both of which bring good luck and prosperity. They say "Gung hay fat choy!" which means, "Happy New Year!"

Making It Work

Invite Chinese students to tell how this holiday is celebrated in their homes. Explore the possibility of asking one of the parents who lived in China to speak to your class about how the Chinese New Year holiday has been adapted for celebration in the United States.

Use the Chinese zodiac to find out the animal that matches each person's birth year. Have each student write a description of that animal's characteristics. (See Chinese zodiac following.)

Learn to write the Chinese characters for "Gung Hay Fat Choy" and make scrolls to decorate the classroom. (See illustrations following.)

Make lion and dragon heads with boxes, paint, and paper. Practice dancing and making a dragon parade. Entertain other classrooms or perform at a school assembly.

Give a New Year's party. Invite parents as guests or ask them to help. Oranges and apples are traditional refreshments. Fortune cookies are always fun. Find a recipe and make your own with fortunes that are appropriate for the students.

Chinese Lunar Calendar and Horoscope

The Chinese Lunar Calendar is a 12-year cycle with a different animal representing each of the 12 years. The animals are believed to influence the year's events as well as the personalities of the people born in that year. Cut out the pieces below and arrange them in a circular calendar that is read counterclockwise, beginning with the rat. Glue the calendar onto another sheet of paper. Use the clues in the Clue Box to help you.

Clue Box

1-rat-1996-thrifty. 8-sheep-2003-artistic. 3-tiger-2010-love of life. 10-rooster-1969-organized.

12-boar-2007-gallant. 9-monkey-1980-clever. 5-dragon-2000-energetic. 11-dog-1994-loyal.

7-horse-1966-talkative. 2-ox-1973-calm. 4-rabbit-1987-peaceful. 6-snake-1977-in-born wisdom.

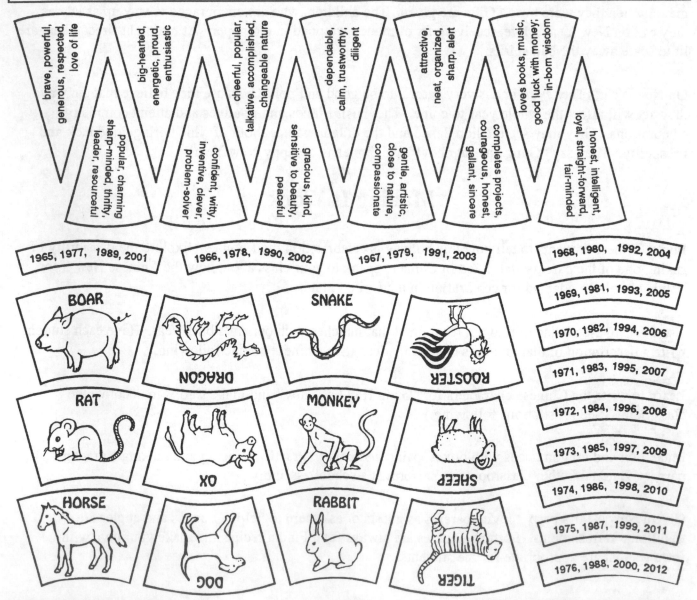

Gung Hay Fat Choy Scroll

Gung Hay Fat Choy means Happy New Year in Chinese. Make a banner that says Happy New Year in Chinese characters. You may use the characters provided below, or you can write the characters yourself. You may want to practice, first tracing along the lines, then drawing the characters freehand in the space provided. You may use paint, markers, or crayons. Use red paper for the background. Glue strips of black paper on the ends to make it look like a scroll.

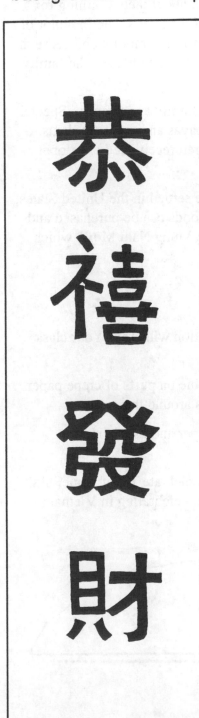  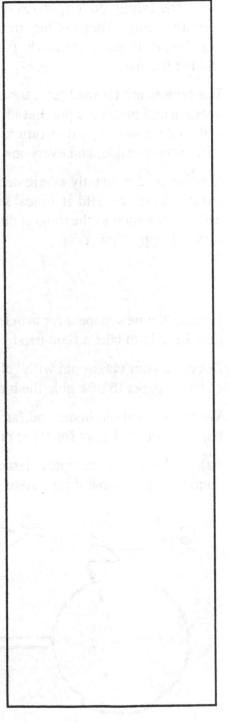

Tet, the Vietnamese New Year

Between January 21 and February 20

Tet is the name of the Vietnamese New Year festival. For the Vietnamese, like the Chinese, the New Year is the most important event of the year. Vietnamese people who are living outside of Vietnam try to reproduce as many of the traditional ceremonies as they can manage.

It is important for families to be together, and of course this is the hardest part for people who have left their families behind in their homeland. People write poems, called *cau doi*, about their yearning for home and family on long strips of red paper and hang them on either side of the altar set up in honor of their ancestors. They put pictures of their ancestors on the altar along with some symbolic objects such as coins, fruit, and candles. Prayers are offered at midnight before this altar for members of the family and for friends.

The houses are cleaned from top to bottom and a great feast is prepared for family and friends. Special noodles and meats are purchased along with fruits such as mangoes and papayas and the ingredients to make rice cakes. The decorations are bong mai, plum blossoms. The children receive red envelopes with money inside, and everyone must be very nice to everyone else.

In some predominantly ethnic neighborhoods where many Vietnamese have settled in the United States, a festival may be held at a local school or shopping center. There, special foods can be purchased and ceremonies such as the dragon dance are performed. Everyone says, "Chuc Mung Nam Moi!" which means Happy New Year.

Making It Work

Consult the newspapers for articles about community events held in connection with Tet. Your class may be able to take a field trip to one of these.

Decorate your classroom with "plum blossoms." Take bare branches and glue on puffs of crepe paper or tissue paper to resemble the blossoms. Display your decorations in vases around the room.

Write poems about home and family. Copy these poems on strips of red paper and use them as a bulletin board display for other members of the class to read.

Ask students of Vietnamese descent to share the ways in which they might celebrate Tet at home. Ask them to explain how these celebrations differ from ones they may remember celebrating in Vietnam.

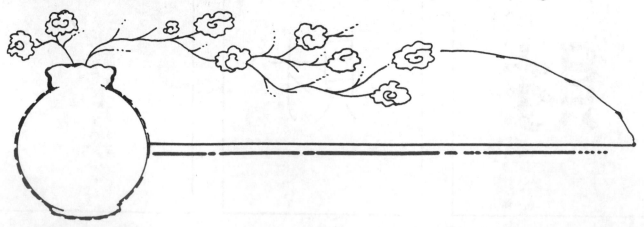

New Year's Dragon Puppet

Paste head here. →

Paste body (on page 132) here. →

New Year's Dragon Puppet (cont.)

Martin Luther King, Jr. Day

Third Monday in January

Dr. Martin Luther King, Jr. was born on January 15, 1929. He grew up in Atlanta, Georgia, with his older sister and younger brother. Martin attended segregated schools. He wanted to be a minister like his father so he studied very hard. He graduated from high school when he was only fifteen years old.

While Martin was at college, he read a book by Mohandas Gandhi. The book told how he used peaceful and nonviolent methods to free his people from British rule. Martin was very impressed with this book. Later, he was to use Gandhi's methods in his struggle to win equal rights for all people. Martin was also influenced by Thoreau's essay, "On Civil Disobedience."

After Martin graduated from college, he went to Boston University to study religion. He received a doctorate and became minister of a Baptist Church in Montgomery, Alabama. There, Martin, who was now called Dr. King, organized a boycott of the city buses to protest the arrest of Mrs. Rosa Parks. Rosa Parks had broken a "Jim Crow," or segregation, law, by refusing to move to the back of a bus. The boycott was successful, and finally the Supreme Court decided that the "Jim Crow" law was unconstitutional.

In order to help people use peaceful means to obtain equal rights, Dr. King formed the Southern Christian Leadership Conference (SCLC). In 1963, he led the March on Washington. The march ended at the Lincoln Memorial where he gave his famous "I Have A Dream" speech to the thousands of people who had marched there with him. Dr. King was awarded the Nobel Peace Prize in 1964. He was the youngest man ever to receive this award.

Dr. King was assassinated in Memphis, Tennessee, on April 4, 1968.

Making It Work

Read King's "I Have A Dream" speech to your class. Discuss the impact this speech had on the people who heard it.

Show a video of the "I Have A Dream" speech as delivered by King at the Lincoln Memorial. Discuss his power as an orator.

Have each student give a speech about a subject that is important to him/her.

Have students write about their dreams for the future.

Tell your students about Gandhi and his struggle to gain independence for India. If appropriate for your class, show the movie, Gandhi, or excerpts from it.

Tell students about Thoreau, what he thought, and how and where he lived.

I Have a Dream

Find a copy of Dr. King's most famous speech, "I Have a Dream . . ." Copy it, or your favorite parts, on the lines below. Memorize the lines that mean the most to you.

Name_____

Martin Luther King, Jr. Wordsearch

Find these terms in the wordsearch below that are associated with Dr. Martin Luther King, Jr. and his civil rights work.

brotherhood	Martin Luther King	nonviolence
I Have a Dream	integration	justice
segregation	peace	assassination
change	civil rights	Nobel Peace Prize
freedom	black Americans	equal rights

```
R J K A A C N O I T A R G E T N I
G N I K R E H T U L N I T R A M C
S O A G E C D M N S O A R E F E V
T I K F G A Z O E T N D K D E G T
H T H O I E Y C U V V J Q A G N E
G A N Q L P I B C P I I H E W A G
I G B R O T H E R H O O D L L H E
R E M C S T H G I R L I V I C C K
L R B U P X M O D E E R F Q Z A H
A G J A S S A S S I N A T I O N L
U E N O B E L P E A C E P R I Z E
Q S I H A V E A D R E A M C R C Z
E S N A C I R E M A K C A L B H M
```

Black History Month

February

Black History Month started in the United States in 1926 as Negro History Week. February had been decided upon because it was the birth month of both Abraham Lincoln and Frederick Douglass. Abraham Lincoln was the U.S. President who freed the slaves and Frederick Douglass was a black man who helped to smuggle slaves out of the South on the "underground railroad."

African Americans are descendants of the only group of people who did not come to America looking for freedom and a better place to live. They were captured by slave-traders and transported by force. They were torn away from their families and homes and sold to the highest bidder to spend their lives in slavery in the South. This period of captivity went on for over two hundred years, so the black people who were freed from slavery during the Civil War had been effectively separated form their heritage by both distance and time. Reclaiming this lost heritage is a major issue among African Americans today.

The historical roots of the descendants of black slaves in the United States can be traced back to the ancient kingdoms of Mali, Ghana, and Saonghai in central and west Africa. These kingdoms were rich in art, literature, and music. This historical reality was purposefully suppressed to support the pro-slavery moral position that depended on the acceptance of the idea that blacks were less than human. This same idea provided a rationalization for the moral position of segregationists and still supports the position of anti-Civil Rights activists. Students need this information. It is also important for them to have the information that many people of the world, at some point in their history, were slaves.

Making It Work

Have students research the major periods other than slavery that influenced African-American culture. These periods are the Civil War, the Reconstruction period, the Harlem Renaissance, segregation, and the civil rights movement. Students should find a description of the period, the dates, and the names of people associated with it. Knowledge of these periods provides the necessary background for reading African-American literature with understanding.

Divide students into groups to research and report on the African kingdoms of Mali, Ghana, and Saonghai.

Have students prepare worksheets to test one another's knowledge of Frederick Douglass and the Underground Railroad. The worksheets may be wordsearches, crossword puzzles, word scrambles, or sets of true/false, matching, or multiple choice questions.

As a class project, make a slavery time line showing different groups of people who have been enslaved and the people who enslaved them.

Make and display African tribal masks as described on pages 137-138.

African Tribal Masks

African tribal masks are regarded as pieces of art as well as symbols of rituals. In Africa, they are carved of wood, but you can make one of paper.

Materials:
- a box, corrugated paper, or heavy paper
- scissors
- newspapers
- glue and water
- masking tape
- tempera paint and paintbrushes
- miscellaneous decorations

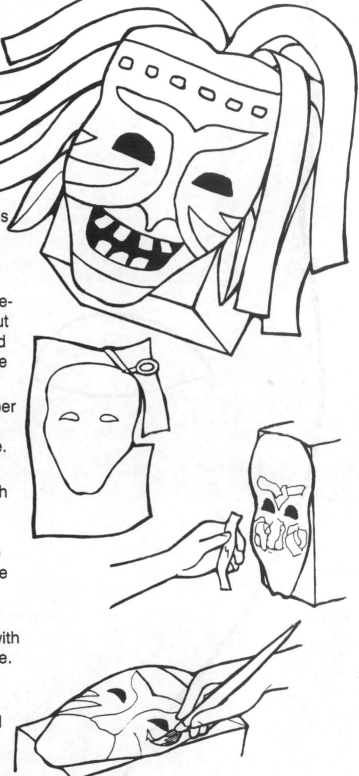

Directions:

1. Look through books to find some examples of various types of African tribal masks. Decide how you would like your finished product to look.

2. Use an inverted box for the base of a three-dimensional mask. For a flat mask, cut out the pattern from page 138 from corrugated or heavy paper. Don't forget to cut out eye holes.

3. Cut shapes from corrugated or heavy paper to extend the mask or make a headdress. Attach the extra pieces with masking tape.

4. To smooth out corners and edges of the mask and to build up facial features, crush pieces of paper to the right shapes and sizes. Hold them in place with strips of newspaper dipped in thin glue. (To make thin glue, mix equal amounts of white glue and water.)

5. When you have constructed the mask to your satisfaction, cover the whole thing with more newspaper strips dipped in thin glue. Allow it to dry thoroughly.

6. Paint your mask with tempera paint. Decorate it with feathers, stones from old costume jewelry, and fabric decorations such as rickrack or sequins.

African Tribal Masks *(cont.)*

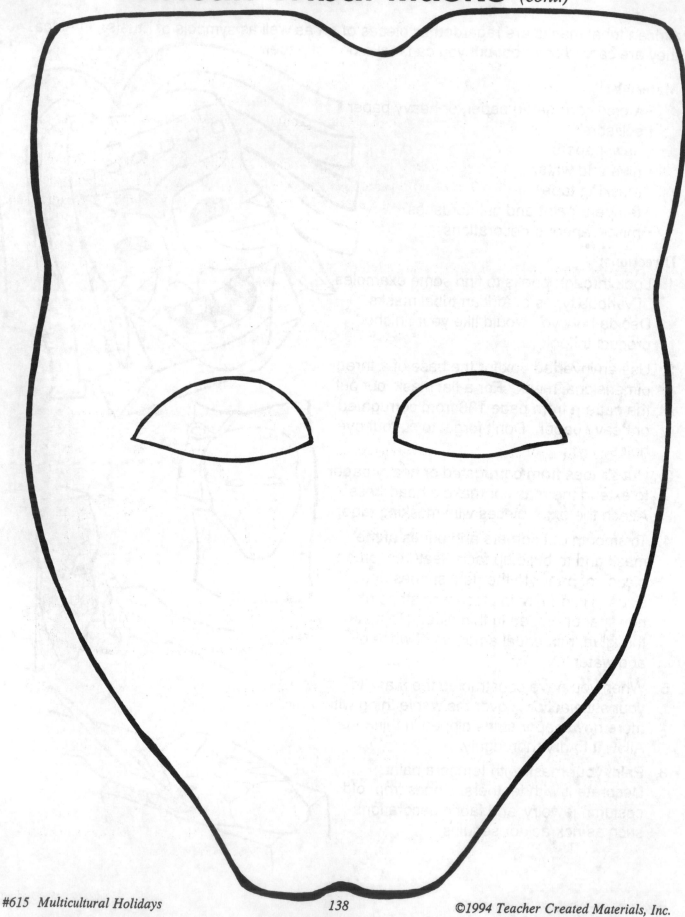

Groundhog Day

February 2

On February 2nd, the groundhog is supposed to wake from his winter sleep and come out of his hole. If he sees his shadow, he will go back into his hole and go to sleep again and winter will last for another six weeks. If he does not see his shadow, he will stay up and winter will be over. In other words, one should hope that the day will be dark and overcast so the groundhog will not see his shadow!

This is a fun day because it is so relaxed. It isn't a deeply meaningful day. You don't have to buy gifts or prepare special food. All you have to do is look for a groundhog or just wait for the media to do it for you. There is an "official" groundhog in the eastern United States who is watched by TV, radio, and newspaper reporters. Check the news and find out what he decided.

This holiday originally hails from Germany and Poland, although the Iroquois Indians have a belief that is very much the same. They watch for bears rather than groundhogs.

Making It Work

The groundhog has another name. Have students find out what else this animal is called.

What does the word "hibernation" mean? What animals beside the groundhog hibernate? What does "estivate" mean? Are there animals who estivate?

Write down the groundhog's weather forecast as reported in today's news. For the six weeks after Groundhog Day mark the weather (sunny, snowy, windy, rainy, cloudy) on the classroom calendar. When the six weeks are over, have students discuss the accuracy of the groundhog's weather forecast. (Meteorologists say that groundhogs are right only about 30 percent of the time.)

Place an outdoor thermometer near your classroom door. Have a student read the temperature at the same time everyday and record it on a graph.

Have students imagine the groundhog's underground house and draw a cut-away picture of the various rooms and furnishings.

Read some animal fables to students. "How The Bear Got His Stumpy Tail" and "Why Mosquitoes Buzz in People's Ears" are good ones that are easy to find. Discuss the stories. Then have students write stories explaining how the groundhog came to be afraid of his own shadow.

What Did the Paper (Radio, TV) Say?

Where was the groundhog sighted?

_____

_____

When was the groundhog sighted?

_____

_____

What is the groundhog's name?

_____

_____

What did the groundhog do?

_____

_____

What does that mean concerning the weather?

_____

_____

Where did you find this information?

_____

_____

140

©1994 Teacher Created Materials, Inc.

Lincoln's Birthday

February 12

Abraham Lincoln was born on February 12, 1809, in a log cabin in the state of Kentucky. He grew up on the American frontier, and in Indiana and Illinois. Although he was poor, he worked hard, and read every book he could find. He walked miles to borrow books and read them by candlelight and firelight after his work was done. Everything he wanted to know, he had to teach himself.

When he was old enough, Lincoln became a lawyer and started his law practice in Illinois. He decided to go into politics, but the first time he ran for office, he lost the election. However, his debates with Stephen A. Douglas made him famous and his political fortunes improved. He was elected President in 1860.

Shortly after Lincoln took office, the Civil War began. Lincoln's main purpose during the war was to save the Union and make the United States one country again. He felt that this country could "not long survive, half slave and half free." On January 1, 1863, he signed the Emancipation Proclamation freeing the slaves in the South. This laid the groundwork for the Thirteenth Amendment to the Constitution which outlawed slavery in 1865 in the whole United States.

When the South was defeated, the people there were very bitter. Their economy crumbled because it was based on slave labor. Lincoln planned to devote himself to making the country whole again, to "bind up the nation's wounds." He planned to stop the people who wanted to get even with the South. But on April 9th of his second term in office, before he could put his plans into action, he was assassinated. He died on April 14, 1865.

Not all of the states celebrate Lincoln's Birthday on February 12th. Some states combine it with Washington's Birthday and call it Presidents' Day. Some of the southern states do not celebrate it at all.

Making It Work

Read selections to your class from Carl Sandburg's biography of Lincoln. This is a beautiful book about which children should know.

Run off outlines of log cabins and let students use them as covers for stories about Lincoln, which can be written on paper of a matching shape. (See pages 142-143.)

Have older students do research to find out some opinions about questions like these:

- Why did Lincoln free the slaves?
- Did everyone appreciate Lincoln's sense of humor?
- Why did Lincoln run the Union Army himself for so long?
- How do people in the South of today feel about Lincoln?

Log Cabin Pattern

1. Cut out two cabin patterns for front and back covers.

2. Add details like a door and windows.

Log Cabin Pattern *(cont.)*

Run off a stack of these pages on which students can copy their Lincoln stories.

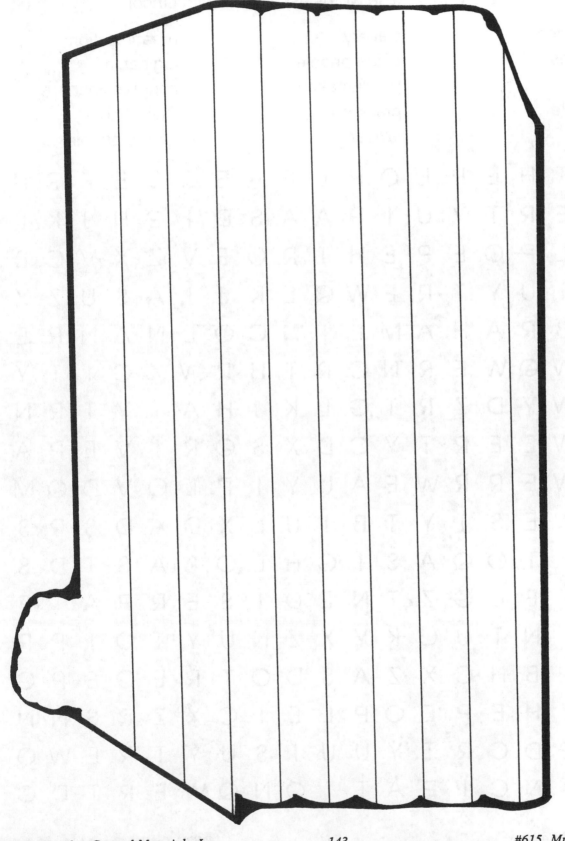

Lincoln Wordsearch

In the wordsearch below, find these words associated with Lincoln.

Abraham Lincoln
United States
poor
by the people
Illinois

slavery
of the people
proclamation
president
lawyer

emancipation
log cabin
congressman
Civil War
for the people

```
B Y T H E P E O P L E A B C D E F G H
Q W E R T Y U I P A A S D I G H J K L
I E L P O E P E H T R O F V Z X V C B
L O I U Y T R E W Q L K J I A S U Z X
P A B R A H A M L I N C O L N A N R E
R A W Q W E R N O R T H R W X C I T Y
O Q W Y D Z R T G L K J H A T Y T R N
C Q W E E R T Y C D X S Q R I V E R A
L Q W E R R W E A U Y I P L O V D Q M
A Q W E S T Y T B I U L X D A D S R S
M H Y T O Q A S I G H L O L A S T D S
A V F E U G Z T N E D I S E R P A T E
T K E N T U C K Y X Z N U Y T O T P R
I M N B H C X Z A S D O T R E O E P G
O F T H E P E O P L E I C X Z R S N N
N S E D C R T Y U U I S U Y T R E W O
E M A N C I P A T I O N Q W E R T D C
```

144

©*1994 Teacher Created Materials, Inc.*

The Lincoln Penny

Fill in the outline of Lincoln's head with U.S. penny rubbings. Put a penny under the paper and rub over it gently with the side of a pencil until the outline of Lincoln's head appears. Move the paper and keep rubbing over the penny until the entire outline is filled.

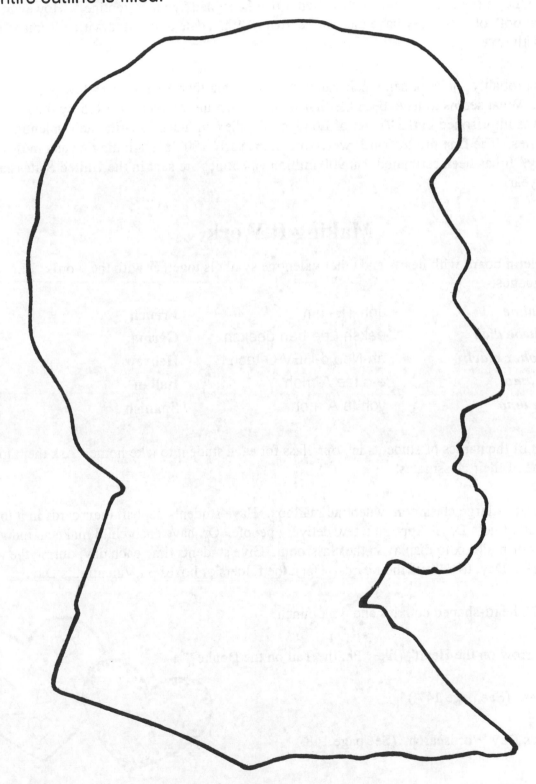

Valentine's Day

February 14

Most people believe that Valentine's Day got its name from one or more men who lived in the 3rd century A.D. They were put in prison and then put to death for being Christians. They were later both named saints. One of them may have written a letter that he signed "your Valentine." However, it is more likely that both of them may have died on February 14th, a date associated with a Roman festival having to do with love.

At first, lovers probably spoke or sang their valentines to one another because very few people could read and write. What seems to have been the first written valentine was sent in 1415 by the Duke of Orleans who was imprisoned in the Tower of London. People continued to write their valentines by hand for centuries. The first printed cards were sold in the early 1800's, beginning a custom that continues today. It has been estimated that 900 million valentines are sent in the United States and Canada every year.

Making It Work

Decorate a bulletin board with hearts and other valentine symbols together with the words "I Love You" in various languages.

Je t'aime	Jeh TE-mm	French
Ich liebe dich	eeksh Lee-bah deeksh	German
Ani ohev otach	ah-Nee o-HEV O-tach	Hebrew
Io ti amo	e-o tee A-moh	Italian
Yo te amo	yoh te A-moh	Spanish

Distribute a list of the names of students in your class for each student to take home. Ask them to give a card to each one of their classmates.

Make and decorate a large classroom valentine mailbox. Have students deposit their cards in it to be delivered on Valentine's Day. Appoint a few delivery people. Or, have each child make an individual valentine folder or mailbox to display in the classroom. Give students time each day, during the week before Valentine's Day, to deliver their cards. Open the folders or boxes on Valentine's Day.

Plan a party with heart-shaped cookies and pink punch.

Play "Pin the Arrow on the Heart" (like "Pin the Tail on the Donkey").

Make Valentines. (See page 147.)

Do a Valentine's Day Wordsearch. (See page 148.)

Pop-Up Hearts Cards

Materials:

- red, white, and pink construction paper
- assorted decorations (glitter, doilies, beads, etc.)
- scissors
- glue
- pen or marker

Directions:

1. Fan-fold paper for pop-up heart (use any color, red, white, or pink).

2. Cut hearts (like paper dolls).

3. Fold hearts.

4. Fold paper for a card in half (use any color, red, white, or pink).

5. Glue inside of card to pop-up when the card is open.

6. Let glue dry before closing. Glue on additional hearts and decorate as desired.

7. Write a valentine message.

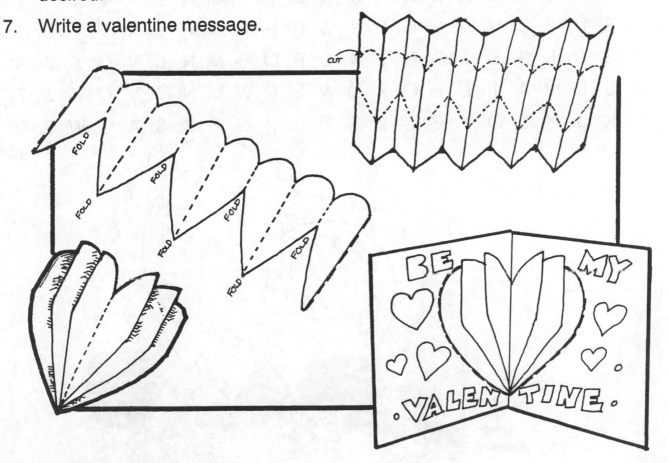

Name_____

Valentine Wordsearch

Find these words in the wordsearch puzzle below.

pink	white	card
love letter	holiday	cupid
candy	red	heart
love	mailbox	sweetheart
Valentine's Day	arrow	

```
A B C S W E E T H E A R T C D E F G H I J K L
M N O P Q H O L I D A Y R U S T U V W X Y Z A
Q W E R T Y U I O P C A S P I N K D F G H J K
L Z X C C W H I T E A V B I N M Q W E R T Y U
A S D V A L E N T I N E S D A Y D F G H J K K
Z X C V R O A B N M D Q W E R Q W E R T Y U I
A S D F D V R E D F Y G H H R Q W E R T Y U I
A S D F G E T G H J K L P O O M N B V C X Z A
A S D M A I L B O X Q W E R W M N B V C X Z Z
L K J H L O V E L E T T E R G F D S A Q W E R
```

Nirvana Day or Buddha's Death

February 15

Buddhism teaches that everyone who dies is reincarnated or reborn and that this cycle continues, over and over, until all of life's lessons are learned and a person reaches enlightenment. A person who reaches enlightenment is free from hatred, desire, and ignorance and has reached a state of "nirvana." Nirvana means death without having to be reborn. Buddha is said to be the first one to have attained this state.

When Buddhists celebrate the anniversary of Buddha's death, it is not a sad thing. They are just remembering that he moved from one state of being to another.

Making It Work

If you have one or more students in your classroom who celebrate Buddha's death on February 15th, ask them to share their first-hand information with their classmates. If you do not have this kind of input, ask student volunteers to call local Buddhist churches and ask for information:

- How is Buddha's death celebrated here?

- How do celebrations held here differ from those held in Japan?

- How does the celebration of Buddha's death differ from the celebrations held on both his birthday, April 8th, and his enlightenment, December 8th?

- What is the relationship between becoming enlightened and attaining nirvana?

- What is "karma"? How does it fit with these ideas?

Have students research the answers to these questions:

- What relationship does Buddhism have to art? Are there any religious rules about what its subject(s) should be?

- What is "zen" or "Zen Buddhism"?

- People meditate in many religions. Is the meditation associated with Buddhism different from other meditation?

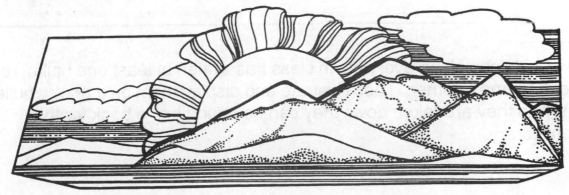

Haiku

Life is a journey
Up and down the tall mountains
And not around them.

The short poem above is a haiku. A haiku is a type of poem that originated in Japan hundreds of years ago. It is a very short poem, consisting of one thought, and seems to reflect the beauty and simplicity of Buddhist ideas. A haiku is usually written about nature but can express one thought about other subjects, too. It is expressed in 17 syllables written in three unrhymed lines. The first and last lines each have five syllables; the middle line has seven.

(5)   Life is a journey

(7)   Up and down the tall mountains

(5)   And not around them.

Check by reading this haiku aloud and "clapping" the syllables. How many claps for Life? (one) For is? (one) For a? (one) For journey? (two) You can continue this process for the other two lines.

Find a book of haiku poetry in the school or public library and read some more examples. Then try a haiku of your own. Don't forget to check the number of syllables by clapping.

_____

_____

_____

Be sure to publish: When everyone in class has written at least one haiku, read them aloud to one another. Then illustrate and display them on a poetry bulletin board. When they are taken down they can be bound into a book for the classroom library.

Washington's Birthday

February 22

Observed on the 3rd Monday in February

George Washington, who was said to be "first in war, first in peace, and first in the hearts of his countrymen," was born on February 22, 1732, in Virginia in what would become the United States. He grew up on the family plantation at Mount Vernon and learned to be a good farmer from his father and half-brother. He inherited Mount Vernon when his half-brother died.

Washington worked as a surveyor for awhile as a young man. Then he joined the army and fought in the French and Indian War. After that war he was elected to the Continental Congress. He married Martha Curtis, a widow with two children.

Washington was very much in favor of declaring independence from England. As the commander-in-chief of the American army, he led the rebellious colonies to victory. He kept the soldiers from losing hope through all of the hardships of the war and was generally regarded as a great hero.

After the Revolutionary War, Washington looked forward to retiring from public life and returning to his beloved Mount Vernon. However, after he helped to write the Constitution, he was elected first President of the new United States in 1781. He made sure that the President was not treated like or addressed as a king and began the custom of having our chief executive addressed as "Mr. President." He also set the precedent for serving only two terms in office.

He was finally able to return to Mount Vernon where he died in 1799. He and his wife, Martha, are buried there.

George Washington is the only President in U.S. history whose birthday was celebrated publicly while he was alive. His birthday is now observed on the third Monday in February to make a three-day-weekend. That day is sometimes also called President's Day.

Making It Work

George Washington was one of two Presidents who was not opposed in his election to office. Have students find out the name of the other one.

Have students find out the name of the only President who ran for more than two terms. Under what circumstances did this happen?

Ask students to:

- Research, draw, and color the flags used during the Revolutionary War by the colonial fighting forces.
- Find the names of the important battles of the War for Independence (another name for the American Revolutionary War).

Name_____

What Do You Know About Washington?

Fill in the blanks in these sentences about George Washington.

1. George Washington was born on _____ in _____.

2. He spent his boyhood at _____ with his half-brother Lawrence Washington.

3. George first worked as a _____.

4. George Washington married _____, a widow with two children.

5. Washington was chosen to be _____ of the American army during the Revolution.

6. Washington crossed the _____ River in 1776 while leading an attack at Trenton, New Jersey.

7. Congress approved the _____ on July 4, 1776.

8. In 1789, George Washington was elected _____ of the United States and served for _____ years.

9. The vice-president under Washington was_____.

10. Washington presided over the convention that wrote the United States _____ in 1787.

11. One of George Washington's acts as President was to establish a _____ for coining money.

12. In 1793, Washington laid the cornerstone of the United States _____ in Washington. D.C.

The Washington Quarter

Fill in the outline of Washington's head with U.S. quarter rubbings. Put a quarter under the paper and rub over it gently with the side of a pencil until the outline of Washington's head appears. Move the paper and keep rubbing over the quarter until the entire outline is filled.

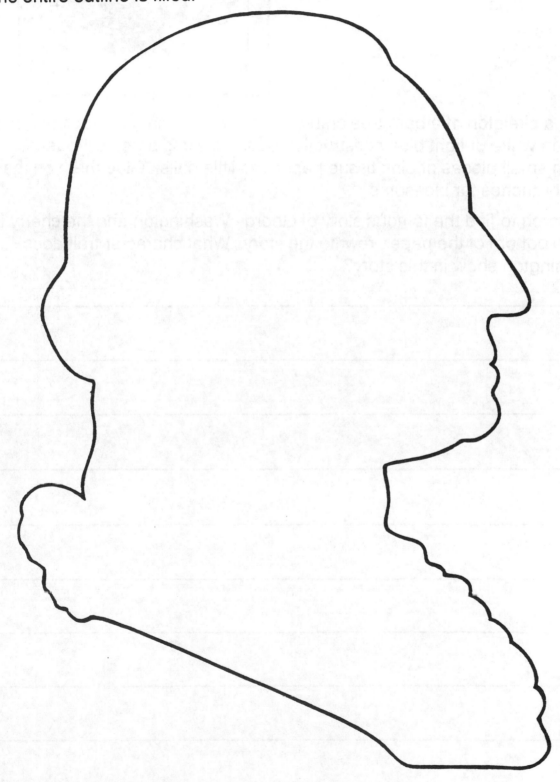

Washington's Cherry Tree

Materials:

- black construction paper
- white or light blue construction paper
- pink tissue paper
- scissors
- glue

Directions:

- Draw a skeleton of a bare tree on black construction paper. Cut it out and glue on white or light blue construction paper, making a tree silhouette. Crush small pieces of pink tissue paper into little balls. Glue them on the bare branches for blossoms.

- Research to find the famous story of George Washington and the cherry tree. At the bottom of the paper, rewrite the story. What character trait does Washington show in this story?

_____

_____

_____

_____

_____

_____

_____

_____

Leap Year Day

February 29

February 29th does not come every year. It happens every four years when we add an extra day to our calendar. We add an extra day every four years because it takes the earth 365 ¼ days to go around the sun. We add the day to catch up with our calendar, and we call it a Leap Year. If we did not do this, our calendar would eventually begin to slip behind the seasons.

Leap Year Day does not really bother anybody except those people who are born on February 29th. Since their birthday will not come again for four years, what are they to do? People make jokes about it, of course. They count their birthdays rather than the years and say it is their third birthday when they are twelve or their fifth birthday when they are twenty. The most practical way of dealing with this is to celebrate the birthday of a Leap Year child on either February 28th or March 1st of the years that are not Leap Years.

There is an old tradition in Scotland and Ireland that women may propose marriage on Leap Year Day. Sometimes this tradition is remembered by having dances to which the girls are supposed to invite the boys.

Making It Work

If you have a Leap Year child in your class, have a special birthday party for him or her. If it happens to be a Leap Year, you can have it on February 29th. If it is a regular year, have it on a date close to the end of February. Play some silly games. A particularly fitting one would be leap frog.

Do the writing activity on page 156. A scoring rubric is on page 26.

Because Leap Year is normally associated with a mix-up in traditional roles, mix things up in your classroom. Have students switch seats. Wear your clothes inside out. Have students do the teachers' and administrators' jobs and vice versa.

Traditionally there has been a great deal of gender stereotyping in careers. We all know it is high time to mix things up! Do a career survey among your students. Find out if their views about career opportunities for men and women are stereotypical or demonstrate an open point of view. Make plans to show films or videos about careers and invite speakers to talk about opportunities for women and men in all areas. Do another survey after you have provided this information to the class.

The Career in My Future

Read the Writing Situation and the Directions for Writing. Then write your piece on the lines provided.

Writing Situation

An anonymous person has offered to pay your way to any college you want to attend if only you can name the career you would like to have and tell why it would make you happy and/or make the world a better place in which to live.

Directions for Writing

Give some thought to the career you would like to have and the reasons you would like to have it. If you have not yet made up your mind, choose something with the idea that you can always change your mind later. Organize your ideas so they will be clear to the reader. Use correct grammar, punctuation, and spelling.

_____

_____

_____

_____

_____

_____

_____

_____

_____

_____

_____

_____

_____

_____

_____

Purim, the Jewish Feast of Lots

February or March

Purim, also called the Feast of Lots, is a happy Jewish festival that includes a great deal of drama. It commemorates the bravery of the good Queen Esther and the downfall of the evil Haman, who tried to persuade King Ahasuerus to cast lots to decide which day would be best to kill the Jews. (If you cast lots, you are deciding something by chance in the same way that you might roll dice or flip a coin.)

The whole story is told in the Book of Esther in the Bible, and this is read aloud on Purim. Sometimes it is even acted out by actors in costume, while people stamp their feet and use noise-makers to drown out the sound of Haman's name. The whole effect is much like the performance of a melodrama where the audience boos and hisses every time the villain appears. This merriment is very welcome at the end of winter.

Purim is celebrated at home with a special banquet, and food is also given to the needy. A traditional food for Purim is a three-cornered cookie designed to look like Haman's hat. It is called Hamantashen.

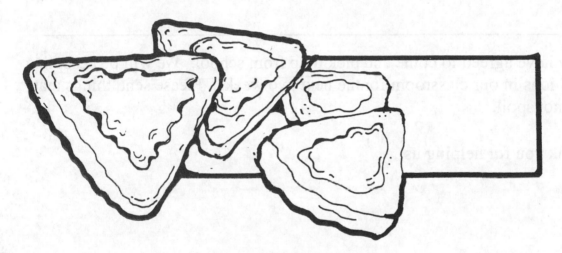

Making It Work

Ask student volunteers to locate a recipe for Hamantashen cookies and make them for the class. Or you may be able to find these cookies in a Jewish bakery at this time of year.

This would be a good time for your class to organize a food drive for needy people in your area. The food collected through the traditional food drives that take place at Thanksgiving and Christmas are probably all used up. Replacements would be welcomed by any agency that distributes food, or maybe you could make a tactful personal donation to somebody of whom you or your students know. Send home a letter asking for donations. Call various agencies to see if someone is available to pick up the food you collect. (See page 158.)

The story of Queen Esther reminds us that good can triumph over evil when people work together. Have each student think of an example of another time in history when good triumphed over evil. Share ideas and discuss.

Purim Food Drive

The teacher can sign the letter below which can then be copied and sent home with students, or each student can write his or her own letter.

Dear Family,

We have been talking about the people who may not have enough to eat at this time of year. We know that the food collected during holiday food drives is probably all gone. We have decided to have a food drive of our own. We are going to give the food we collect to

They have agreed to come and pick it up from school. We will be accepting donations in our classroom for the next two weeks. Please send things that will not spoil.

Thank you for helping us.

_____
Student Signature

_____
Teacher Signature

Spring Holidays

March

Birthstone: Bloodstone

Flower: Daffodil

March was named in honor of Mars, the Roman god of war. Until 46 B.C., when the Julian calendar was adopted, March was the first month of the year.

April

Birthstone: Diamond

Flower: Sweet Pea

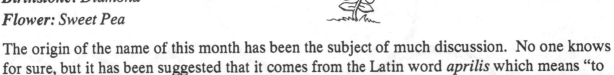

The origin of the name of this month has been the subject of much discussion. No one knows for sure, but it has been suggested that it comes from the Latin word *aprilis* which means "to open" and may refer to the opening of buds in the springtime.

May

Birthstone: Emerald

Flower: Lily of the Valley

May was probably named for Maia, the Roman goddess of growth and fertility.

The word "spring" means to leap or jump up, and that is what the plants do in this season. Spring arrives in the northern hemisphere on March 21st during most years. The spring (or vernal) equinox is the day when the hours of light and darkness are equal. The hours of daylight will then get longer until the summer solstice arrives. (Just as in the fall, the seasons are reversed in the southern hemisphere. When the northern hemisphere welcomes spring, the southern hemisphere is greeting the season of fall.)

The traditional idea of spring includes melting snow, warming weather, and sprouting plants and budding trees. However, many people live in areas that do not experience this kind of dramatic change from one season to another. In many areas it just gets a little warmer, but the idea of new life and growth is still there. Most of the spring holidays include the idea of rebirth and new life. For this reason, eggs have become a symbol of the season. Many cultures also celebrate their New Year at this time.

This is an upper grade contract to be used in connection with the spring holidays. You can run it off and distribute it your students. Use the part of this page below the line as a cover and the two following pages as an instructional packet and sign-up slip to keep track of student presentations.

Spring Holiday Contract

Spring Holiday Contract *(cont.)*

1. Choose the spring holiday in which you are most interested. If you (or your family) are from another country, please consider sharing your own customs and traditions with the class.

(Note: Many spring holidays celebrate a variety of things.)

2. Research your spring holiday. You may use all kinds of reference books and encyclopedias. You may also consult primary sources — people with first-hand, personal knowledge. Interview your parents, older relatives, and family friends. Just be sure to write down where you got your information.

3. Your report will be due during the two-week period from _____ to _____. Make an appointment so your presentation can be scheduled. Try not to wait until the last minute.

4. Here is what to do for your report/presentation:

    a. Write an information paper to be turned in. Here are some things to include (though you may think of many more):

       • What is the name of your holiday?
       • What is the theme of your holiday? Birth? New growth? A fresh start? A new year? Giving thanks?
       • When is it celebrated?
       • Where is it celebrated? In public? At home?
       • Is it celebrated differently in different countries?
       • Have the customs of your holiday become well-known or are they practiced only by a special group of people?
       • Does your holiday have a religious significance?
       • Are there costumes? Parades? Dances? Special foods?
       • Is your holiday for everyone? Just for children? Just for adults?

    b. Include a bibliography. Don't forget to list any primary sources.

    c. Do at least _____ of the following:

       • Plan and then tape (audio or video) an interview with an older relative or friend. This interview should focus on memories associated with your holiday. (You will play the tape for the class as part of your final presentation, so be sure to get permission for this from the person you interview.)

Spring Holiday Contract *(cont.)*

- Research a traditional menu for the celebration of your holiday. Write and illustrate your menu on a large poster board. If possible, include recipes for some of the most unusual dishes.

- Create a simple holiday word search for a primary class and have enough copies run off so the teacher of the class won't need to do any extra work. Include an answer key.

- Learn how to make a variety of paper flowers. Teach this skill to your own class and/or another class. Decorate your classroom with the flowers.

- Write and illustrate a poem about your holiday. Use many different kinds of figurative language: simile, metaphor, personification, etc.

- Make an appropriate door decoration and display it on your classroom door. Take it home in time to use for your own celebration.

  Create your own activity. Check with the teacher first.

d. Be prepared to make an oral presentation to describe and display the activities you have completed for your holiday contract. Don't forget to reserve a tape player or TV/VCR to play your taped interview if you did one. Plan to read your information paper aloud to the class.

e. Optional: Bring the class a food treat representing your holiday. Distribute it at the end of your presentation.

If you schedule your presentation early enough, you may invite your parents to come and be part of the audience. (If you wait until the last minute, we will not be able to guarantee a definite time.)

Fill out the form below, clip it off, and return it to the teacher.

- -

Name_____

The holiday I have chosen is _____ .

I would like to schedule my presentation on _____ .

This is a primary grade contract to be used in connection with the spring holidays. You can run it off and distribute it your students. Use the part of this page below the line as a cover and the two following pages as an instructional packet and sign-up slip to keep track of student presentations.

Spring Holiday Contract

Spring Holiday Contract *(cont.)*

1. Choose the spring holiday in which you are most interested.

   (Note: Spring holidays celebrate many different things.)

2. Find out about your spring holiday. You may use all kinds of reference books and encyclopedias. You may also ask people who have first-hand, personal knowledge. Talk to your parents, older relatives, and family friends. Just be sure to write down where you got your information.

3. Your report will be due during the two-week period from _____ to _____. Make an appointment with the teacher so your report can be scheduled. Try not to wait until the last minute.

4. Here is what to do for your report/representation:

   a. Write an information paper to be turned in. You may ask your parents for help. Here are some things you may want to include (though you may think of many more):

      • What is the name of your holiday?
      • What does it celebrate? Birth? New growth? A fresh start? A new year? Giving thanks?
      • When is it celebrated?
      • Where is it celebrated? In public? At home?
      • Is it celebrated differently in different countries?
      • Does almost everyone in this country celebrate your holiday?
      • Does your holiday have a religious meaning?
      • Are there costumes? Parades? Dances? Special foods?
      • Is your holiday for everyone? Just for children? Just for adults.

   b. Include a bibliography. Don't forget to list any people to whom you spoke.

   c. Do at least _____ of the following:

      • Ask your parents to help you plan and then tape (audio or video) an interview with an older relative or friend. This interview should be about the person's memories of the holiday you chose. (You will play the tape for the class as part of your final presentation, so be sure to get permission for this from the person you interview.)

Spring Holiday Contract *(cont.)*

- Make a poster showing the foods that go with your holiday. You may draw the foods or cut pictures from magazines. Label each food with its traditional name.

- Create a holiday wordsearch. Make enough copies for your class. Include an answer key for the teacher.

- Learn how to make several different kinds of paper flowers. Teach the rest of the class what you learned. Decorate your classroom with the flowers.

- Write a poem about your holiday. Copy it in your best handwriting and draw a picture to go with it so the teacher can make a spring poetry bulletin board.

- Make an appropriate door decoration and display it on your classroom door. Take it home in time to use it for your own celebration.

d. Be prepared to make an oral presentation to describe and display the activities you have completed for your holiday contract. Don't forget to reserve a tape player or TV/VCR to play your taped interview if you did one. Plan to read your information paper aloud to the class.

e. Optional: Bring the class a food treat representing your holiday. Distribute it at the end of your presentation.

If you schedule your presentation early enough, you may invite your parents to come and be part of the audience. (If you wait until the last minute, we will not be able to guarantee a definite time.)

Fill out the form below, clip it off, and return it to the teacher.

- -

Name _____

The holiday I have chosen is _____ .

I would like to schedule my presentation on _____ .

Parent signature _____

International Women's Day

March 8

The first protest march against the terrible conditions under which women worked in the textile and garment industries of the United States was held on March 8, 1857, in New York City. American women have decided that the anniversary of this march is a good time to honor women's achievements and remember women's goals.

Women in the United States no longer fight for the right to vote. They have pretty much proved that they can be elected to and hold public office, although some campaigns waged against them often have sexist overtones. They are still fighting the language bias, insisting on chairperson instead of chairman and humankind instead of mankind, and rejecting the automatic use of masculine pronouns. Even though this battle has been called silly and superficial, it seems to be responsible for a great deal of consciousness-raising.

However, women must still engage in other battles. In the present day, there is supposed to be legal protection for the right of women to receive equal pay for equal work, but these laws are not always enforced. Women must still fight this battle. Discrimination against women in the hiring and promotion process is against the law also, but there still exists the "glass ceiling" in upper-level jobs and plain old prejudice in lower-level ones. Women are fighting the battle of sexual harassment, too, at work, in school, and in public places. These and other battles wage on.

Because it has been enthusiastically adopted by women in socialist countries, some people have tried to discredit the celebration of International Women's Day. It is still, however, a meaningful holiday in the United States and Canada. It can be a time for women of those countries to give thought to helping the causes of women in other lands, women who are still disenfranchised or not considered equal to men in other ways.

Making It Work

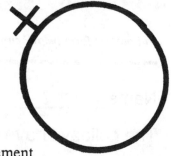

Have students do some research on the Women's Movement and find out:

- names of women who have been important or influential in the movement

- names of organizations that are associated with the movement

- titles and authors of books that have been important influences in the movement

Have interested students create posters and/or slogans that would be appropriate for use on International Women's Day.

Name_____

International Women's Day Theme Song

1. Make up a song that women can feel good about singing on International Women's Day.

    - Some song writers like to have the melody first. You can make it up or use one that is well-known.

    - Other song writers like to write the words first and then fit the melody to the words.

2. Write the words on the lines below. Make a note of the tune if it is familiar. If you make up the tune, record it on tape.

3. Teach the words to volunteers and perform it for your class (or for the school).

Song for International Women's Day

_____ Sung to the tune of _____ .

or

_____ Tape of original melody attached.

_____

_____

_____

_____

_____

_____

_____

_____

Mardi Gras or Carnival

February or March

Mardi Gras or Carnival is the celebration before the Christian penitential season of Lent. Although Mardi Gras literally means "Fat Tuesday" in French and refers to the day before Ash Wednesday, the celebration takes up more than just that one day. In New Orleans, for example, it lasts for a week or more.

In the countries of South America, Carnival (as it is called there) is the most important holiday of the year. This is doubly true of Brazil where the celebration lasts longer every year. The "samba schools," which are the groups in charge of the Carnival parades, would have already spent months in the preparation of the costumes for the parades. Thousands of these costumed samba dancers compete for prizes.

All over Europe, too, this celebration, known by a variety of names, goes on. Germans call it *Fasching*; Poles call it *Zapusty*; and Hungarians call it *Farsang*.

Mardi Gras or Carnival is, traditionally, a period of indulgence in rich foods and rowdy behavior. Christians were once required by their churches to observe a strict fast during Lent, very often giving up the use of meat and even fats, eggs, and dairy products. Because of this, people tried to use everything up in the days before Lent began. The word "carnival" comes from Latin words that mean "taking away meat." Christians no longer observe fasts that are as strict as they were in the past. They do, however, often offer a sacrifice by abstaining from some food of which they are really fond.

The date of Mardi Gras or Carnival depends on the beginning date of Lent. And the beginning date of Lent depends on when Easter occurs in any particular year. (See "The Christian Calendar," page 261.)

Making It Work

Ask students to discuss the following questions:

- What similarities do you see between Christianity and other religions? What differences?
- Why did people feel that they needed to use up the foods they would not be eating during Lent?

Have students do some research to find out what this season is called in England and why. What contest is associated with the English name? How did it begin?

Creating Carnival Costumes

1. Meet as a class to brainstorm a theme for your costumes.

2. Work with a group to decide how to interpret the theme.

3. Locate reference books and look at pictures of some Carnival costumes.

4. Sketch your costume in the space below. Indicate colors you would like to use.

5. If there is time, actually construct the costume using crepe paper and a stapler. You might fit it on a member of your group.

6. Compare designs with the other groups. Discuss outcomes and problems. Are you pleased with your results? If you were going to start over, would you do anything differently?

Ash Wednesday and Lent, the Christian Penitential Season

February or March

Ash Wednesday is the first day of Lent, the Christian penitential season that starts forty days before Easter, not counting Sundays. On Ash Wednesday, Catholics and some other Christians go to church and have ashes put on their foreheads in the form of a cross to remind them of their mortality and their sinful nature.

The whole season of Lent used to be a period of strict fasting in commemoration of the forty days Jesus spent in the wilderness. It is still observed but not as strictly. Instead of "giving up" something for Lent as a sacrifice, many people prefer to do something positive. Someone might choose to give extra money to help those in need, while someone else might visit people who are sick.

Lent culminates in Holy Week, the week preceding Easter. The Sunday before Easter Sunday and the last three days of Holy Week have special names: Palm Sunday, Holy Thursday, Good Friday, and Holy Saturday. Palm Sunday commemorates the day that Jesus entered Jerusalem. On that day people lined the street and waved palm branches. Many Christian churches pass out palm leaves in memory of that occasion. Holy Thursday commemorates the day of the Last Supper which has been the subject of many famous paintings. Good Friday commemorates the day on which Jesus was crucified and died. Holy Saturday is symbolic of the day Jesus lay in the tomb waiting for Easter Sunday.

Christians who spend Holy Week in Jerusalem walk the paths that Jesus was said to walk on Palm Sunday and again on Good Friday. On Good Friday, the walk they take is called the Way of the Cross. Christians elsewhere can choose to attend many different special church services on these days.

Making It Work

Ask students:

- If you were going to give up something as a sacrifice, what would it be? How would you decide on it? Could it be something you didn't like anyway?

- If you were going to do something positive, what would it be? Could it be something you enjoy doing?

Have students compare the Christian season of Lent with the Moslem month of Ramaden. What are the similarities? What are the differences? (See page 264.)

Treat your students to hot cross buns, traditional sweet rolls that are served on Good Friday. They have a cross made of icing on the top.

Lent and Ramadan

List the similarities:

Lent	Ramadan

List the differences:

Lent	Ramadan

Draw a conclusion:

_____

_____

_____

St. Patrick's Day

March 17

Saint Patrick was a man who went to Ireland in 432 A.D. to spread the Christian faith. He became a Bishop and the patron saint of Ireland. Legend has it that Patrick drove the snakes from Ireland, but scientists believe that Ireland was always free from snakes. Some people believe that Patrick's "snakes" were the pagan beliefs he wanted to replace with Christianity.

This holiday, which is celebrated wherever people from Ireland have settled, is associated with several popular symbols. Shamrocks became symbols of this holiday because Saint Patrick used their leaves, which are divided into three parts, to explain the doctrine of the Trinity. Leprechauns are the "little people" of Ireland. They are like fairies or gnomes in other countries but smarter and more mischievous. They also own pots of gold that can be taken from them by really clever and lucky mortals. The color green goes with Saint Patrick's Day, too. Green is Ireland's color and people speak of "the wearin' of the green" because this was forbidden by English law for many years. (Maybe you have forgotten to wear green on Saint Patrick's Day and were pinched by a friend!)

Saint Patrick's Day, which is still an important religious holiday in Ireland, is celebrated publicly in the United States with parades. This is largely because the U.S. is home to millions of people who were either born in Ireland or are the descendants of those born there. The biggest parade is in New York City, and it has been held since 1762. It is celebrated privately with special foods, cards, parties, and all kinds of merry-making.

Making It Work

Ask students to share their own St. Patrick's Day celebrations. Do they attend church services? Do they eat special foods? What are they? Do they send or receive cards? Did anyone in their family come from Ireland? Who? Do they wear green to school? Do their parents wear green to work?

Read an assortment of Leprechaun stories to the class. Then have students write their own stories entitled "How To Catch a Leprechaun." Use them for a bulletin board display with shamrocks and pots of gold.

Have a Saint Patrick's Day party. Serve green punch and cupcakes frosted with green icing.

Enjoy a Saint Patrick's Day art project. (See directions and patterns for a Leprechaun Marionette on pages 173-175.)

Leprechaun Marionette

Materials:

- patterns on pages 174–175
- index or stiff paper
- paper towel tube
- 11' (4m) string or yarn
- glue or tape
- scissors
- hole punch
- markers or crayons

Directions:

1. Reproduce pattern onto index paper. Color and cut out.
2. Fold over head; punch hole in hat.
3. Roll the body into a tube shape and fold tab in; attach the back together.
4. Reproduce strips on the bottom of this page four times. Glue or tape together two strips for each arm and each leg. Accordion fold legs and arms.
5. Punch holes in hands and feet and attach them to the ends of arms and legs.
6. Tape or glue head by attaching the face to the front of the body and the neck inside the back of the body. Attach arms and legs to body with tape or glue.
7. Tie a 15" (38 cm) length of string around the middle of the paper towel tube and attach it to the leprechaun's hat.
8. Tie a 3' (1 m) length of string to right side of the paper towel tube and attach ti to the leprechaun's left foot. Do the same for the right foot.
9. Tie an 18" (46 cm) length to the left side of the paper towel tube and attach it to the leprechaun's left hand. Do the same for the right hand.
10. Manipulate the marionette by raising and lowering the string.

Leprechaun Marionette Pattern

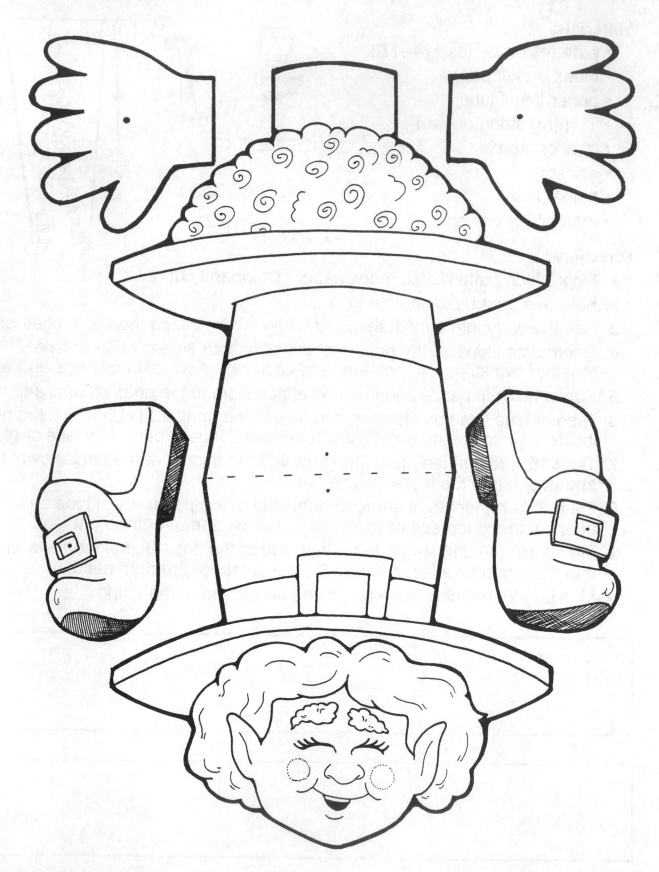

Leprechaun Marionette Pattern *(cont.)*

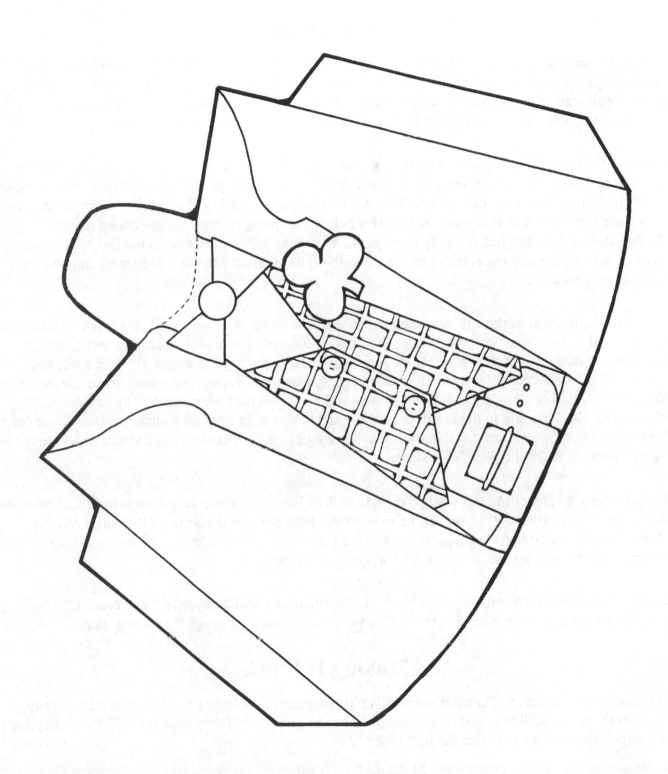

Noruz, the Middle Eastern New Year

March 21

Noruz, which is sometimes spelled Now Ruz, means new day. It is the Middle Eastern New Year celebration. This celebration goes on for two weeks, ending on the thirteenth day after Noruz with another celebration called Sizdar-Bedah. Noruz is celebrated by people of every religion in most of the Middle East. It is a national holiday in Iran and is often called the Iranian New Year.

Families start to get ready for the holiday about two weeks ahead of time. They travel long distances to be together with as many members of the family as they can. They put lentils or wheat seeds in shallow bowls of water where they can sprout. They are entertained at public gatherings in the community by a clown who pokes fun at everyone. A few days before the spring equinox, on the eve of the last Wednesday of the year, fire-jumping takes place. Everyone jumps over a small bonfire. Some people say this is to burn away the sorrows of the old year, while others say that it will help the sun win over the darkness of winter.

At the exact moment of the equinox, the family celebration begins. They either sit around a cloth on the floor or gather around a table set with seven symbolic objects. These objects change with time and changing conditions, but they can include sprouted seeds, coins, sugar, vinegar, flowers, fruit, and spices. Other symbolic objects are an orange, an egg, candles, a mirror, and a holy book. Everyone says, "May you live a hundred years!" Grown children go to visit their parents. Then other visiting starts. The oldest people in the family stay home and the younger ones go around visiting. Since the New Year lasts for so many days, there is time for a lot of visits. Pastries such as baklava are served to every visitor to make the New Year sweet.

People who are celebrating this festival outside of their homeland try to keep it as authentic as possible. Members of a family travel to stay at the same destination, perhaps the home of the oldest relative. Once there, they perform the preparations and the ceremonies. They often make great sacrifices to take this trip, and those who are unable to go feel lonely and displaced.

Sizdar-Bedah, the thirteenth day after Noruz, is the end of the Middle Eastern New Year. It is considered unlucky to stay inside on that day, so it is customary for people to go on a picnic.

Making It Work

Do you have students in your class who will celebrate Noruz? Will they travel to join other family members? Where will they go? How long will they be gone? Will they miss school? Have they had this experience before or is this the first time?

Celebrate Noruz in your classroom. Make the New Year sweet for your class by serving baklava.

Sprinkle seeds in water in a shallow bowl and allow them to sprout. How long will it take? Keep a written record.

Name_____

The Names Have Changed

Many countries in the world have changed their names in the 20th century. Quite a few have changed in the last few years. Have a classroom contest and see who can identify the most countries that have changed their names. One has been done for you.

1. _____*Iran*_____ was _____*Persia*_____
2. _____ was _____
3. _____ was _____
4. _____ was _____
5. _____ was _____
6. _____ was _____
7. _____ was _____
8. _____ was _____
9. _____ was _____
10. _____ was _____
11. _____ was _____
12. _____ was _____
13. _____ was _____
14. _____ was _____
15. _____ was _____
16. _____ was _____
17. _____ was _____
18. _____ was _____
19. _____ was _____
20. _____ was _____
21. _____ was _____
22. _____ was _____

Holi, the Indian Spring Festival

March

Holi is a favorite holiday among the children in India. It is connected with the spring equinox and celebrates the beginning of spring. It is also a harvest festival in northern India because March is when the winter crop is ready. But these are not the reasons that the children love this holiday best. They love it because it is a time when they can squirt or splash everyone, friends, neighbors, and even strangers, with brightly colored water!

Bonfires are lighted on the eve of this holiday. These fires are intended to help the sun get stronger and the days longer after the equinox. People sing and dance around the bonfires until morning when the fires are put out — with water. This begins the water part of the festival, and people begin to throw water at one another. The fun often continues for three days. People visit one another and eat sweets together to symbolize friendship. Special foods are prepared and eaten, and candies are given to the children.

The religious background of this festival commemorates the time when Krishna came to earth and played with the colors of life. So people make offerings of colored powders to Krishna, and children make these same offerings to their parents. But the fun of the festival includes people of all social classes and of all religions. When they are laughing and playing and pouring colored water on each other, it is hard to tell them apart.

Hindus have adapted this festival to life outside of their homeland by celebrating it more quietly in homes and temples. People often invite groups of friends to their homes to enjoy the special foods and to share the joy of a party with singing and dancing.

Making It Work

If you have students from India in your class, ask them to share the customs associated with Holi. How have families adapted their celebrations to life here? How do your students celebrate the holiday?

Look for an Indian market that stocks the special foods eaten as a part of this festival. Purchase some of the sweets for your students to try. Are these sweets like American candies? What is different about these foods?

Have students look up and share some of the Indian legends that explain the customs of Holi.

Experiment with colored powders (tempera paints), water, and liquid starch to create fingerpainting projects as described on page 179.

Projects With Colored Powders and Water

Capture the feeling of Holi by mixing up your own paint solution and then using it to fingerpaint. Follow this recipe to make the paint:

Mix 1 tablespoon (15 mL) vinegar and 2 tablespoons (30 mL) baking soda. Add 1 teaspoon (5 mL) water, 1 tablespoon (15 mL) corn starch, 1/2 teaspoon (2.5 mL) glycerin, and any desired food coloring. Stir.

Once you have made the paint, take big sheets of paper and let your imagination run wild. The resulting pictures should have the happy feeling of spring.

Dry the finger paintings and use them for a variety of projects:

- Cut silhouettes of temple dancers from black paper and mount them on the finger paintings.
- Cut silhouettes of temple dancers from the finger paintings and mount them on black paper.
- Use brushes and tempera to paint a scene using a finger painting as a background.
- Use finger paintings to back a bulletin board.
- Cut letters for a bulletin board from the finger-painted paper.
- Cut, fold, and make cards from the finger-painted paper. Paste or paint a decoration on the front and write a message inside.
- Cut flower petals from the finger painted-paper and make a bulletin board display by adding stems and leaves cut from green construction paper.
- Write a poem or a short paragraph telling something about Holi. Letter it carefully on a finger painting that goes with what you wrote. Hang it up so other class members can read it.
- Look at each other's paintings. Try to interpret their meaning. Of what do they remind you? Do other students see what you see in your paintings?
- If you were to do this project again, would you do it the same way or differently? What did you learn?

Easter, the Resurrection of Jesus Christ

Between March 22 and April 21

Easter is a holiday that moves each year. But it always falls on the first Sunday after the first full moon of spring. Several other holidays and observances depend on when Easter falls in any given year. Ash Wednesday, which is the beginning of the season of Lent, occurs 40 days before Easter. Mardi Gras, which is the Tuesday before Ash Wednesday, therefore changes every year as well. Since many countries celebrate "Carnival" before Lent begins, these festivals also happen at different times each year. (See "The Christian Calendar" page 261.)

Easter Sunday is the holiest day in the Christian year since it celebrates the resurrection of Jesus Christ. This means that Jesus rose from the dead. Many people think that Easter probably came to be celebrated in the spring because of the prevailing theme of new life as the earth returns from the darkness and cold of winter. Church services held at sunrise also symbolize the triumph of light over darkness. The name of the holiday itself comes from Eostre, a Roman goddess of spring and fertility.

Easter has also moved into the area of a traditional holiday. Many people who are not involved in its religious observance celebrate Easter with feasting, family parties, and a visit from the Easter Bunny. The goddess Eostre favored the hare, an animal like a rabbit, and this may be the origin of the Easter Bunny. Easter eggs are traditional in many parts of the world, but they are not always brought by a bunny. In some places they are brought by doves, cranes, or foxes. The children of France believe that they are brought by the church bells.

Making It Work

Write and illustrate poems and stories about spring. Use them as the basis for a seasonal bulletin board.

Do an Easter art project. (See page 181.)

Do research to find out how people in different countries decorate their Easter eggs. Some of these are real art forms that are displayed in museums.

Decorate real eggs. Use food coloring, paints, sequins, beads, yarn, etc. Attach pieces of ribbon to the decorated eggs and use them to trim an attractively shaped bare branch for display in the classroom. (Blow the contents of the eggs out first by making a small hole in each end of the shell and blowing through one hole. Wash and drain the shells before decorating.

Make Easter cards. (See page 183.)

Baby Chick Surprise Egg

Materials:

- 8 ½" x 11" (22 cm x 28 cm) white construction paper
- 5" x 5" (13 cm x 13 cm) yellow construction paper
- crayons or markers
- colored paper scraps
- scissors
- glue
- brass fastener

Directions:

Trace the egg pattern on page 182 onto the white paper. Decorate the egg with crayons, markers, paper scraps, etc., then cut it out. Overlap the scalloped edges and hook them together by putting the brad through the two holes. Trace the baby chick pattern onto the yellow paper. Add features as desired. Glue the baby chick so that it sticks up in back of the lower section of the egg (see illustration).

Baby Chick Surprise Egg *(cont.)*

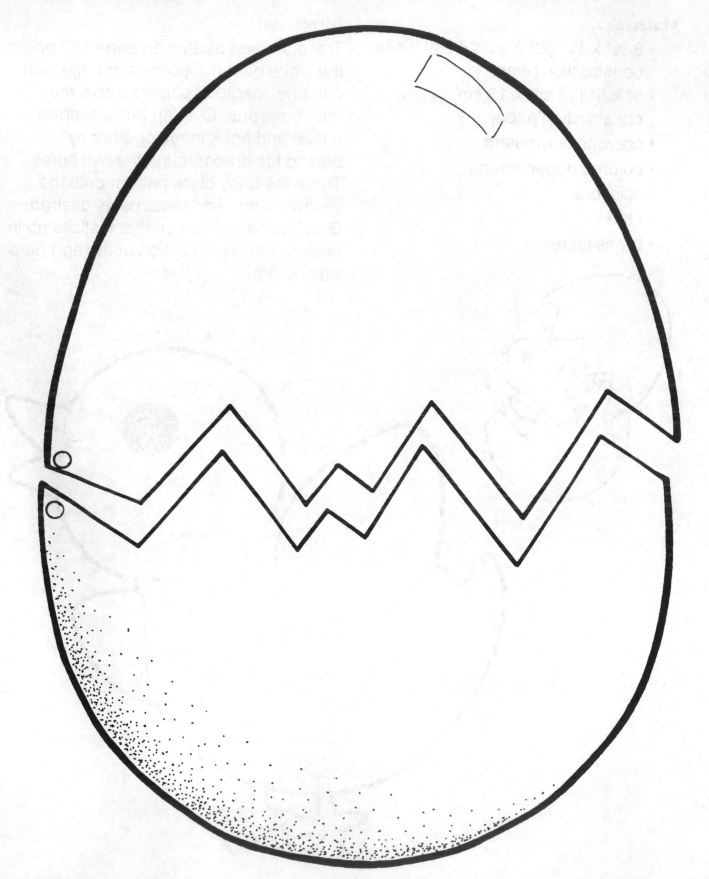

Bunny Cards

Materials:
- construction paper
- scissors
- glue
- crayons or markers
- cottonball

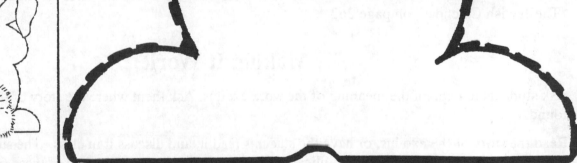

Directions:
Fold paper of any desired springtime color in half to make a card. Cut out bunny shape pattern and make two on white paper. Glue one bunny to the front of the card and one to the back. Decorate the front bunny as desired. Glue a cottonball to the back bunny for its tail. Write an Easter message inside the card.

Passover, the Jewish Festival of Freedom

March or April

Passover, also known as the Festival of Freedom, is a Jewish holiday that celebrates the exodus, the deliverance from slavery of the Hebrews in Egypt over 3,000 years ago. The holiday lasts for eight days. It begins with a special meal, the Seder. The story of the exodus is read from a book called *Haggadah.*

The Passover symbols are placed on the Seder plate in the middle of the dinner table. A roasted lamb bone recalls the sacrificial lambs of the first Passover. A hard-boiled egg is a symbol of new life. Parsley or celery is a reminder that Passover comes in spring when everything begins to grow. A bitter herb such as horseradish is used to symbolize slavery. Charoset, made of apples, nuts, wine, sugar, and cinnamon, represents the mortar the Jews made as they built cities for the Egyptians.

In addition to the Seder Plate, salt water, wine, and matzoh are also on the dinner table. Salt water represents the tears of the Jews as slaves in Egypt. Wine symbolizes the sweetness of life. Matzoh, which is unleavened bread, is a reminder of the Jews' hurried departure from Egypt with no time for bread to rise.

An extra goblet is put on the table for the eagerly awaited guest, Elijah, the prophet of hope and faith.

During the Seder, the youngest child asks the four Questions beginning with "Why is this night different from all other nights?" The questions are answered in the narrative of Haggadah.

Passover is a movable festival. For more detailed information about the dates on which it falls, refer to "The Jewish Calendar" on page 262.

Making It Work

Ask students to explain the meaning of the word exodus. Ask them where the story of the exodus can be found.

Read the story of the exodus, or have the students read it, and discuss it in class. The story has been included in many of Hollywood's biblical epics. You might like to show one of these (or part of one) in video form to give the feeling of the time and place.

Many Jewish festivals and religious ceremonies are centered in the home. Ask students to share their customs and describe the ways in which they celebrate.

Make a Seder Plate using the pattern on page 185, and discuss the meanings of the symbols that are used. Depending on time, resources, and grade level, teachers may share the information given above or ask students to do their own research on the Passover symbols.

Seder Plate

Make a Seder Plate to learn about the Passover symbols. Color the Seder Plate pictured below and cut it out. Then cut along the bold lines to divide the Seder Plate into sections. Next, cut a circle the same size as the Seder Plate out of a separate sheet of paper. Attach the centers of the two circles with glue or a brass fastener. Finally, lift up each section of the Seder Plate and on the paper under it, write a brief description of the food that is pictured and what it symbolizes.

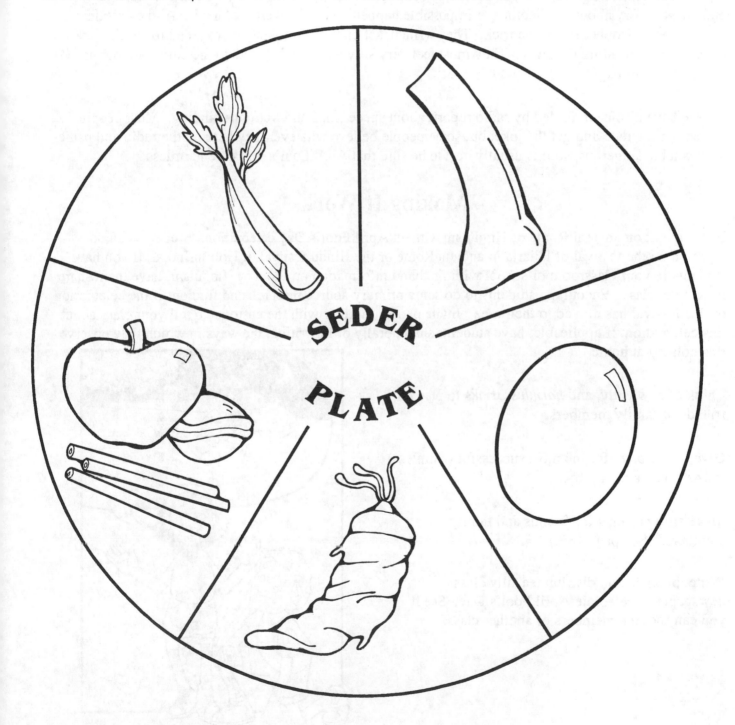

April Fool's Day
April 1

April Fool's Day has its roots in many cultures. It is related to the ancient Roman festival of Hilaria and the Hindu festival of Holi (or Huli). It is celebrated in Europe, Canada, and the United States today in much the same way.

The idea of April Fool's Day is, of course, to trick someone. Almost every year some newspaper publishes a story about a ridiculous or impossible happening as if it were real news. And every time this happens, people fall for the trick. They write upset or even angry letters to the editor of the newspaper, protesting the story. They must feel very silly when their letters to the editor are published on the editorial page.

People have also been fooled by radio reports about space ships and Martians landing. Most people remember the date and get the joke, but some people believe whatever they hear on the radio and panic. This can be dangerous, so it is usually best to be sure that April Fool's jokes are harmless.

Making It Work

Begin a unit on ancient Rome or Hinduism with an April Fool's Day celebration. Students can do research on the festival of Hilaria in ancient Rome or the Hindu festival of Holi in India. If you have students in your classroom or school with firsthand information on India or Hinduism, have them share it with the class. Encourage students to do some primary-source research and find out if the celebration of this festival has moved to their area. Invite people familiar with the customs to tell your class about this celebration. If applicable, have students share, orally or in writing, the ways in which they observe this holiday at home.

Think of new, silly, and *harmless* tricks to play on friends or family members.

Give a silly prize for the most successful (harmless) trick of the day.

Make silly presents for friends and family members. (See page 187.)

Write, publish, and distribute a silly class newspaper to celebrate April Fool's Day. See if you can fool the members of another class.

Make a Silly Weather Worm

Materials:

- 17" (43cm) lengths of yarn (any color; as many as needed for any desired thickness)
- three smaller lengths of yarn for tying
- plastic craft (doll) eyes or ones made of paper
- glue

Directions:

- Bunch together as many lengths of yarn as desired and tie about 1 inch (2.5 cm) from the top.
- Tie the lengths together again about 2 inches (5 cm) from that.
- Braid the yarn the rest of the length until you reach about 1 inch (2.5 cm) from the bottom, and tie the braid off with a smaller length.
- Glue the eyes onto the 2 inch (5 cm) opening. That will be the head of the worm, and the tuft above it is its hair.

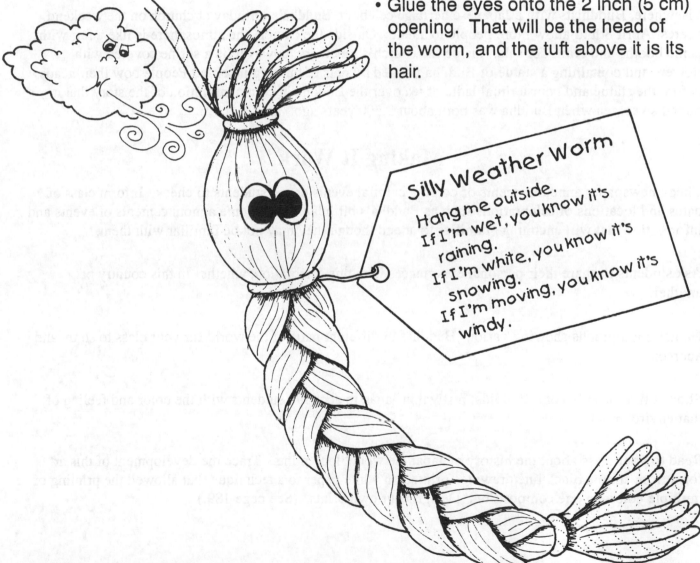

Silly Weather Worm

Hang me outside.
If I'm wet, you know it's raining.
If I'm white, you know it's snowing.
If I'm moving, you know it's windy.

Hana Matsuri or Buddha's Birthday

April 8

All Buddhists celebrate the three main events of Buddha's life: his birth, his enlightenment, and his death.

The Buddhists of Japan celebrate these events separately. They recognize Buddha's birthday on April 8th, his enlightenment on December 8th (Bodhi Day), and his death on February 15th (Nirvana Day). In Japan, Buddha's birthday is called Hana Matsuri. There, people walk in parades and take fresh flowers to shrines.

In Southeast Asia people combine Buddha's birthday with the celebration of his enlightenment and death in the most important triple holiday of the Buddhist year, Vesak. (See pages 212-214.)

Elsewhere, Buddhists with a Japanese heritage celebrate Buddha's birthday at church on the weekend nearest April 8th to allow more people to attend. Outside the church, the atmosphere is like a fair with game booths and crafts for sale. Inside the church's sanctuary, however, is a shrine covered with flowers and containing a statue of Buddha flanked by pots of burning incense. People bow their heads before the statue and pour a ritual ladle of tea over the Buddha in commemoration of the story that it rained sweet tea when Buddha was born about 2,500 years ago.

Making It Work

Check newspaper announcements of coming cultural events or ask students to check. Inform class of dates and locations of celebrations such as Buddha's birthday. Send home announcements of events and information that will encourage families to attend though they may not be familiar with them.

Ask students to share their personal experiences with this celebration, whether in this country or another.

Gather photographs showing various Buddhas in different parts of the world for your class to study and appreciate.

Show a film or video of a Buddhist festival in Japan to acquaint students with the color and feeling of that environment.

Read to your class about the history of Japanese woodblock prints. Trace the development of this art form from simple black line drawings printed on white paper to a technique that allowed the printing of multiple colors in one composition. Design your own prints. (See page 189.)

Making Prints

Japanese artists often organize a series of prints around a single theme. You and your classmates may each want to make an image of Buddha. Each person will probably see him differently. This is fine because Buddhism encourages people to have open minds.

Materials:
- 2 plastic foam meat trays
- scissors
- water-soluble marking pen
- stick or ball-point pen
- newspaper
- printing ink, various colors
- roller
- rice paper
- other types of paper as desired

Directions for making the printing plate or block:
1. Cut the curved edges off a plastic foam tray from the meat department of your grocery store. When you finish, you should have a flat, rectangular surface that is completely smooth on one side.

2. Sketch a design or figure very lightly on the smooth side using water-soluble marking pens.

3. Use a stick or a ball-point pen to "carve" your design or figure into the surface of the foam tray.

Directions for printing on paper with your block:
1. Cover your inking and printing areas with newspaper.

2. Squeeze some printing ink into a foam tray. Run a roller back and forth over the ink.

3. Roll the inked roller over your block. Cover the uncarved areas completely.

4. Lay rice paper on top of the inked block and rub firmly with your hands. (Rice paper lets enough light come through so you can see what you are doing.)

5. Peel the print off the block and hang to dry. Try several colors and other types of paper. Wash your block between prints.

Arbor Day

First Celebrated April 10, 1872

Although Arbor Day is usually celebrated in April, there is no set day for it across the whole United States. It was first celebrated in Nebraska in 1872. Julius Sterling Morton, a settler in that state, was convinced that planting trees would help to conserve water and save the topsoil of the prairies. He persuaded the state of Nebraska to set aside a day for tree planting, and on that first Arbor Day more than a million trees were planted.

Many cultures around the world bring their own tradition of tree planting with them to the United States. Bolivians plant trees in October (spring in the southern hemisphere), Koreans and Russians in April. Jews in Israel plant trees in late winter. Jews living in other, less temperate climates, arrange to have trees planted in Israel for them.

Most states in the United States have an Arbor Day. It is very often celebrated in school. Children may put on a program or pageant, and a civic group often presents a designated grade level with a tiny tree to take home and plant.

As Julius Sterling Morton said, "Other holidays repose upon the past, Arbor Day proposes for the future."

Making It Work

Have students go to the library and find as many poems as they can about trees. Have copies of these poems available for the class to read. Each student can:

- pick a favorite poem
- copy it on paper
- illustrate it
- memorize it

It is fun (and a good experience) for students to recite the poems they memorized for each other, for another class, at an assembly, or for parents who are invited to the classroom for the occasion. You can then use the illustrated poems for a bulletin board display, or bind them into a book for your classroom library.

Have students do some research into the current conflict between conservationists and the logging industry. Make lists of how both sides feel about various issues. Compare and discuss. (Will how a person feels be influenced by where he/she lives? Why or why not?)

Ask students to consider in what way Arbor Day is a holiday dedicated to the future. Can you think of any other holidays that are also dedicated to the future?

Arbor Day Book

Start a book of your own about trees. Some pages follow that will help you get started, but you can add many ideas of your own. Color this page for your cover or draw your own, and mount it on a piece of folded construction paper.

Name_____

Arbor Day Around the World

Research to find out how Arbor Day (or the idea behind it) is celebrated in these countries around the world.

Country	How It Is Celebrated
Canada	
Iceland	
India	
Israel	
Japan	
Russia	
Yugoslavia	

Name_____

Trees That Grow Where I Live

Research to find out the names of trees in your area. Describe them by how they look, feel, and smell.

Name of Tree	Description
1.	
2.	
3.	
4.	
5.	
6.	
7.	
8.	
9.	
10.	

Solar New Year in Southeast Asia

April 13 or 14

Songkran:	Thailand
Bun-Pi-Mai-Lao:	Laos
Thingyan:	Burma
Bon Chol Chhnam:	Kampuchea (Cambodia)
Baisakhi:	Sri Lanka
Baisakhi:	Bangladesh
Baisakhi:	India

Most of Southeast Asia celebrates the Solar New Year by one name or another. Most of the festivals involve water since this is the hottest time of the year in these countries. The water that is thrown by the bucketful at everybody is intended to bless them and to wash off the troubles of the old year.

There are many other New Year's rituals to be observed, also. Houses are cleaned, new fires are kindled, old wrongs are righted, new clothes are worn, gifts are exchanged, and special foods are prepared and eaten. The images of Buddha in the temples are ceremonially washed with a mixture of perfumed water and flower petals.

Outside of Southeast Asia, people from each of these countries adapt their celebrations to new conditions. Most of them gather in public places like colleges and community recreation centers where there will be room for everybody. Their main purpose in celebrating the New Year is to pass on their culture to their children. A secondary, but still important purpose, is to refresh themselves with a breath of home in a strange land. Adults and children alike are mesmerized by the dances, the music, and the smells of traditional foods.

Making It Work

Check newspapers (or ask students to check) for announcements of Solar New Year celebrations in your area. Remember, there may be variations in the spelling of the names of these festivals in the newspapers. Keep parents informed by sending home a class newsletter with this kind of information.

Ask students to share with the class first-hand reports of celebrations they attend. Where was the festival they attended? Which ethnic, national, or religious group put it on? Did they attend as a family? What did they see? Hear? Do? Eat?

Stick-Figure Dolls in Traditional Clothing

Materials:

- pens
- pencils
- paper
- markers
- scissors
- fabric glue
- white glue
- clay
- craft or popsicle sticks
- fabrics scraps, felt scraps
- decorations: beads, sequins buttons
- reference books

Directions:

Make a stick person and add a head and face. This can be as simple as a circle cut from paper: just add drawn-on features and glue at the end of the stick that forms the body. Or, it can be a realistic head and face modeled from clay.

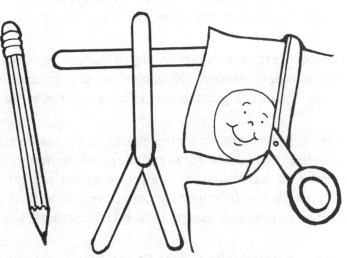

Look through reference books for colored pictures of people who are wearing traditional clothing of a country in Southeast Asia. Encyclopedias often have this information. Decide on a country and style to depict.

Choose scraps of material that compliment the style of clothing you have chosen. Cut, glue, and decorate costumes, working right on the stick figure.

Allow to dry, and display on a bulletin board. Include a map of the region and use yarn to connect the costumed stick figure to its country of origin.

Earth Day

April 22

Earth Day was started in the 1960's. It was one of the first attempts to make people aware of the earth as their environment and of their responsibility to take care of it. When Earth Day started, it focused on pollution, particularly of the air and water. Young people were often frustrated and sometimes frightened by pollution because they felt powerless to improve the situation. They heard so much about air and water pollution that they were afraid to breathe the air or drink the water.

Although the whole subject is still controversial, a lot has been done to improve the condition of the air and water since the beginning of Earth Day. Also, our approach to the improvement of our environment has become more positive, more responsive to the efforts of young people.

We are concerned with preserving our natural resources, and scientists are busily looking for alternative fuels and other materials. However, our natural resources can also be preserved by recycling materials, and this is something that students can do just as efficiently as can scientists.

We are still concerned with the quality of the air we breathe, but a lot has been done by requiring certain limits to be met for harmful emissions from both vehicles and factories. We have also remembered that air quality is affected by the number of trees and other green plants in an area, and young people can help here by doing everything from paying for the preservation of a piece of rainforest to planting trees in their own backyards, schools, and neighborhood parks.

We are concerned with the condition of the earth's oceans, and people are still arguing about how much garbage we can dump in these oceans without upsetting their ability to clean themselves. In the meantime, however, young people have learned not to disturb the sea animals in tidepools and have joined in the effort to keep our beaches clean.

The celebration of Earth Day in 1992 was made memorable by an international conference held in Rio de Janeiro, Brazil. The leaders of most of earth's nations attended this conference. Many people feel that not much was accomplished there. However, the attention of the world's people has been drawn to the problems of the environment, and this should make future progress easier.

Making It Work

Encourage students to establish a recycling center for newspapers and aluminum cans. Use the proceeds to pay for school events, or send the money off to buy an acre of rainforest or to save an animal on the endangered species list.

Establish a club to keep your own schoolyard beautiful. Pick up litter, plant flower beds and trees, and immediately repaint surfaces marked with graffiti.

Save the Earth Newspaper

Plan to write and publish a newspaper about ways to improve the environment. You can do this yourself, or you can enlist the help of a group of interested friends. You can do it on your own time, or you can ask your teacher to let you do it as a school project. Unless you have your own computer, it might be easier to do it in school where you could probably use the computer facilities that are available there. The whole job will be easier and more fun with the appropriate word-processing software and easy access to a printer.

1. If you plan to write and publish a newspaper with a group, your first job will be to decide on the jobs and then match a person with each job title.

   Job titles you might consider are editor, publisher, reporter, researcher, and paste-up artist. Brainstorm for other job titles you might want to have. Then write a job description for each job title. A job description is a definition of the job. It tells what the person who has that job will be doing. Finally, decide who will do the jobs. (See page 198.)

2. Next, you should establish a list of topics or departments for your newspaper. Brainstorm as many article ideas as you can for each department. Some of the department's titles might be "Endangered Animals," "Trees and Forests," "Water Wasters and Savers," "Famous Environmentalists," and "Current Events in Conservation." There are many more. Choose the ones in which you are most interested. (See page 199.)

3. After you are organized with job titles and ideas for articles, people will begin to write. If you are using a page-maker or desktop-publishing software, follow the directions that come with it. If you are planning to paste up your newspaper, follow these steps:

   • Have your writers print out their stories in newspaper column width. Trim neatly with a paper cutter.

   • Lay out the stories attractively on the paper you plan to use for your newspaper.

   • Use some kind of fixative or tape to keep them positioned.

   • Add headlines and art work.

   • Make copies and distribute. You can give a sample paper away free to get people's interest, and then if your school policy allows it, charge a fee to cover your paper costs.

Save the Earth Newspaper *(cont.)*

Job Title	Job Description	Person

Save the Earth Newspaper *(cont.)*

Department Title	Article Ideas

Earth Day Wordsearch

Find these words in the wordsearch below.

animals	conservation	environment	organic
Arbor Day	Earth Day	garden	pollution
birds	ecology	litter	soil erosion
compost	endangered	nature	spring

```
S O I L E R O S I O N E Q C T A A
P X L D R Y R B N B V N M K O N P
R Z I A Q W G I U T Y V P L K I F
I J T F H G A R D E N I I U N M M
N A T U R E N D E E A R T H D A Y
G R E R D S I S X C V O A S D L E
Q B R W E Y C O I J V N Q W E S C
C O C O M P O S T C O M Q E D C O
O R D G J E N D A N G E R E D E L
I D E R T Y U I O P K N L N B C O
A A E T Y U P O L L U T I O N E G
S Y C O N S E R V A T I O N E R Y
```

May Day

May 1

May Day has been celebrated for thousands of years. The Druids and the ancient Romans probably started this festival in which trees were worshipped. Much later, the English substituted a tall pole for the tree. A "Maypole," which was erected in the middle of a village was decorated with long trailing ribbons that hung from the very top. Dancers held the ends of the ribbons and danced around the pole, weaving the ribbons into patterns. A May Queen was chosen to rule over the festival.

May is the time when spring is turning into summer. It has been associated with flowers since the Romans worshipped Flora as their goddess of spring. When this holiday became so popular in England, the custom of gathering and giving flowers became popular, too. People went out early in the morning of May 1st to gather flowers and tree branches. This was called "bringing in the May." The flowers and branches were used as decorations for their homes and as gifts to be delivered in May Baskets.

Since the late 1800's, May Day has also been a day dedicated to labor. It is an international celebration of the worker and is celebrated in many socialist countries. However, the United States honors labor in September on Labor Day (see page 22).

Today, May Day is often celebrated with Maypole dances and the giving of May Baskets. These are small baskets filled with flowers or candy. Children leave them on a friend's doorstep, ring the doorbell, and run quickly around the house before they can be caught and kissed.

Making It Work

Create your own Maypole dance around a flagpole or tetherball pole. Attach an even number of crepe paper ribbons to the top. The ribbons should alternate in length: short, long, short, etc., the difference being just enough to notice. To wind the Maypole, have students hold the ends of the ribbons (one ribbon per student). Students with short ribbons should form a circle just inside the circle of students with long ribbons. Have the two circles of students walk around the Maypole in opposite directions, alternately stepping to the outside and raising their arms and then stepping inside and ducking under the arms of others, causing the ribbons to be woven in an over/under pattern. Reverse directions to unwind the Maypole. After a few practices, add music and have the students skip or dance as they wind and unwind the Maypole. Options: You may want to decorate the top of the Maypole with flowers. The colors of the ribbons can be varied to create different looks. The weaving patterns can be varied, such as two over, one under.

Ask students if they have ever made and delivered May Baskets. To whom did they give the baskets? How did they deliver the baskets? What was in the baskets?

Make May Baskets according to the directions on pages 202-203, then share them.

May Baskets

1. Use green plastic berry baskets from the market. Weave a ribbon through the holes, leaving enough extra at both ends to tie a bow at the top as a handle. Weave more ribbon in a pleasing design around the sides if desired. Stuff the bottom with damp, crumpled paper towels or wet moss, and fill with short-stemmed flowers.

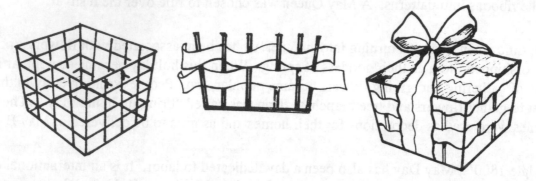

2. Start with a plain paper cup. Decorate it with crayons or markers, or cut designs from paper and glue them on the cup. Another option is to cover it with colored paper. Cut the paper a little "taller" than the cup so you can cut fringe for the top and bottom edges as shown below. Add a pipe cleaner handle. Fill with flowers or candy.

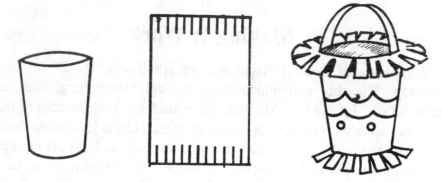

3. Fold a square of fabric or paper in half diagonally. Add flowers that have long stems. Tie or staple the top corners together as a handle.

May Baskets *(cont.)*

Cut out the basket and color it. Fold along the dotted line. Glue or staple the sides together. Fill with flowers or candy.

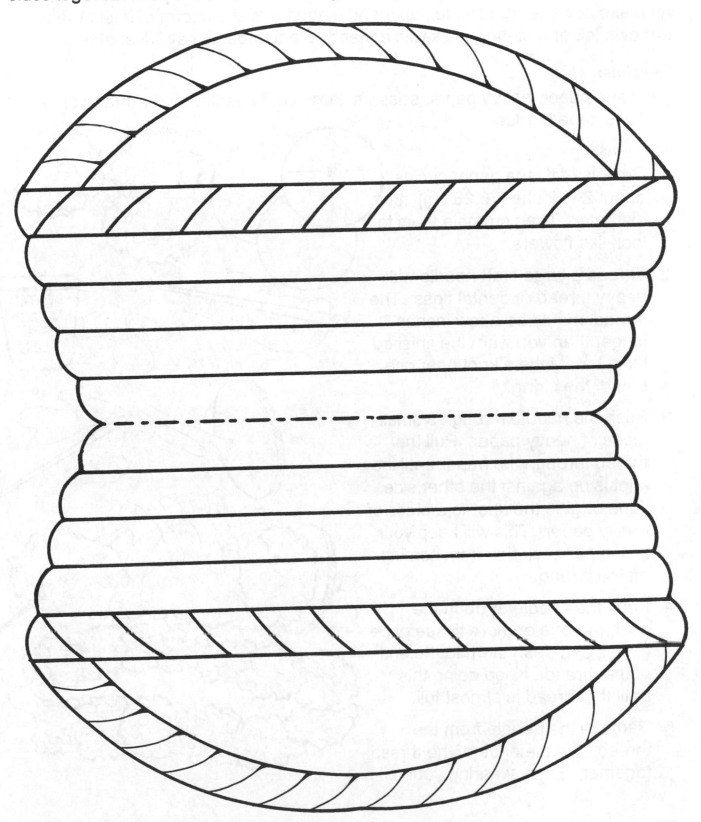

Lei Day in Hawaii

May Day has a special meaning in Hawaii. Hawaiians make, display, and wear leis. Lei-making contests are held, and traditional dances are performed. You can make flowers from tissue paper and string them in the form of a lei. Wear your own lei, or exchange leis with a friend. Remember to say, "Aloha!"

Materials:

- tissue paper, heavy paper, scissors, large craft needle, heavy thread or dental floss, tape or glue

Directions:

1. Cut lots of tissue paper circles about 2 ½ inches (6.25 cm) in diameter. Then crumple them to look like flowers.

2. Thread a large craft needle with heavy thread or dental floss. The thread should be a few inches longer than you want the finished lei to be. Make a knot near one end of the string.

3. Push the needle through a small piece of heavy paper. Pull the thread through the paper until the knot is up against the other side. Tape or glue the knot to a piece of heavy paper. This will keep your tissue paper circles from coming off the thread.

4. Poke the needle through the center of one or more tissue paper circles and push them to the end of the thread. Keep doing this until the thread is almost full.

5. Remove the needle from the thread. Tie the ends of the thread together. Enjoy wearing your lei!

Cinco De Mayo, the Fifth of May Mexican Victory

May 5

On May 5th, Mexicans celebrate their 1862 victory over the French army. The French planned to capture Mexico City and take over the country. But Mexican peasants in the town of Puebla rose up and defeated the well-trained and well-equipped French. This day is a national holiday in Mexico. Mock battles take place, ending with giant firework displays.

In the United States where there is a large number of Mexican immigrants, Cinco De Mayo has become a day to celebrate Mexican heritage. Many elementary schools set aside May as Hispanic Heritage Month. It is a day of festivity, especially in the southwestern United States, and is the occasion for many parades and mariachi concerts.

More over, people of all ethnic backgrounds have begun to celebrate Cinco De Mayo just for fun, in much the same way that everyone celebrates Saint Patrick's Day. People have parties, eat Mexican food, and generally enjoy the day.

Making It Work

Many women took part in the Battle of Puebla. They are recognized in the mock battles in Mexico. Have students debate the issue of women serving actively in the armed services in wartime. This is currently an issue of some controversy in the western world.

Have students research the events surrounding Cinco De Mayo and the Battle of Puebla. How did the French army manage to get involved in the first place? Where did they go when they retreated?

If you have students from Mexico or of Mexican heritage in your classroom, ask them to share Cinco De Mayo celebrations they have experienced. How have their celebrations adapted to living here?

Ask students of other ethnic backgrounds if their families do anything to celebrate Cinco de Mayo. Do they have a party or eat any special foods?

Use a map to demonstrate the extent of Mexico's former holdings in the United States. What states were once part of Mexico? How did these became part of the U.S.?

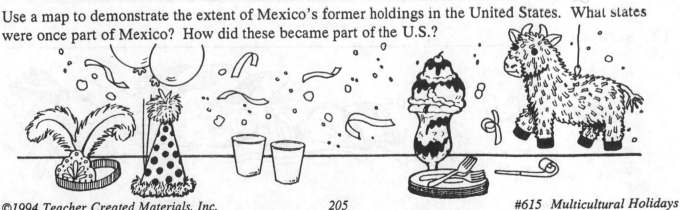

Do You Know These Words?

Many Spanish words have crossed the Mexican borders into other countries. These words have become part of the English language. Write down what you think they mean and then look them up in the dictionary to check yourself.

Hint: These are all foods.

1. chili _____

2. guacamole _____

3. tortilla _____

4. plantain _____

5. taco _____

6. enchilada _____

7. paella _____

Hint: These are all articles of clothing.

8. sombrero _____

9. poncho _____

10. bolero _____

11. mantilla _____

12. serape _____

Children's Day

May 5

May 5th used to be Boys' Day in Japan, but it is now a day for all children, boys and girls. On this day, Japanese parents honor their children and take them to Shinto shrines to be blessed by the priests.

The carp was the symbol of the Boys' Day festival. A family would hang carp-shaped kites, one for each son, from tall poles in their gardens. This fish still stands for the characteristics parents want for their children. The carp symbolizes strength, courage, and determination because it can swim upstream against the current.

May 5th is also Children's Day in the Republic of South Korea. It is a real holiday for children. They do not have school on that day. Many zoos, museums, and theaters admit them free. There are special sporting events and competitions for them to enter. Their parents give them candy and gifts.

Many other countries also celebrate a special day for children. Children's Day is November 14th in India, April 23rd in Turkey, May 27th in Nigeria, June 17th in Indonesia, August 16th in Uruguay, and October 12th in Brazil. In China, Poland, Germany, and Russia, it is on June 1st. The United States does not celebrate a day for children. When children ask their parents about this, the most common response is, "Everyday is children's day in this country."

Making It Work

In 1946, the United Nations established UNICEF, the United Nations International Children's Emergency Fund, to help children who had suffered in World War II. Since then, UNICEF has extended its programs to help children in developing countries. Children can help children through UNICEF. To request more information about UNICEF, write to

> *UN Department of Public Relations*
> United Nations
> New York City, NY 10017

Help students to gather and deliver clothing to homeless children in your area.

Ask students to research ways in which Children's Day is celebrated in other countries. Have them present their findings to the class in ways that reflect the celebrations. For instance, they may perform a play, make a craft project, sing a song, or share a recipe. Whatever the activity, they should explain the significance of the activity and of the country's overall celebration.

Have students work in groups to plan a Children's Day celebration for the United States. Ask them to decide when and how it should be celebrated.

Make a carp kite in recognition of Children's Day in Japan. Directions are given on page 208.

Making a Japanese Carp Kite

Materials:

- large paper cup (plain or waxed)
- markers or crayons
- colored paper
- crepe paper for streamers
- glue or stapler
- string

Directions:

1. Draw the head of a carp on the paper cup, or design the head of a carp using colored paper and attach it to a paper cup. Include eyes and mouth. (The mouth should be near the bottom of the cup.) Use any colors that you like.

2. Cut a dozen streamers from crepe paper. Glue or staple them to the open end of the cup.

3. Poke four tiny holes around the bottom of the cup as shown.

4. Cut four 12" pieces of string, and make a knot in one end of each. Pull the strings through the four holes in the cup from the inside out. Tie the four ends together to make the kite's bridle. Attach a longer string to the bridle to hold.

Mother's Day

The Second Sunday in May

Mother's Day was first celebrated as an American holiday in 1872. It was called a Mother's Day for Peace and was suggested by Julia Ward Howe, who is best known for writing "The Battle Hymn Of The Republic." She had nursed the wounded during the Civil War and was determined to put an end to war. She wanted to set aside a day dedicated not only to mothers but also to peace.

Later, in 1907, Anna Jarvis started a campaign for a national Mother's Day. She arranged to hold a church service in Philadelphia on the anniversary of her own mother's death and started the custom of wearing a carnation. This custom is still observed. In some places it is now the custom to wear a red carnation if your mother is living and a white carnation if she has died.

By 1915, Jarvis' campaign had become so successful that President Woodrow Wilson proclaimed the second Sunday in May to be Mother's Day in the United States. Mothers are honored in many other countries as well, on different days and with different customs. However, mothers the world over like to receive flowers and candy in honor of their day.

Making It Work

Make individual Mother's Day collages. Cut pictures of women and children from magazines, combine and mount them attractively, and finish with a spray of shellac or other fixative. They can serve as gifts and make nice place mats for a Mother's Day meal.

Make "carnations" from crepe paper. Give mother a single flower or make her a bouquet.

Write essays or poems about what it means to be a mother. Students may want to write about their own mothers. The results of these writing projects can be copied and made into cards for Mother's Day.

Ask students how they celebrate Mother's Day at home. Are other female family members such as grandmothers and aunts honored as well as mother? Are there ethnic differences in the way Mother's Day is celebrated within different cultures in the United States, or is this really an "American" holiday?

Research Mother's Day customs in other countries. Ask volunteers to report their findings to the class. You might want to mount facts on a bulletin board entitled "Mother's Day Around the World."

Give a Mother's Day Tea. Invite mothers to visit school during May. Read aloud the things you have written about mothers and serve cookies and punch.

Mother's Day Coupon Book

Color carefully, cut out, and staple the coupons into book form. (Personalize blank coupons if you would like.) Give to Mother for a present on Mother's Day.

Happy Mother's Day

from _____

Good for 1 hug.

Good for 1 errand.

Good for 1 job of your choice.

Good for playing with the baby.

Good for feeding a pet.

Mother's Day Coupon Book *(cont.)*

Good for pulling weeds.

Good for yard work—watering or raking leaves.

Good for setting the table.

Good for folding clothes.

Good for helping with dinner.

Good for being cheerful all day.

Vesak: Buddha's Birth, Death, and Enlightenment

Around the Second Sunday in May

Vesak is the festival that combines Buddha's birth, enlightenment, and death into one celebration. It is the most important festival in the Buddhist year. Many Buddhists who have already celebrated these events separately (see Hana Matsuri, Bodhi Day, and Nirvana Day) also take part in Vesak.

Buddha was born Prince Siddhartha in about 563 B.C. in northern India. As a young man, he was so unhappy about the suffering he saw around him in the world that he gave up everything and set out to see what he could do. He finally decided to meditate. At about the age of 35, as he sat under the famous Bo Tree, he reached a state of enlightenment. (This means he remembered all of his past lives.) After that he was known as Buddha, which means "the Enlightened One." He taught his method of reaching enlightenment until he died at the age of 80.

On Vesak, Buddhists go to temples for ceremonies. They decorate homes and buildings with lights and paper lanterns. In Laos, people shoot off rockets. In Vietnam, people buy caged animals and set them free. In Sri Lanka and Korea, people have special lantern parades. In the United States and Canada, people gather together to celebrate the cultural as well as the religious aspects of the day. They keep the rituals, decorations, and foods as true to those they had in their home countries as they can, so their children will have the experience. The changes they make are for convenience. Holidays may be celebrated on the closest weekend so more people can attend. Ceremonies that used to take place within families may take place at temples, churches, or community centers because many people who emigrated left their families behind.

Making It Work

Check the newspaper (or have students check) to find announcements of cultural and religious observances in your area. Send home information about these events so people of different backgrounds will be more apt to attend.

If you have one or more students in your classroom who celebrate Vesak, ask them to share their first-hand information with their classmates.

Ask students to invite their parents to come to school and share their memories and experiences with the class. They may be able to bring photographs or examples of traditional clothing.

Show a film or video of holiday celebrations in Southeast Asia to give students a feeling for the color and sounds of the region.

Make special Vesak lanterns using the patterns and directions on pages 213-214.

Vesak Lanterns

Since lanterns are used for so many of the Vesak celebrations, to make your own would be a fitting activity in honor of Vesak.

Materials:
- pattern, page 214
- stiff paper, four times the size of the pattern
- one more sheet of stiff paper, 7" (17.5 cm) square
- ink pen
- tape
- string

Directions:
- Cut out the pattern on page 214. Also cut out the shaded areas around the figure of Buddha. Using the cut-out shape as a pattern, trace it four times across on the stiff paper, as illustrated. Cut out. Ink in details as desired. Cut out one more plain 7" (17.5 cm) square. This will be the base of the lantern. Tape all sides together as shown to make a five-sided box. Make holes in the middle of the top edges of each side panel, and put string through them. Knot string together and hang your lantern.

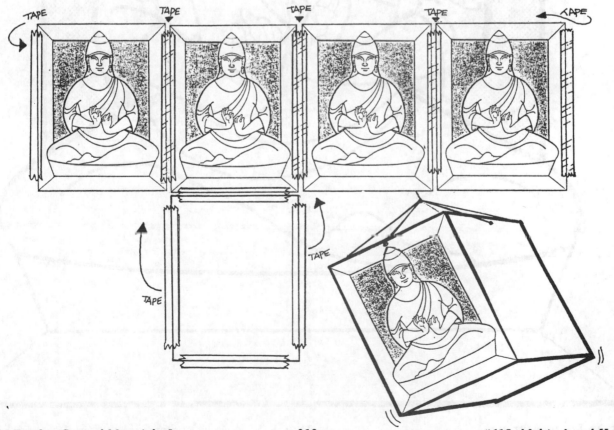

Vesak Lanterns (cont.)

Memorial Day
May 30 or Last Monday of May

Memorial Day is the day on which Americans honor those who have died for their country. It is celebrated on May 30th, or on the last Monday in May in order to make a three-day weekend. (On the calendar you may see "Traditional Memorial Day" on May 30th and "Memorial Day Observed" on the last Monday.) It is a legal holiday in most states. And, even though it falls in May, it is usually considered to be the mark of the beginning of summer.

Memorial Day was originally called Decoration Day because it was the day women in the South chose to decorate the graves of men who had died in the Civil War. These women honored the dead of both armies, Union and Confederate. It is thought that Cassandra Oliver Moncure, a Virginia woman of French ancestry, started the movement.

In the northern states, the Grand Army of the Republic, which was an organization of veterans of the Union Army during the Civil War, was in charge of Memorial Day celebrations. The American Legion took over this responsibility after World War I. Today they sell small artificial red poppies around Memorial Day to raise money to help disabled veterans.

Military parades are held on Memorial Day and special programs take place at Gettysburg and at Arlington National Cemetery. A highlight of these programs is often the reading of President Abraham Lincoln's Gettysburg Address.

Making It Work

Ask your students if any have gone to a cemetery to decorate a grave. Was it a military cemetery? Was it the grave of someone who died in a war? Allow students to share experiences.

Ask students who come from different homelands to tell about ceremonies that honor the people who died in wars in the countries where they used to live. They may have first-hand experiences or they may wish to interview an older relative to get this information. Students may be interested in building an oral history of their family by tape-recording these interviews. (Make sure they get permission before recording an interview, even with a family member.)

If there are no representatives of other backgrounds in your classroom, have students do some research in the library to find out how other countries honor those who died in wars. Students can write reports or give oral reports to the class.

Read Lincoln's Gettysburg Address to your students. Encourage them to memorize it. (See page 216.)

Find out about the American Legion and its use of red poppies. Often the American Legion holds competitions concerning patriotism, and poppies are a common theme. Find out if there is one such competition in your area.

The Gettysburg Address

In 1863, Abraham Lincoln gave a short but moving speech that has come to be known as the "Gettysburg Address." The time was two years before the end of the Civil War, and he was dedicating a cemetery at the town of Gettysburg. Legend has it that he wrote out his remarks on the back of an old envelope while riding to Gettysburg in a train. Whether or not this is true, his remarks have gone down in history as one of the most powerful speeches ever given. Following is the complete text of the speech as it has been recorded.

Fourscore and seven years ago our fathers brought forth on this continent a new nation, conceived in liberty and dedicated to the proposition that all men are created equal.

Now we are engaged in a great civil war, testing whether that nation or any nation so conceived and so dedicated can long endure. We are met on a great battle field of that war. We have come to dedicate a portion of that field, as a final resting place for those who here gave their lives that that nation might live. It is altogether fitting and proper that we should do this.

But, in a larger sense, we cannot dedicate—we cannot consecrate—we cannot hallow — this ground. The brave men, living and dead, who struggled here, have consecrated it, far above our poor power to add or detract. The world will little note, nor long remember, what we say here, but it can never forget what they did here. It is for us the living, rather to be dedicated here to the unfinished work which they who fought here have thus far so nobly advanced. It is rather for us to be here dedicated to the great task remaining before us—that from these honored dead we take increased devotion to that cause for which they gave the last full measure of devotion—that we here highly resolve that these dead shall not have died in vain—that this nation, under God, shall have a new birth of freedom—and that government of the people, by the people, for the people, shall not perish from the earth.

Summer Holidays

June

Birthstone: Pearl

Flower: Rose

Although there is some disagreement about where June got its name, most scholars think that it was named to honor Juno. Juno was the wife of Jupiter, king of the Roman gods.

July

Birthstone: Ruby

Flower: Larkspur

July was named to honor Julius Caesar. Its named was changed from Quintilis, the Latin word for "fifth" in 44 B.C., the year Caesar was assassinated.

August

Birthstone: Sardonyx

Flower: Poppy

August was renamed by the Roman Senate to honor Augustus Caesar. He took a day from February and added it to his month so no other month would be longer than his.

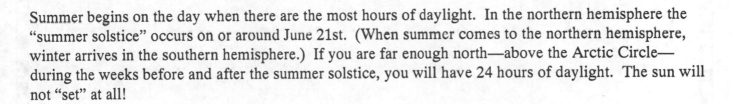

Summer begins on the day when there are the most hours of daylight. In the northern hemisphere the "summer solstice" occurs on or around June 21st. (When summer comes to the northern hemisphere, winter arrives in the southern hemisphere.) If you are far enough north—above the Arctic Circle—during the weeks before and after the summer solstice, you will have 24 hours of daylight. The sun will not "set" at all!

People traditionally travel during the summer because that is the time when most of us take our annual vacations. We go to visit friends and relatives or just to look at interesting places and things. Some people always return to the same summer place, and others go to a different place every year.

Summer is the time for outdoor celebrations and entertainment. It is the time for food festivals. Your own community may have an annual Strawberry Festival or Garlic Festival or Fish Fry. Many of these celebrations include parades and contests and carnival games as well as opportunities to feast on the featured food.

Also, with the increasingly common adoption of year-round school, summer celebrations will very likely become more mainstream since children will be in school when these events are observed.

Summer Holidays

This is an upper grade contract to be used in connection with the summer holidays. If you are in year-round school, it can be used as a regular contract. If the students have their vacation in the summer, they can take it home for enrichment, reinforcement, extra credit, or just for fun. Use the part of this page below the line as a cover and the two following pages as an instructional packet. Send it home a week before vacation and have parents sign and return the slip at the end of the last page to verify that they received it.

Summer Holiday Contract

Summer Holiday Contract *(cont.)*

1. Choose the summer holiday in which you are most interested. If you (or your family) are from another country, please consider basing your research and activities on your own customs and traditions.

2. Research your summer holiday. You may use all kinds of reference books and encyclopedias. You may also consult primary sources — people with first-hand, personal knowledge. Interview your parents, older relatives, and family friends. (You can also include your personal experiences as part of your research.) Just be sure to write down where you got your information.

3. Here is what to do for your holiday research/activities.

   a. Write an information paper to be turned in. Here are some of the things you might want to include (though you may think of many more):

      • What is the name of your holiday?
      • What is the theme of your holiday?
      • When is it celebrated?
      • Where is it celebrated? In public? At home?
      • Is it celebrated differently in different countries?
      • Have the customs of your holiday become well-known or are they practiced only by a special group of people?
      • Does your holiday have a religious significance?
      • What are the symbols of your holiday?
      • Are there costumes? Parades? Dances? Special foods?
      • Is your holiday for everyone? Just for children? Just for adults?

   b. Include a bibliography. Don't forget to list any primary sources.

   c. Do at least _____ of the following:

      • Keep a scrapbook/journal about your holiday. Your information paper will be the first thing you enter. Take some pictures and include them along with anything of interest you find in the newspapers or magazines you have at home. Write a description of the celebrations, events, and so on that you attend.
      • Add to your scrapbook with articles (and pictures) about other celebrations that are held in your community during the summer. Save programs, ticket stubs, brochures, and pamphlets from everywhere you go — fairs, exhibits, food festivals, etc. — at home or away.

Summer Holiday Contract (cont.)

- Write a letter to your teacher describing your holiday or one of your summer activities. Keep a copy of the letter in your scrapbook.

_____

Teacher's Name

_____

Street Address

_____

City   *State*   *Zip Code*

- Plant a garden in your backyard or in a planter on a patio, balcony, or windowsill. Herbs are a good choice. Start with seeds and keep a careful day-by-day record of how your garden grows. Write down your observations and make sketches. Be sure to date all of your observations and sketches.

- Start a collection of picture postcards. Add to it every time you go somewhere.

- Make simple puppets from paper bags or socks and a puppet theater from a large carton. Use them to tell the story of your holiday. Entertain a primary class or the little kids in your neighborhood.

- Prepare dinner for your family. Treat them to some of the foods that are associated with your holiday. Find recipes in your family's collection of cookbooks or at the library.

- Write about where you would go on vacation if you could go anywhere in the world. Find the place on a map. Figure out how far away it is from where you live.

- Create your own activity. Check with the teacher first.

  d. Share your research and activities with your classmates and teacher.

Fill out the form below, clip it off, and return it to the teacher before the last day of school.

━━

Name _____

The holiday I have chosen is _____ .

Parent signature _____

This is a primary grade contract to be used in connection with the summer holidays. If you are in year-round school, it can be used as a regular contract. If the students have their vacation in the summer, they can take it home for enrichment, reinforcement, extra credit, or just for fun. Use the part of this page below the line as a cover and the two following pages as an instructional packet. Send it home a week before vacation and have parents sign and return the slip at the end of the last page to verify that they received it.

Summer Holiday Contract

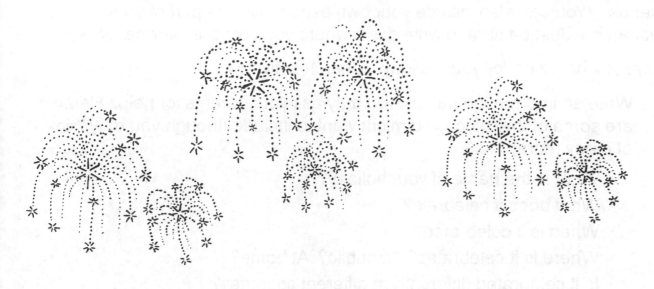

Summer Holiday Contract *(cont.)*

1. Choose the summer holiday in which you are most interested. If you (or your family) are from another country, please consider basing your research and activities on your own customs and traditions.

2. Find out about your summer holiday. You may use all kinds of reference books and encyclopedias. You may also talk to people with first-hand, personal knowledge. Interview your parents, older relatives, and family friends. (You can also include your own experiences as part of your research.) Just be sure to write down where you got your information.

3. Here is what to do for your holiday research/activities.

    a. Write an information paper. You may ask your parents for help. Here are some of the things you might want to include (though you may think of many more):

     - What is the name of your holiday?
     - What does it celebrate?
     - When is it celebrated?
     - Where is it celebrated? In public? At home?
     - Is it celebrated differently in different countries?
     - Does almost everyone in this country celebrate your holiday?
     - Does your holiday have a religious significance?
     - What are the symbols of your holiday?
     - Are there costumes? Parades? Dances? Special foods?
     - Is your holiday for everyone? Just for children? Just for adults?

    b. Include a bibliography. Don't forget to list any people to whom you spoke.

    c. Do at least _____ of the following:

     - Ask your parents to get you a scrapbook or help you to make one. (A simple way to do this is to punch holes in sheets of construction paper and tie them together with yarn or string.) They can also help you to get started keeping a scrapbook/journal about your holiday. Your information paper will be the first thing you enter. Take some pictures and include them along with anything of interest you find in the newspapers or magazines you have at home. Write a description of the celebrations, events, and so on that you attend.

Summer Holiday Contract *(cont.)*

- Add to your scrapbook with articles (and pictures) about other summer celebrations. Save programs, ticket stubs, brochures, and pamphlets from everywhere you go — fairs, exhibits, food festivals, etc. — at home or away.

- Write a letter to your teacher describing your holiday or one of your summer activities. Keep a copy of the letter in your scrapbook.

_____
Teacher's Name

_____
Street Address

_____
City   *State*   *Zip Code*

- Plant a garden in your backyard or in a planter on a patio, balcony, or windowsill. Herbs are a good choice. Every week, draw a sketch of your garden. Date your sketches.

- Start a collection of picture postcards. Add to it every time you go somewhere.

- Ask your parents to help you find a recipe for a special food that goes with your holiday. Make it (or buy it at an ethnic market) to surprise your family.

- Write about where you would go on vacation if you could go anywhere in the world. Find the place on a map. Figure out how far away it is from where you live.

  d. Share your research and activities with your classmates and teachers.

Parents:

Please feel free to help your child with the activities in this summertime contract. Read it over. Then fill out the slip below, clip it off, and return it to the teacher before the last day of school.

- -

Name _____

The holiday I have chosen is _____

Parent signature _____

Summer Festivals

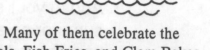

All Summer

Festivals are held all over the United States during the summer months. Many of them celebrate the food of an area or region. There are Garlic Festivals, Strawberry Festivals, Fish Fries, and Clam Bakes. Here are a few real examples:

- ### *Black-Eyed Pea Festival*

  This celebration is held in Athens, Texas, in the middle of July. It features events such as "pea-poppin', pea-eatin', and pea-shellin'" and ends with a black-eyed pea cook-off.

- ### *Dinosaur Days*

  Adults and kids can tour the fossil quarries in Grand Junction, Colorado, toward the end of July.

- ### *Lion's Fish Fry*

  This is a yearly fish feast and old-time parade and carnival held in Costa Mesa, California, on the Memorial Day Weekend.

- ### *Pufferbelly Days*

  Of special interest to both kids and train buffs, you can see model railroad cars and even take a ride on a steam-driven train near the beginning of September in Boone, Iowa.

- ### *Rockwood Old-Fashioned Ice-Cream Festival*

  This festival has a Victorian theme with crafts such as glass blowing and lots of home-made ice cream. It is held in Wilmington, Delaware, near the beginning of July.

- ### *Valparaiso Popcorn Festival*

  At the beginning of September in Valparaiso, Indiana, you can visit a craft fair, listen to music, and see a parade with floats made out of popcorn.

Attendance at festivals such as these used to be strictly a family affair but now with more and more year-round schools, summer festivals can become part of the school experience as well.

Making It Work

Have kids search the newspapers, watch for signs, and ask family and friends to watch for festival announcements. Prepare and send home a weekly newsletter keeping people informed about what is going on in your area.

Take a field trip to a nearby festival. Learn how it started.

Name_____

Summer Festivals in the United States

Use reference books to look up the foods listed below. Find out something about their history. Were they discovered/grown/invented in America or brought here from some other country? Do they have other names in different parts of the United States? In other countries?

Squash _____

_____

Hominy grits _____

_____

Corn _____

_____

Pancakes_____

_____

Waffles_____

_____

Tomatoes_____

_____

Hot dogs _____

_____

Ice cream cones _____

_____

Pizza _____

_____

Shoo-fly pie _____

_____

Summer Festivals *(cont.)*

Sandwiches _____

_____

French fries _____

_____

Barbecue _____

_____

Clam chowder _____

_____

Hamburger _____

_____

Apple pie _____

_____

Pasta _____

_____

Tacos _____

_____

Sushi _____

_____

Sukyaki _____

_____

Guacamole _____

_____

Chow Mein _____

226 ©*1994 Teacher Created Materials, Inc.*

Native American Ceremonial Dances

All Summer

Music and dancing have always been significant in the lives of Native Americans. Traditional dances have always played a vital role in religious rituals and other ceremonies.

Some traditional dances began as ways to guarantee the success of hunts. The Deer Dance of the Yaqui Indians and the Bear Dance of the Sioux are examples of this kind of dance. The dancers represent the animals to be hunted. They shake ceremonial rattles or scrape rasps while the drums keep the rhythm of the dance.

The Green Corn Dance, whose tradition is shared by many Native American tribes, combines celebrations for thanksgiving and the new year. The celebration is a time of feasting and merry-making. It occurs at the time of the first ripe corn.

Before the European settlement of the North American continent, the Sun Dance was the major religious ceremony of all of the Plains Indians. The Sun Dance involved fasting, dancing, and ceremonial drumming in an effort to establish a connection between the participants — and the people they represented — and the Great Spirit. This ceremony was widely suppressed by Christian missionaries, but some members of those tribes managed to preserve it and pass it on.

All of these ceremonies are being performed today in the United States as the Native American tribes reclaim their culture and customs. In some places outsiders are welcomed, while in other places, they are not.

Making It Work

Contact individual Tribal Bureaus for information about the Native American ceremonies that are open to visitors.

Introduce students to the history of the Native Americans from their point-of-view.

Divide students into groups to find out about the lifestyles of various Native American tribes on reservations today. What kinds of work do they do? What foods do they eat? What clothes do they wear? What kinds of homes do they have? What are the structures of their families? What religious practices do they follow? What are their leisure-time activities? What provisions are made for education? What provisions are made for health care?

Native American Musical Instruments

Drums

Music plays an important part in the lives of Native Americans. From the time they are born until they die, their lives are marked by dances and ceremonies. The drum provides the rhythm and is often joined by rattles and rasps to furnish the background for the chants and dances accompanying tribal ceremonies.

Drums

There are four major types of drums:

1. The small hand drum which could be carried into battle

2. The larger drum usually made from a hollowed log

3. The water drum used by the Apache

4. The basket drum used by Southwestern tribes

Native Americans make drum heads from animal hides. The drums are decorated with printed symbols and designs having significant meanings. The Native American never plays the hide drums by tapping with his hands, as is done in Africa. A drumstick is always used.

Quick and Easy Drums

1. Coffee cans with plastic lids are instant drum material. First remove the metal bottom for a better sound. Cover with construction paper. Add Native American symbols and designs.

2. Oatmeal boxes, salt boxes, or paper ice cream containers make drums with a different sound.

3. Pottery jars, flower pots, and metal buckets also make excellent drums. Attach a head of light 100% cotton canvas by using a rubber band or tightly tied string. Dampen the fabric to shrink it. When struck it will make a drum-like sound.

   These drums should be struck with drumsticks. Wooden kitchen spoons with painted Native American designs work well.

4. For a basket drum, use any size woven basket. Turn it over. This can be struck by hand or with pine needles to make a whisk-like sound.

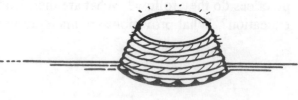

Native American Musical Instruments *(cont.)*

Drums With Paper and Cloth Drumhead

Materials:
- heavy brown paper sack
- scissors
- cheesecloth
- pencil
- ruler
- shellac
- brush
- wrapping twine
- rubber band
- coffee can for frame (open at both ends)
- can opener

Directions:

1. Use a can opener to remove the bottom from a coffee can so it is open at both ends.

2. Cut a heavy brown paper sack open and spread it flat.

3. Center the coffee can on the paper sack and trace around it.

4. Using a ruler and a pencil, make marks 2" (5 cm) outside the circle. Join these marks, making a second, larger circle. Cut out this larger circle.

5. Using the paper circle as a pattern, cut a matching circle from the cheesecloth.

6. Hold the paper and cheesecloth circles together under running water to dampen them.

7. Place the cheesecloth circle on top of the paper circle. Put both circles on top of the coffee can. Hold them in place with a rubber band.

8. Tie wrapping twine tightly over the rubber band. Leave a loop for a handle if desired.

9. Allow the paper and cheesecloth circles to dry thoroughly.

10. Apply 3 coats of shellac to the drumhead, allowing it to dry after each coat. (White glue may be used instead of shellac, but the sound is not as resonant.)

11. Decorate the drum with Native American symbols and designs.

Native American Musical Instruments *(cont.)*

Rattles

Rattles were very important to the Native Americans and they used many different types. Medicine men shook special rattles in ceremonies and healing rituals. Rattles were used as musical instruments during dances and as background to singing. A birchbark rattle accompanied the mournful chant of a Northwest tribal funeral. The Navajo used a combination drumstick and rattle. It was made from rawhide soaked around sand and pebbles, which could give a drum and rattle sound. Bright paint, feathers, colored ribbon, beads, and shells were used to beautify these instruments.

Nineteenth-century Native Americans prized the empty metal spice boxes used by the settlers. Tin cans and other metal containers were used for rattles, also.

Quick and Easy Rattles

1. Make a rattle from a cardboard tube. Tape one end of the tube (paper towel, etc.) closed. Place beans inside. Shake to determine the sound. Add beans until the desired sound is achieved. Tape open end closed. Decorate with marking pens.

2. Use a metal box (a candy or bandage box works well). Put in beans and experiment with sound. Tape box lid closed. Decorate with paper and markers or paint.

Soda Pop Can Rattle

Materials:
- Aluminum soda pop can (clean and dry)
- 10" (25 cm) dowel, 1/2" (1.3 cm) diameter
- masking tape
- beans
- construction paper, scissors, marking pens
- hammer and nail

Directions:
1. Obtain empty soda pop can. Be sure it's very dry inside (otherwise beans can mold).

2. Insert dowel at the opening. Secure dowel with a nail at the top of can.

3. At bottom opening, insert beans until you have a good sound. The type of bean, rice or popcorn will vary the sound.

4. When you have a sound you like, tape the opening securely.

5. Cover the can with construction paper.

6. Use marking pens and decorate with Native American symbols and/or designs.

Native American
Musical Instruments *(cont.)*

Rasps

The rasp (a notched stick) is used by many Native American tribes. By notching sticks in different ways, tribes can vary the sounds and create new sounds to accompany their dances and ceremonies.

The Sioux were able to create the angry bear sound used in the Bear Dance by rubbing a short, heavy rasp with another stick. This was done over a metal sheet covering a hole in the ground. Using this sounding chamber, they created a growl representing the angry spirit of a charging bear.

Quick and Easy Rasp

Use a piece of corrugated cardboard as shown and strike it with a pencil or small stick.

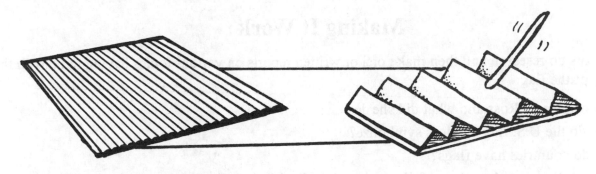

Traditional Rasp   *(needs adult help and supervision)*

Materials:

- 1 dowel, 1" (2.5 cm) diameter by 12" (30 cm)
- 1 dowel, ¼" (.6 cm) diameter by 8" (20 cm)
- saw (coping saw works well)
- pocketknife (adult use only!)
- pencil
- sandpaper

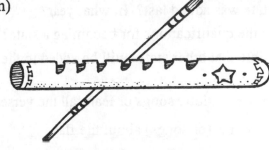

Directions:

1. On the longer dowel, make a pencil mark every 3/8" (1 cm) from one end, leaving 4" (10 cm) for holding at the other end.

2. With saw, cut straight down into dowel at each pencil mark.

3. Have an adult notch a "V" with pocketknife 3/16" (.5 cm) from each cut.

4. Sand rough edges.

To Play: Rub shorter dowel along the notched dowel.

Flag Day

June 14th

On June 14th, the United States commemorates the day in 1777 when the Continental Congress adopted a resolution saying that the flag of the United States would consist of "...13 stripes, alternate red and white, that the 'Union' be 13 stars, within a blue field..." The resolution did not describe the arrangement of the stars or allow for the changes that would be necessary as more states joined the Union. When Kentucky and Vermont became part of the country, a new resolution was passed in 1794, giving the flag 15 stars and 15 stripes.

Fortunately, Captain Samuel C. Reid of the U.S. Navy realized that the flag would soon be a very strange shape if a stripe were added for each state. He brought this to the attention of Congress and in 1818 a law was passed. It stated that the stripes on the U.S. flag would stay the same (13) to represent the 13 original colonies, and a new star would be added for each state as it joined the Union. The flag has changed many times since then.

Making It Work

Have students do research and then make oral or written reports on various topics having to do with the history of the flag:

- Who was Betsy Ross and what did she do?
- What do the U.S. flag's colors symbolize?
- Why do countries have flags?
- What are the rules Americans follow when they display their flag? What are these rules called?
- Is the American flag ever flown upside-down?
- Which star represents the state in which you live (if you live in the U.S.)? In what year was it added?
- Which state was added last? In what year?
- What are the qualifications for becoming a state?
- Is it possible that other states will be added to the Union?

Learn one or more patriotic songs or learn all the verses of "The Star Spangled Banner" (see page 251).

Write patriotic poems (or songs) about the flag.

Learn what all the words in the "Pledge of Allegiance" mean. Rewrite the pledge using your own words.

Combine your songs, poems, and reports into a patriotic program. Give it for another class or for the whole school.

Do a colorful art project honoring the flag. (See page 233.)

Do the same kind of research on flags from countries other than the United States.

Patriotic Stars

Materials:
- white paper
- red and blue crayons, markers, or ink pens
- red or blue paper

Directions:

1. Draw some stars in red or blue on white paper.

2. Outline each blue star with red and each red star with blue. Keep going until the paper is filled, alternating colors as you go.

3. Mount on red or blue paper for a colorful, patriotic art bulletin board.

Juneteenth

June 19th

Juneteenth is a slang contraction of June and nineteenth. It commemorates the day in 1865 when the slaves in Texas finally got the news of President Lincoln's "Emancipation Proclamation"—two and a half years after it was issued. Celebrations broke out all over the state. The day was celebrated annually until the 1960's when civil-rights leaders were trying to become more a part of mainstream America. The festival was gradually revived and Texas legislators made the day a state holiday in 1979.

The day is now celebrated as a black freedom festival across the United States. It is seen as a way to preserve the heritage of black Americans as well as an opportunity to fill a cultural and social void. In many places, community celebrations featuring entertainment, games, barbecue, and African-American art are hosted by local chapters of the NAACP and other organizations that promote preservation of the heritage of black Americans.

Making It Work

Have students research the history of slavery in the world and in the United States. Have them make an illustrated timeline based on this research. Post the timeline around the room above the bulletin boards.

Assign groups to study and report to the class on historical topics associated with slavery such as the Civil War, Abraham Lincoln, the Underground Railroad, Harriet Tubman, and Sojourner Truth. You may also want to include noteworthy contemporary black Americans such as Alex Haley, Jesse Jackson, Thurgood Marshall, Marian Anderson, and Ralphe Bunche. Your students will discover many more. (See pages 235-239.)

Read the "Emancipation Proclamation" to the class. Discuss.

Call a local college or university and arrange for someone from the black studies department to come and talk to your class about the influence of slavery on modern America.

Ask a local African-American artist to talk to your class about ethnic influences in arts and crafts. Allow students to create ethnic art for display.

Take your class on a field trip to a local Juneteenth celebration. If this is not possible, have students create and host their own celebration.

Name_____

Black Biographies

Use an encyclopedia or other reference books to find information for a brief biographical sketch of each of the following famous black Americans. Then find their names in the wordsearch that follows. Add other names as desired.

Hank Aaron _____

_____

_____

_____

Muhammad Ali_____

_____

_____

_____

Marian Anderson _____

_____

_____

_____

Louis Armstrong _____

_____

_____

_____

Name_____

Black Biographies *(cont.)*

Gwendolyn Brooks _____

_____

_____

_____

Jim Brown _____

_____

_____

_____

Ralph Bunche _____

_____

_____

_____

George Washington Carver _____

_____

_____

_____

Name_____

Black Biographies *(cont.)*

Charles Drew_____

_____

_____

_____

_____

Paul Lawrence Dunbar _____

_____

_____

_____

_____

Alex Haley _____

_____

_____

_____

_____

Matthew Alexander Henson _____

_____

_____

_____

_____

Black Biographies *(cont.)*

Jesse Jackson _____

_____

_____

_____

_____

Scott Joplin _____

_____

_____

_____

_____

Martin Luther King, Jr. _____

_____

_____

_____

_____

Thurgood Marshall _____

_____

_____

_____

_____

©1994 Teacher Created Materials, Inc.

Name_____

Black Biographies (cont.)

Leontyne Price _____

_____

_____

_____

_____

Harriet Tubman _____

_____

_____

_____

_____

Booker T. Washington _____

_____

_____

_____

_____

Phyllis Wheatley _____

_____

_____

_____

_____

Juneteenth Wordsearch

Find the following names of black Americans in this wordsearch.

Hank Aaron	Ralph Bunche	Jesse Jackson
Muhammad Ali	George Washington Carver	Scott Joplin
Marian Anderson	Charles Drew	Martin Luther King, Jr.
Louis Armstrong	Paul Lawrence Dunbar	Thurgood Marshall
Gwendolyn Brooks	Alex Haley	Leontyne Price
Jim Brown	Matthew Alexander Henson	Harriet Tubman
Booker T. Washington	Phyllis Wheatley	

```
G H A N K A A R O N Q W E M U H A M M A D A L I R T
E Y L Y U I O P L O U I S A R M S T R O N G A S D F
O D E F G H J K L Z X C V R A A B H N M Q W W E R T
R Q X W E H R T Y U I O P I L T A U S D F E F G H J
G Z H X C A V B N M Q W E A P T R R T Y U N A S D F
E Q A W E R R T Y U I O P N H H A G S D F D B G H M
W Z L X C R V B N M Q W E A B E R O T Y U O O Q W A
A A E S D I F G H J K L Q N U W W O E R T L O Y U R
S Z Y X C E V B N M Q W E D N A R D T Y U Y K U I T
H L E O N T Y N E P R I C E C L A M S D D N E Q W I
I Z X C V T Q W E R T Y U R H E A A J I M B R O W N
N Z X C V U Q W E R T Y U S E X A R E S D R T Q W L
G Z X C V B A S D F G H J O Q A Q S S A S O W R T U
T C V B N M Q W E R T Y U N Q N Q H S Q W O A Q W T
O Z X C V A Z X C V B N M Q W D R A E A S K S C V H
N L K J H N G F D S A P O I U E Y L J T R S H E W E
C H A R L E S D R E W A S D F R Q L A Z X C I Q W R
A A S D F G H J K L P I U Y T H Q W C E R T N U I K
R Z P H I L L I S W H E A T L E Y Q K W E R G T Y I
V D F G G S C O T T J O P L I N P O S L K J T H G N
E Q W E R T Y U I O P L K J H S H G O F D S O S D G
R Z X C V B N M L K J H G F D O D S N A Q W N E R J
A P A U L L A W R E N C E D U N B A R Q W E R T R R
```

The Summer Solstice

June 20, 21, or 22

The summer solstice is the longest day of the year in the northern hemisphere. That is, it is the day on which the sun shines for the greatest number of hours. It occurs exactly six months after the winter solstice, the shortest day of the year. The farther north you go, the more hours of daylight there are.

Ancient people had many ceremonies to honor the sun as it reached its fullest strength. Many modern people participate in rituals that continue this tradition. Modern pagans—witches and druids—participate in spiritual rites that include an offering of bread and a ceremonial fire. In Sweden, the Land of the Midnight Sun, and where the summer solstice is an important holiday, people celebrate with folk dancing and traditional Swedish food. Swedish Midsummer's Eve Festivals are very popular in Sweden as well as other places with large Swedish populations. Needless to say, surfers, beach people, and the general population of sun worshippers say that the day is even better than Christmas.

Making It Work

Have student volunteers research and build models of the stone structures in Stonehenge, England, and Saskatchewan, Canada. They can make reports to the class to share their information. What is the apparent connection between these structures and the summer solstice?

Read about some of the superstitions connected with Midsummer's Eve and Midsummer's Day, both festivals connected with magic and fairies. Most of the superstitions have to do with foretelling the future and finding out the identity of one's true love or one's future husband or wife.

Ask students to find information on midsummer fires, bonfires that are lit in honor of the sun. See how many different customs associated with these fires can be found. Do people still light them? Why? Where? For what are the ashes used?

Show a classic surfing film like *The Endless Summer*. Discuss. Then have students write about how they would spend an ideal summer if they could go anywhere and do anything.

Have a class picnic in a nearby park. Play games, fly kites, and celebrate the coming of summer.

Make a summer bulletin board full of flowers and butterflies. (See page 242.)

The Summer Solstice

Making Tissue Paper Flowers

Materials:
- four 9" x 9" (23 cm x 23 cm) squares of tissue paper
- string
- scissors

Directions:

1. Stack the pieces of tissue paper on top of each other and fold together like a fan or accordion.

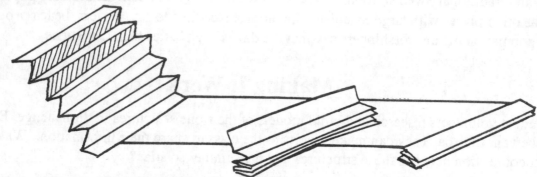

2. Tie the piece of string around the middle. Do not gather. Round the corners on each end of the folded paper.

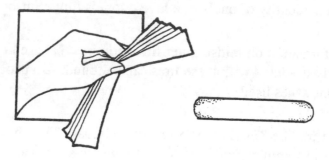

3. Spread each side like opening a fan. Carefully separate each layer, gently pulling to the center.

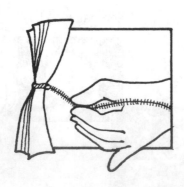
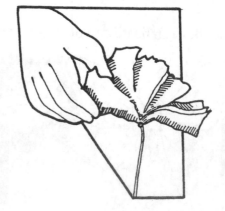

Father's Day

Third Sunday in June

Father's Day, as we are used to celebrating it, is observed in both the United States and Canada. It began in the United States, but no one knows where it started or who started it. Some sources credit the holiday to Mrs. John Dowd of West Virginia, and others to Mrs. John Bruce Dodd of Seattle, Washington. Many people think it was started to make fathers feel just as important as all the mothers who were honored on Mother's Day, the second Sunday in May.

In the United States, it is customary for children to give gifts and cards to their fathers on Father's Day. In other countries such as Yugoslavia, Father's Day (and Mother's Day, too) are celebrated differently. In Yugoslavia, children sneak up on their parents and tie their feet to their chair. The parent must then pay a ransom in the form of a gift to the child in order to get untied.

Father's Day is taken more seriously than that in North America! In fact, a national Father's Day Committee was founded in 1936. This group meets in New York City. Each year it chooses a Father of the Year. Many famous men have received this honor. Among them are Presidents Dwight D. Eisenhower and Harry S. Truman.

Making It Work

Have children write essays nominating their own father (or someone who fills that role for them) for the honor of Father of the Year. Mount these essays attractively and encourage the students to give them as Father's Day gifts.

Students can make a Father's Day collage as a personalized gift for each of their fathers. Cut out profile silhouettes of a man's head from heavy paper. You might have several kinds, varying the hair style to provide for individual differences. Have students go through magazines and cut out pictures that pertain to their father's interests. Assemble a collage from the cut-outs and either use it for the gift itself or as a decoration for the top of a gift box.

Brainstorm lists of all the special qualities of a good father. Discuss.

Run off copies of the certificate on page 244. Students can fill them in, color them, and present them to their fathers or paternal caretakers on Father's Day.

This certifies that

_____

deserves to be honored on

FATHER'S DAY

June _____, 19 _____

_____   _____
Signature   *Date*

Canada Day

July 1

Canada Day is Canada's birthday party just as the Fourth of July is the birthday party of the United States. It is celebrated in ways that are as different as the various parts of Canada are different, but no matter where you are in Canada, the celebration ends with fireworks. In the most northern parts of Canada, the sun does not set at this time of year so they have special fireworks with lots of colored smoke. The cities of Windsor, Ontario, in Canada and Detroit, Michigan, in the United States join together to have a celebration called the International Freedom Festival on July 2nd. This combination birthday party for two countries has the biggest fireworks display of all.

Canada is a very big country and one that most Americans know very little about. It stretches from the Atlantic Ocean to the Pacific Ocean just as the United States does. Its official name is the Dominion of Canada, and it is divided into areas called provinces. Canada has two official languages, English and French, and a large immigrant population.

Some of the world's most beautiful scenery is in Canada, and many tourists visit just to look at it. In the Canadian Rockies, for example, one can see glaciers and mountain goats in person. The skiing is famous around the world.

Making It Work

If your class contains one or more Canadians, you can get some first-hand information about Canada. Of course, if you are in Canada this will be no trouble. Otherwise, have students consult an encyclopedia.

1. How does Canadian money differ from U.S. money? What is a loonie?

2. What problems have Canadians had with two languages in their country? What other countries in the world have more than one official language?

3. How did Canada come to have two languages?

4. Which Canadian city is farthest south? Which is farthest north?

5. What are the average winter temperatures in the larger Canadian cities? What thermometer is used? Do the summers ever get hot? How hot?

6. What is the system of Canadian government? Describe it.

7. What are some favorite Canadian pastimes?

8. What are the largest immigrant groups in Canada?

Use the map on the next page to get better acquainted with Canada.

Canada

Use the map below to get better acquainted with Canada. Mark and label the provinces. Locate and label at least two major cities in each province. Add any other details that are of interest to you. Use an atlas, an encyclopedia, or a textbook to help you.

Name_____

Canada's Flag

Find a picture of Canada's flag. Sketch it in the space below. Do Canadians and Americans feel the same about flags? How do you know? How can you find out?

Write the words to the Canadian national anthem below. Practice singing it.

_____

_____

_____

_____

_____

_____

_____

_____

4th Of July or Independence Day

July 4

The Fourth of July is the birthday of the United States of America. It was on this day in 1776 that representatives of twelve of the thirteen original colonies approved the final draft of the *Declaration of Independence*, written by Thomas Jefferson. In taking this action, they severed all ties with England and started the Revolutionary War.

Besides taking their liberty into their own hands, the colonists gave strength to people around the world to break their chains and be free. People who were not able to make their own countries free, now at least had a place to come. This has been the magic of the United States of America since it began.

The *Declaration of Independence* was first read to the public in Philadelphia, where it was celebrated with bells that rang all night long. Bell-ringing is still a part of the Fourth of July celebrations, as are parades, band concerts, picnics, and firework displays.

Making It Work

Read the *Declaration of Independence* aloud to the class. Ask students to comment, choosing the words that they find most meaningful.

Have students read about Thomas Jefferson. Why do people think of him as such an unusual man? What did he do besides write the *Declaration of Independence*? He is often called a Renaissance man. What does that mean?

Ask students to find the answers to these questions:

1. Who were the Sons of Liberty?

2. Where did they live?

3. What did they do?

4. What was the Boston Tea Party?

5. Why did it take place?

Have students look up the roles of the following people in the Revolutionary War:

- George Washington
- Benjamin Franklin
- Patrick Henry

- Samuel Adams
- Paul Revere
- John Adams

Put on a patriotic program including some famous patriotic songs. The word to three songs are given on pages 249-251.

Patriotic Songs

People who love their country enjoy singing patriotic songs. There are many patriotic songs in the United States. If you are a United States citizen, you may already know some of them.

Read the words of the patriotic songs found here and on the next two pages. Think about what each song means. Discuss the words and their meaning with others. If you are not a United States citizen, write down the words of a patriotic song from your country and what it means to you. How does the song make you feel?

As a class, you and your fellow students can research into patriotic songs from around the world and learn to sing them. Put on a school-wide celebration where you celebrate your country as well as the countries around the world by singing their patriotic songs.

Here is one song from America:

America The Beautiful
by Katherine Lee Bates

O beautiful for spacious skies,
For amber waves of grain,
For purple mountain majesties
Above the fruited plain!
America! America!
God shed His grace on thee
And crown thy good with brotherhood
From sea to shining sea!

O beautiful for pilgrim feet,
Whose stern, impassioned stress
A thoroughfare for freedom beat
Across the wilderness!
America! America!
God mend thine every flaw,
Confirm thy soul in self-control,
Thy liberty in law!

O beautiful for heroes proved
In liberating strife,
Who more than self their country loved,
And mercy more than life!
America! America!
May God thy gold refine
Till all success be nobleness,
And every gain divine!

O beautiful for patriot dream
That sees beyond the years
Thine alabaster cities gleam
Undimmed by human tears!
America! America!
God shed His grace on thee
And crown thy good with brotherhood
From sea to shining sea!

Patriotic Songs (cont.)

Read and discuss these words to one of the United States' popular patriotic songs.

America

by Samuel Francis Smith

My country, 'tis of thee,
Sweet land of liberty,
Of thee I sing;
Land where my fathers died,
Land of the pilgrim's pride,
From every mountain-side
Let freedom ring.

Let music swell the breeze,
And ring from all the trees
Sweet freedom's song;
Let mortal tongues awake,
Let all that breathe partake,
Let rocks their silence break
The sound prolong.

My native country, thee,
Land of the noble free,
Thy name I love;
I love thy rocks and rills,
Thy woods and templed hills;
My heart with rapture thrills
Like that above.

Our father's God, to Thee,
Author of liberty,
To Thee we sing;
Long may our land be bright
With freedom's holy light;
Protect us by Thy might,
Great God, our King.

Patriotic Songs (cont.)

Read and discuss these words of the American National Anthem.

The Star-Spangled Banner

by Francis Scott Key

O say! can you see, by the dawn's early light,
What so proudly we hail'd at the twilight's last gleaming?
Whose broad stripes and bright stars, thro' the perilous fight,
O'er the ramparts we watch'd, were so gallantly streaming?
And the rocket's red glare, the bombs bursting in air,
Gave proof thro' the night that our flag was still there.
O say, does that Star-Spangled Banner yet wave
O'er the land of the free and the home of the brave!

On the shore, dimly seen thro' the mists of the deep,
Where the foe's haughty host in dread silence reposes,
What is that which the breeze, o'er the towering steep,
As it fitfully blows, half conceals, half discloses?
Now it catches the gleam of the morning's first beam,
In full glory reflected now shines on the stream;
"Tis the Star-spangled Banner, O long may it wave
O'er the land of the free and the home of the brave!

O thus be it ever when freemen shall stand
Between their loved homes and the war's desolation!
Blest with vict'ry and peace, may the heav'n rescued land
Praise the Pow'r that hath made and preserved us a nation!
Then conquer we must, when our cause it is just,
And this be our motto; "In God is our trust!"
And the Star-spangled Banner in triumph shall wave
O'er the land of the free and the home of the brave!

Bastille Day

July 14

The French Revolution began on July 14, 1789, with the storming of the Bastille by the people of Paris. The Bastille was a royal prison that had become a symbol of the king's absolute power. When the people of Paris took it over, they released the king's political prisoners and razed the building itself to the ground.

The French Revolution was inspired by the success of the American Revolution. The French had watched and helped the American colonists win their battle to achieve independence from England. But the French Revolution was different because it was fought by the citizens of France against their own resident monarch. The American Revolution had been fought against an "absentee" king who lived far across the Atlantic Ocean. It was probably because of this that the French Revolution became incredibly bloody. The French national anthem, "La Marseillaise," commemorates the fact that it was the people of Paris who stormed the Bastille. It begins with the words, "To arms, citizens!"

In France, Bastille Day is celebrated in much the same way that people in the United States celebrate the Fourth of July and those of Canada celebrate Canada Day. There are parades and fireworks, speeches and flag-waving. The mood is very celebrational.

French people who have moved to other nations often recognize their special holiday with private celebrations put on by families and semi-public ones sponsored by organizations.

Making It Work

Ask members of your class if any of them came from France or have relatives who came from France. What customs do they observe in connection with Bastille Day?

Ask students to find the answers to these and similar questions:

1. How did the French help the American colonists during the American Revolution?

2. What famous Frenchmen are associated with the American Revolution?

3. What instrument of execution was made famous by the French Revolution?

4. What famous symbol of the United States was a gift from the people of France?

5. How has France been important to the development of Canada?

Ask students: What was "the shot heard round the world"? What conncection does this reference have to the French Revolution?

Name_____

The French Flag

Use reference books to find out what the French flag looks like and the significance of its design and colors. Use the space below to show and write about what you find.

Obon

July 15

Obon is a religious observance in which Japanese Buddhists show their respect for loved ones who have passed away. The Obon Odori is a series of colorful folk dances performed at Buddhist temples in connection with this observance. These dances, accompanied by the rhythm of a taiko drum, are passed on from one generation to another so that the tradition, brought here from Japan, will live on in the United States. Some of the dancers wear kimonos, but this isn't necessary. Many people wear casual American clothes when they dance.

According to legend, Maudgalyayana, one of Buddha's followers, had a vision in which he saw his dead mother unable to eat in the afterlife. He told Buddha about this vision. Buddha advised him to give offerings of food to the monks. Maudgalyayana followed this advice, his mother was saved, and everybody danced. This is the dance that is commemorated in the Obon Odori. Food is still a part of the festival, too, but people no longer make a food offering. Rather, various foods—sushi, teriyaki, and other Japanese dishes—are sold as a part of the Obon festival to raise money for the temple. Finally, lanterns are also associated with this festival.

(Vietnamese Buddhists call this festival Vu Lan. Chinese Buddhists also celebrate a festival that is very much like the Japanese and Vietnamese ones.)

Making It Work

Ask students to keep the class informed about the times and places where one can attend celebrations of festivals such as Odon.

Invite local Japanese Buddhists to come to your classroom to explain, demonstrate, and maybe even teach the folk dances associated with this festival.

Have groups of students write their own original legends that involve a dance. They can make up drum rhythms and dance steps and perform their dances for one another.

Buy some recordings of folk dance music (with instructions for the steps) and learn some dances from other cultures.

Ask students whose families still have traditional kimonos to show them to the class. Perhaps a parent or grandparent of a student will describe the clothing and how it is worn.

Make paper lanterns and hang them up to decorate your classroom.

Paper Lanterns

Materials:
18" x 16" (46 cm x 40 cm) paper; scissors; glue; string

Directions:

1. Draw three lines the long way on a long paper rectangle and score as shown in the sketch. (To score place a ruler next to the line and run the tip of a scissors along the paper against the ruler.)

2. Draw short lines from the top scored line to the bottom scored line, an even distance apart.

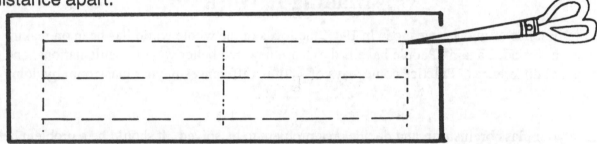

3. Fold on the middle scored line. Cut on the short lines as shown.

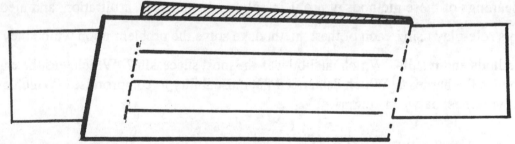

4. Open up. Roll into a tube and glue ends together. Make two holes and hang with string.

Hiroshima Day

August 6

At 8:15 a.m. on August 6, 1945, the first nuclear weapon in the history of the world exploded over Hiroshima. Now every year at that time, everything stops in that city and people bow their heads in a minute of silence to remember the 140,000 people who died in the atomic blast.

Ground zero of the 1945 bombing is now the site of Peace Memorial Park where the dome of a preserved bombed-out building looms in the background. Speaking there in 1993, the mayor of Hiroshima called upon world leaders to eliminate nuclear weapons. Noting that nuclear weapons have not been used since 1945, the mayor said, "Yet there is no guarantee that such things will never happen in the future."

Hiroshima Day is always noted around the world as a day to work for peace. However, since it falls in the summer, it has not been celebrated in schools. Now, with more and more year-round schools in operation, there is a good chance it can become more popular.

Making It Work

Since the first use of nuclear weapons in 1945, the focus of the whole world has been on making sure they were never used again. People have had to learn new and better ways to settle national and international differences. Practice some ways of settling differences in your classroom by doing this exercise:

1. Have your class brainstorm and decide on a problem to be solved. It should be a problem between people that could occur in their own lives.

2. Learn the meanings of these methods of problem-solving: negotiation, arbitration, and mediation.

3. Have students role-play using each of these methods to solve the problem upon which they decided.

4. Compare methods and results. Which method was the most successful? Which was the easiest to use? Which was the hardest? Which demanded the most ability to compromise? Which one do you think would work best between countries?

Write to The Lion and the Lamb Peace Arts Center, Bluffton College, Bluffton, OH 45817 for information and materials about promotion of peace and international understanding through the arts and literature for children.

Name_____

The Nobel Peace Prize

Consult an encyclopedia to learn about Alfred Nobel and the Nobel Peace Prize. Then find out why the people listed below were recipients.

Mother Teresa (1979)

_____

_____

Archbishop Desmond Tutu (1984)

_____

_____

Teddy Roosevelt (1906)

_____

_____

Woodrow Wilson (1919)

_____

_____

Jane Addams (1931)

_____

_____

Name_____

The Nobel Peace Prize *(cont.)*

George C. Marshall (1953)

_____

_____

Dr. Martin Luther King, Jr. (1964)

_____

_____

Henry Kissinger (1973)

_____

_____

Ralph J. Bunche (1950)

_____

_____

Albert Schweitzer (1952)

_____

_____

Linus Pauling (1962)

_____

_____

Elihu Root (1912)

_____

_____

Movable & Personal Special Days

Movable Feasts

Many holidays move around because of the way people have tried to reconcile lunar (moon) and solar (sun) calendars with the actual solar year, the time it takes for the earth to make one revolution around the sun. Western people who use the Gregorian calendar simply add a day every four years, or more precisely, to every year whose date is divisible by four, and the year comes out almost even. (The only people who really care are those who are born on February 29th, Leap Year Day. They must figure out when to celebrate their birthday in the years when there is no February 29th!) The Gregorian calendar more or less ignores what the moon is doing.

Most of the people who follow a lunar calendar or a lunisolar calendar have found ways to make everything come out evenly, too. Extra days, called intercalary days, are added according to various plans. The Jewish calendar, for instance, adds a "leap month" at certain intervals in a seventeen-year cycle.

Many of these calendars, the ways in which solar and lunar time are fitted together, and the dates of important movable holidays are discussed in greater detail on the following pages. The movable holidays themselves are included in the main portion of this book, because even though they move, they start in the same month or at least in the same season of the year.

The only important calendar that makes no attempt whatsoever to adjust lunar and solar time is the Islamic calendar. Islam uses a lunar calendar. All of Islam's special days drop back 11 days each solar year because there is an eleven-day difference between the solar year and the lunar year. All of the special days of Islam are described in this part of the book because they have no fixed connection with any part of the solar year and no relationship with the seasons.

Personal Days

Personal days and the ways in which they are celebrated are described in this part of the book, too, since they can happen at any time of the year. Even those special personal days that have become associated with certain times of the year can, if necessary or desirable, happen at any other time. Weddings and graduations, for example, can happen just as well in March or July or December as in the more traditional June. These days and the ways in which they are celebrated are described more fully on pages 279 through 282.

Different Calendars

Calendars in General

There are, in general, three kinds of calendars: solar, lunar, and lunisolar. The solar calendar is based on the sun. The lunar calendar is based on the moon. In the lunisolar calendar, the year is based on the sun and the months are based on the moon. The solar year is 11 days longer than the lunar year.

The Gregorian Calendar

The calendar commonly used today is the Gregorian calendar. It is named after Pope Gregory XIII who corrected the Julian calendar (which had been named after Julius Caesar) in the 16th century. He corrected it by skipping ten days. Many people were very upset about this (probably because they missed their birthdays!) and some countries waited hundreds of years to make the change. Some countries have never changed.

Nevertheless, the Gregorian calendar is now used in almost every country of the world for convenience in the everyday workings of business and government. It is a solar calendar; that is, it is based on the length of time it takes the earth to travel around the sun. It is kept "on time" by the addition of a Leap Year Day at the end of February in every fourth year. Solar calendars are useful in agricultural societies because the dates and the seasons stay matched up from year to year. But even though people like to use the Gregorian calendar for keeping track of practical things, they also like to use various kinds of lunar or lunisolar calendars for keeping track of religious festivals. This is why so many holidays move around.

There is an 11-day difference between the lunar year and the solar year. Most calendars add extra (intercalary) days or months so that festivals stay more or less in the same season of the year. Some, however, do not, and festivals move right around the year, appearing sometimes in winter and sometimes in summer.

The Buddhist Calendar

The Buddhist calendar is lunisolar. They calculate the New Year by the position of the sun and the months by the moon. The Solar New Year is celebrated in the month of April. An extra day is occasionally added to the seventh month and an extra month is added every few years. Buddhists traditionally observe the anniversaries of Buddha's birth, enlightenment, and death.

Different Calendars *(cont.)*

The Chinese Calendar

The Chinese calendar is lunisolar. It consists of 12 lunar months of 29 or 30 days. An extra (intercalary) month is added every few years. There is also a solar calendar divided into 24 periods of 15 days each. These periods are named for seasonal changes. Most holidays and festivals are calculated on the lunar cycle.

Between 1994 and 2000, the Chinese New Year falls on the following dates on the Gregorian calendar:

February 10, 1994	February 7, 1997
January 31, 1995	January 28, 1998
February 19, 1996	February 16, 1999
	February 5, 2000

The Christian Calendar

The Christian calendar uses the Gregorian calendar for the most part, although church traditions vary in their interpretation of the dates. Western churches start their year on the first Sunday of Advent. Eastern Orthodox churches begin their year in September. Easter takes the lunar aspects of the calendar into account. It occurs on the first Sunday after the first full moon after the vernal equinox, so the date is different from year to year. The forty days before Easter are called Lent, a penitential period which changes its starting date in relation to Easter's date in any given year.

The last day before Lent (Carnival in Latin American countries and Mardi Gras in France and the United States) is a festival that is celebrated around the world. Between 1994 and 2000, Carnival or Mardi Gras falls on the following dates:

February 15, 1994	February 11, 1997
February 28, 1995	February 24, 1998
February 20, 1996	February 16, 1999
	March 7, 2000

Between 1994 and 2000, Easter falls on the following dates:

April 3, 1994	March 30, 1997
April 16, 1995	April 12, 1998
April 7, 1996	April 4, 1999
	April 23, 2000

The Hindu Calendar

There are a number of different Hindu calendars. Some Hindus celebrate the Solar New Year in April as do the Buddhists. Others celebrate at different times according to lunar calendars that measure the months from full moon to full moon. The same festivals may be celebrated at different times depending on the calendar that is used in a region.

Different Calendars *(cont.)*

The Islamic Calendar

The Islamic calendar is totally lunar. It is never adjusted to match the solar year, so it drops back 11 days each solar year. The day begins at sunset, so holidays begin on the eve of the date on which they are observed. Eid al-Fitr and Eid al-Adha are the only two holidays observed by all Muslims because they were set by the Prophet Muhammad. Eid al-Fitr comes at the end of Ramadan. It is in March during 1993, 1994, and 1995. It drops back to February in 1996 and 1997, and then to January in 1998, 1999, and 2000.

The Jewish Calendar

The Jewish calendar is lunisolar, calculating its year by the sun and its months by the moon. A "leap month" is added seven times during each 19-year cycle. The day begins at sunset, as does the Islamic day. Three of the most important holidays on the Jewish calendar are Rosh Hashanah, Passover, and Hanukkah.

Between 1994 and 2000, Rosh Hashanah falls on the following dates on the Gregorian calendar:

September 6, 1994	October 2, 1997
September 25, 1995	September 21, 1998
September 14, 1996	September 11, 1999
	September 30, 2000

Between 1994 and 2000, Passover falls on the following dates on the Gregorian calendar:

March 27, 1994	April 22, 1997
April 16, 1995	April 11, 1998
April 7, 1996	April 1, 1999
	April 20, 2000

Between 1994 and 2000, Hanukkah falls on the following dates on the Gregorian calendar:

November 28, 1994	December 14, 1998
December 18, 1995	December 4, 1999
December 6, 1996	December 22, 2000
December 24, 1997	

Muslim Special Days

Who Are the Muslims?

Muslims are followers of the Islamic religion. Islam is one of the world's major religions. Muslims believe in one God whose Arabic name is Allah. Muhammad is the important prophet of the Islamic faith. The teachings of Allah to Muhammad are recorded in the *Koran* (or Qur'an) which is the holy book of Islam, as the *Bible* is the holy book of Christianity and Judaism.

The two main branches of Islam are the Sunni Muslims and the Shia Muslims. Although they do not have major differences in doctrine, they choose their leaders differently. All Muslims must observe the forms of worship called the Five Pillars of Islam: reciting the Creed, praying five times a day, giving alms to the poor, fasting during Ramadan, and making the pilgrimage to Mecca (the Hajj). Even though followers of Islam include people from a wide diversity of countries, wealth, climate, and culture, their shared form of worship encourages a strong sense of brotherhood.

What Special Days Are Celebrated in Islam?

There are only two official festivals in Islam. These are Eid al-Fitr (sometimes spelled Eed al-Fitr or 'Id al-Fitr) and Eid al-Adha (sometimes spelled Eed al-Adha or 'Id al-Adha). Both of these festivals are connected with the Pillars of Islam, the five prescribed forms of Islamic worship. Eid al-Fitr is celebrated at the end of the fast of Ramadan. Eid al-Adha is celebrated toward the end of the last month of the Islamic year, the month in which people undertake the Hajj or pilgrimage to Mecca.

In addition to these religious festivals which are celebrated by all Muslims, there are other celebrations connected with Islamic history. These occasions may or may not be celebrated by Muslims in various parts of the world. They are Milad-an-Nabi, the Birthday of the Prophet Muhammed; Lailatul Bara'at, the Night of Deliverance; Lailatul Mi'raj, the Night of the Ascent; 'Ashura, a tradtional day of fasting; and Muharram, the Muslim New Year's Day.

Two features of the completely lunar Islamic calendar have a profound effect on the Muslim festivals: Each new month begins with the appearance of the new moon. And, since the festivals drop back 11 days each solar year, they have no connection with the seasons.

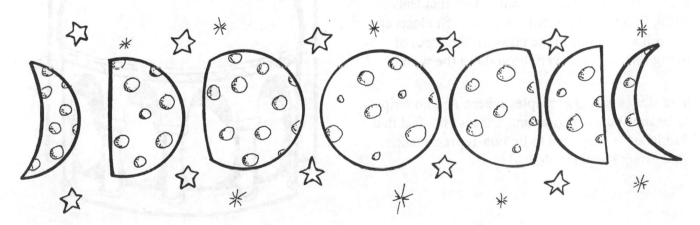

Ramadan

9th Month of the Islamic Lunar Calendar

Ramadan is the 9th month of the Muslim year. It begins, as does each lunar month, when the new moon is sighted. Since the dates of the lunar calendar drop back 11 days each solar year, Ramadan can and does occur in both winter and summer (as well as spring and fall). It is an important month. Muslims believe that the *Koran* was first revealed to Muhammad during the month of Ramadan. It is also the month when the Battle of Badr is remembered. This battle resulted in victory for the Muslims.

Ramadan is also the month of fasting. Fasting from dawn to sunset is compulsory for every Muslim over the age of twelve, with the exception of the old, the sick, travelers, pregnant women, and nursing mothers. Children are encouraged to ease into the fast by going without food and drink for a few hours of the day or for a few days during the month. The Ramadan fast is very strict, excluding even water. A meal called *suhur* is taken before dawn to provide nourishment for the day. The fast ends each day at sunset. The meal taken to break the fast is called *iftar*. In the winter when the nights are long and the weather is cool, the Ramadan fast is less difficult than it is in the summer when the days are not only hot but long, with many hours stretching between dawn and sunset.

The twenty-seventh night of Ramadan is celebrated as the most likely date on which the *Koran* was revealed to Muhammad. Because no one is sure exactly when this happened, Muslims spend the last ten nights of Ramadan praying and reading the *Koran*.

Making It Work

Ask student volunteers to bring Korans to school to show and explain to the class. Have students observe Arabic script. Point out that there are no vowels as such. Vowel sounds are indicated by dots. Notice that the book is read (from the traditional Western view, at least) from back to front, bottom to top, and right to left.

Discuss fasting. Have students share incidents of fasting in religions other than Islam. Students can research and report to the class on the types of fasting that are observed throughout the world.

Have students find examples where Arabic script has been used as decoration. Discuss the fact that Islamic art is supposed to be non-representational. What effect has that rule had?

Using Decorative Script

Islamic artists use Arabic script to make beautiful designs. You can make designs from your cursive signature or even your printed name. Here's how:

1. Fold a piece of paper in half the long way and write your name along the fold. Use big, flowing letters. Then go over the letters in dark crayon or very soft pencil.

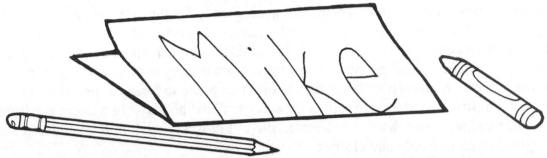

2. Fold the paper again so the writing is inside, and rub hard with a ruler or the side of a book to transfer the writing to the other side of the paper. Open the paper and turn it so your name goes up and down and makes a pattern.

3. Add to the pattern if you want and add color.

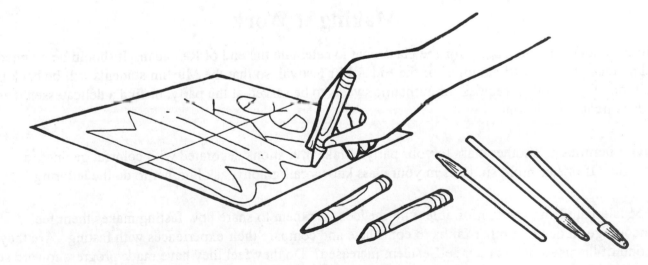

Eid al-Fitr

1st Day of the 10th Month of the Islamic Lunar Calendar

Eid al-Fitr (or 'Id al-Fitr) is the festival that marks the end of the fast of Ramadan, so it is celebrated on the first day of the tenth month of the Islamic year. It begins when the new moon is sighted, and it is a time of great rejoicing.

People spend most of the month of Ramadan getting ready for the celebration—decorating the house, buying gifts, and sending cards to friends and relatives. Many stores stay open all night during Ramadan to give people more time to shop for the Eid al-Fitr celebration. On the day itself, everyone gets up early to offer special prayers. These prayers are usually held in large open spaces such as parks. When the prayers are over, people go visiting or return home to feast on special foods. In Muslim countries the festival is celebrated with a three-day national holiday. In western countries Muslims take the day off from work or school to celebrate. Eid al-Fitr is a special time for children who receive many gifts as well as candy and clothes.

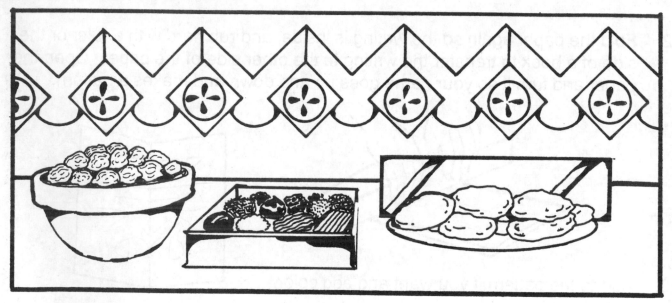

Making It Work

Help students to plan a party for the classroom to celebrate the end of Ramadan. It should be planned to take place after the official time for the Eid al-Fitr festival, so that the Muslim students will be back in school. Try to collect recipes for authentic sweets to be served at the party, or find a delicatessen that stocks treats of this kind.

Invite families or another class to your party. Make invitations decorated with colorful geometric designs. If one or more students in your class knows calligraphy, ask him/her to do the lettering.

If Muslim students are comfortable with the idea, ask them to share how fasting makes them feel. Encourage students of other faiths to contribute and compare their experiences with fasting. Are they proud of themselves? Is their self-esteem increased? Do they feel they have made progress toward self-discipline? Did experiencing hunger make them feel more compassion toward the poor?

Sample Stylized Designs

Artists who practice the Islamic religion have become adept at using non-representational designs to beautify their surroundings.

Look at the sample below and then complete your design on the next page. This design was made by cutting small figures out of heavy paper and tracing around them to create a pattern that interconnects.

Your Stylized Designs

Use your own cut-out shapes (or existing objects such as coins) to create your own non-representational design in the space below. The more complicated the design and the more the parts interconnect, the more interesting your design will be. Try your hand at a stylized design to be used as the front of an invitation. Draw it first in black and white. Your teacher may duplicate some of the designs for everyone to color.

Eid al-Adha

10th Day of the 12th Month of the Islamic Lunar Calendar

Eid al-Adha is the festival of sacrifice. It commemorates the example of obedience and faith set by Abraham when God asked him to sacrifice his son, Ishmael. God told Abraham to stop at the last minute, and Abraham thankfully sacrificed a ram instead. Now, Muslims sacrifice animals to God as part of the Eid al-Adha festival to symbolize their willingness to give up anything for the cause of God.

Eid al-Adha is celebrated much like Eid al-Fitr, with the addition of the animal sacrifice. In Muslim countries the animals are sacrificed at home by a senior member of the family. In western countries where licenses are required to slaughter animals, people who have licenses go to the slaughterhouse and sacrifice the animals in the name of the community as a whole. The meat is divided into three portions. One part is kept and cooked for the family. A second part is given to friends and relatives. A third part is donated to feed the poor.

Making It Work

Have students research the idea and practice of animal sacrifice. Do other modern religions incorporate this practice in their rituals or festivals?

Ask students to look up Abraham and read the whole story of his sacrifice. Have them share their information with each other.

What connection does this festival have with the pilgrimage to Mecca that is required of every Muslim once in his life? What is the pilgrimage called? What title is given to a person who has made the pilgrimage? What is the sacred building at Mecca called? What are the clothes worn by pilgrims to Mecca called? Of what do these clothes consist? Are the same type of clothes worn by both men and women? In what country is Mecca located? Have students locate Mecca on a map.

In what country is Medina located? Why is this city important to Muslims? Have students locate Medina on a map.

Name_____

Muslim Words

Define each of these words and then find them in the wordsearch on page 272:

1. Muhammad _____

_____

2. Mecca _____

_____

3. Medina _____

_____

4. Abraham _____

_____

5. Ishmael _____

_____

6. Hajj _____

_____

7. Hajji _____

_____

8. Zamzam _____

_____

9. Koran _____

_____

10. Ka'ba _____

_____

Muslim Words *(cont.)*

11. Pillars of Satan _____

_____

12. Pilgrimage _____

_____

13. Sacrifice _____

_____

14. Saudi Arabia _____

_____

15. Miqat _____

_____

16. Ihram _____

_____

17. Hagar _____

_____

18. The Prophet's Mosque _____

_____

19. Allah _____

_____

20. Plain of Arafat _____

_____

Name_____

Muslim Wordsearch

Find these words that have to do with Muslims in the wordsearch below.

Muhammad	Mecca	Medina	Abraham
Ishmael	Hajj	Hajji	Zamzam
Koran	Ka'ba	Pillars of Satan	Pilgrimage
Sacrifice	Saudi Arabia	Miqat	Ihram
Hagar	The Prophets Mosque	Allah	Plain of Arafat

```
Q W E R T Y U M E C C A I O H A J J I P A P Q W E
S D F G H J K E L Z X B C V B N M Q W K E I R T Y
M U H A M M A D O P A R S D H F S G H O J L Y U I
K L Z X C V B I N M Z A M Z A M A Q W R E L R T Y
Q W E R T Y U N U I O H P A J S U D K A B A D F G
F G H J K L Z A P X C A V B J N D M Q N W R E R T
Y U I O P A S D I S H M A E L F I G H J K S L Z X
C V B N M Q W P L A I N O F A R A F A T E O R T Y
U I O P A S D F G G H J K L Z X R C V B N M F M Q W
Q W E R T Y U I R O P A S D F G A H J K L S Z X C
A S D F G H J M I Q A T K L Z X B C V B H A G A R
S Z A Q W S X C M D E R F V B G I T Y U I T O L P
M N B V C X Z S A C R I F I C E A Z I H R A M L Q
L K J H G F D S G A P O I U Y T R E W Q S N D A F
F R T G H Y U J E B G H N M J Y T R E W Q E R H T
T H E P R O P H E T S M O S Q U E C V G H U I O P
```

Milad-an-Nabi, the Birthday of the Prophet Muhammad

12th Day of the 3rd Month of the Islamic Lunar Calendar

Muhammad was born in Mecca in late August, 570 A.D., according to the Gregorian calendar. He lived for over forty years of his life as a camel-driver and trader before he was surprised to begin receiving messages from God. When he began to act on these revelations, he not only established one of the world's major religions but also brought a unified purpose to many of the independent, nomadic Arab tribes.

Muhammad's birthday is a big holiday in the Middle East. There are fireworks and processions. In the west, the birthday of the prophet is celebrated at home and in the mosque where stories are told about his life, his character, his mission, and his successes. Gifts are given and traditional candies are served.

Making It Work

Display a world map in the classroom so that discussions of the life of Mohammad can be related to place names and to modern times.

Ask students to share their experiences in celebrating Muhammad's Birthday both in this country and in other countries. Has the celebration changed as it has adapted to life in the western world? How?

Provide a timeline for students to complete by adding the dates of events in the life of Mohammad and in the spread of Islam, together with pictures to illustrate these events. Pictures may be drawn by students or consist of illustrations duplicated from books.

Discuss the Hegira, the name given to Muhammad's flight from Mecca to Medina.

Show films or videos of the Middle East to give students a feeling for the area, the climate, the architecture, the lifestyle, the standard of living, etc. If you have students from the Middle East in your classroom, ask them to critique and expand on the visual materials for the class. Are they accurate? Are they biased? In what way?

Begin a collection of books about Islam, Islamic art, and so on for your classroom library.

Weaving

Small rugs are very important to the members of a nomadic culture. They serve a variety of purposes and can easily be rolled up and transported.

You can use a simple loom to weave a tiny rug for yourself. Follow these directions.

Materials:

- stiff cardboard, about 6x8 inches (15 cm x 20 cm)
- 10-12 feet (3-4 m) of string or yarn for warp
- scissors
- thick yarn for weaving
- interesting materials to add texture (fabric strips, ribbon, straw, etc.)

Directions:

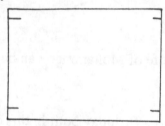

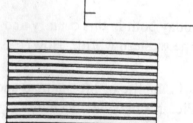

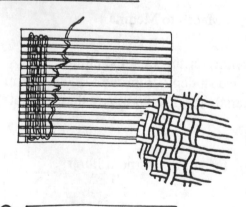

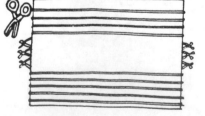

1. Cut slits in the top and bottom of the cardboard about 1 inch (2.5 cm) in from both sides.

2. Make a knot in one end of the warp string and catch it in the upper left-hand slit. Then pull it down and through the lower left-hand slit.

3. Using the first warp string as a guide, wrap the rest of the warp string around the cardboard leaving ½ -1 inch (1.25 cm-2.5 cm) between warps.

4. When you get to the right-hand slits, catch the warp thread in the top slit and then the bottom one, making a knot to hold the string tight.

5. Start to weave by threading the weaving material over and under the warp threads. Alternate the over and under in each row until full. Work on only one side of the loom.

6. Turn the loom over. Starting in the center, cut the warp threads in the middle, two at a time, and tie them off at the top and bottom starting with the center. Cut the threads evenly to make a fringe.

Celebrating the Historical Events of Islam

Lailatul Bara'At, the Night of Deliverance

The Middle of the 8th Month of the Islamic Lunar Calendar

On this night Muslims ask Allah for forgiveness for people who have died. They may spend the night reading the *Koran*, praying in mosques, and visiting graveyards to pray for family and friends. In doing this they are imitating Mohammad, who was in the habit of fasting and praying for several nights during this month which preceeds Ramadan. Women prepare special foods for friends and family. They also give food to the poor and hungry. Halvah is a traditional food for this night.

Lailatul Mi'Raj, the Night of the Ascent

27th Day of the 7th Month of the Islamic Lunar Year

On this night Muslims commemorate the miraculous journey of the Prophet Muhammad to Heaven. According to Islamic belief, Muhammad was given a winged horse named Buraq by the Angel Gabriel, and led from Mecca to Jerusalem to the seven heavens of the Islamic faith. There, Allah gave him the prayers that all Muslims say every day. Muslims spend this night praying and reading the *Koran*.

'Ashura, a Traditional Day of Fasting

10th Day of the 1st Month of the Islamic Lunar Calendar

'Ashura was regarded as a traditional day of fasting even before Islam. Muslims believe that on this day Noah left the Ark after the flood, and Moses freed the Jews and brought them out of Egypt. Muslims in many countries keep a voluntary fast on this day and prepare special foods to celebrate the end of the fast. It is the principal festival of the Shi'ite sect.

Muharram, the Muslim New Year's Day

1st Day of the 1st Month of the Islamic Lunar Calendar

This holiday is connected to Muhammad's flight from Mecca to Medina. Many of his followers joined him, and because they were able to worship freely, the Islamic religion began to grow. This flight, called the Hegira, is considered the first major event in the development of Islam, and the calendar is dated from it. Dates after the Hegira are called A.H. in much the same way that dates on the Gregorian calendar are dated A.D.

Celebrating the Historical Events of Islam *(cont.)*

Making It Work

Have students compare the Muslim observance of Lailatul Bara'at with ceremonies honoring or interceding for the dead that take place in other religions and in other parts of the world. All Saint's Day and All Soul's Day are celebrated in the Catholic church and have been secularized into Halloween (All Hallows' Eve) in many countries. People from Hispanic countries celebrate the Day(s) of the Dead which may last three days: October 31st, November 1st, and November 2nd. These are the dates of the Eve of All Saint's Day, All Saint's Day itself, and All Soul's Day. Many people in the Far East offer prayers and food to their ancestors at their New Year's celebrations.

Find out the words of the Muslim prayers recited by the faithful five times a day. What is a "muezzin"? What is a "minaret"? What is a "mosque"? What is the relationship among the three words? Why do Muslims use a prayer rug when they pray? What are these rugs called?

Ask students to research the answers to these questions: What is a Whirling Dervish? How are they related to Islam? Can you describe what they did? What they wore? Where they lived? Who started the movement?

Get a book illustrating Arabic script for students to examine and enjoy. Ask a caligraphy expert to come to your classroom and get your students started with this artistic hobby. Try to provide students with caligraphy materials or ask them to get their own. Make cards, invitations, and awards more special with this fancy writing.

Arabic is the official language of at least sixteen countries. Do some research to find out which countries they are. Where are they located? Is the Islamic religion important in all of them? Define democracy. Are any of them democracies? What is a theocracy? Are any of them theocracies?

The crescent moon and the evening star are used as symbols on the flags of many countries in the Middle East. What is the meaning of these symbols? What countries use these symbols on their flags? Are they the same countries where Arabic is spoken as the official language?

The Kaleidescope

A kaleidescope makes a constantly changing pattern out of many different pieces. This could be a symbol of Islam. Finish and or color the pattern below. Create your own on the next page.

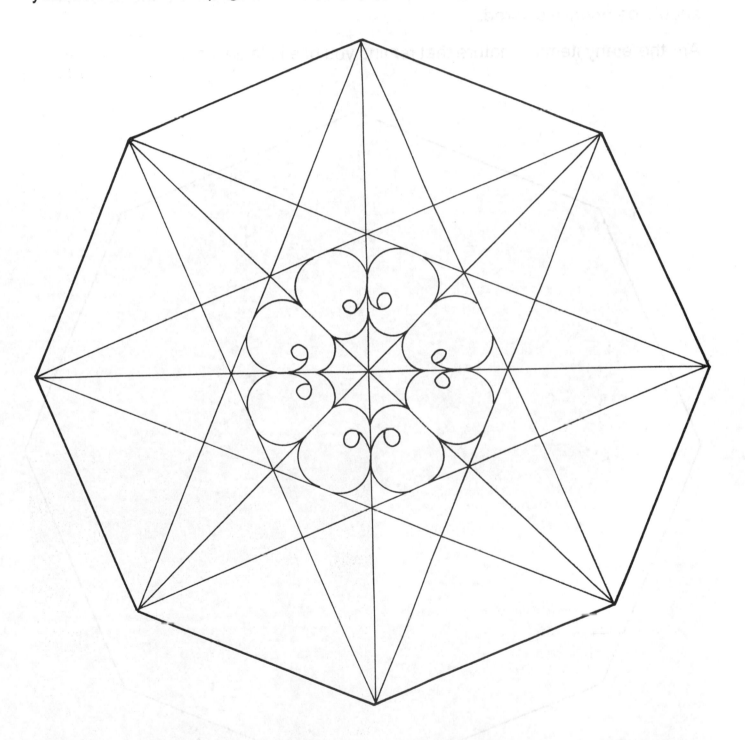

Draw identical shapes/lines at 90° angles to one another to complete the pattern.

Name_____

Create a Kaleidescope

Experiment with the sample on the preceding page. Then create your own pattern in the space below. Each space should be a replication of the other. All should be brightly colored.

Are there any items in nature that remind you of a kaleidescope?

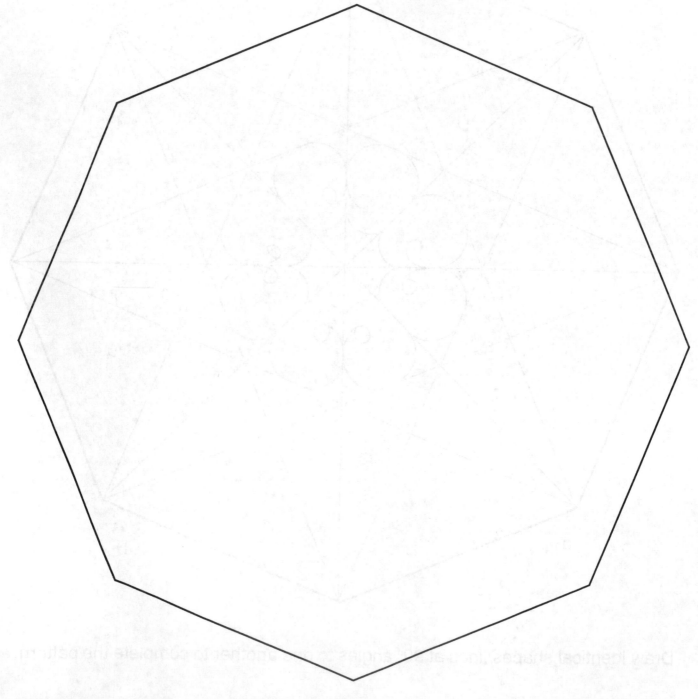

Personal Special Days

What Are Personal Days?

Personal days are days that are dedicated to just one person. They may be celebrated with large numbers of friends and family members, but they do not have to be. You could celebrate a personal day all by yourself, and while it might not be as much fun, it would still have the same meaning. Your birthday is the day that you were born, whether or not you have a party.

What Makes a Day Special?

A day is special because it marks a special event, both when it is happening and often on its anniversary (yearly date). Included in the list of personal special days are birthdays, name days, baptisms, confirmations, Bar Mitzvahs, Bat Mitzvahs, graduations, and weddings. Some of these days have a religious significance—baptisms, confirmations, Bar Mitzvahs, Bat Mitzvahs—and some are secular or not religious—birthdays and graduations. Some can be either or both—name days and weddings.

How Is a Personal Special Day Celebrated?

The way people celebrate their personal special day varies from person to person and from family to family, as well as from country to country. People in the United States don't often celebrate name days while people in Europe often do. Some families make a big fuss over every event while other families are very casual about all occasions. Some individuals who belong to families that like to celebrate may hate to be the center of attention. And, of course, some people who would just love to celebrate belong to families that just do not.

All in all, personal special days can be celebrated many different ways. Children do not have much choice, but as an adult, you can take control of your own special days and celebrate them just about any way you want. It is up to you.

Birthdays

Your birthday, of course, is the anniversary of the day on which you were born. You celebrate the anniversary of that date each year—unless, of course, you were a Leap Year baby born on February 29th, or unless you are from an Asian country where everyone gets a year older on New Year's Day. This can be very confusing when you move to another country and go to enroll in school. Unless you learn a new way to figure your age, you may be put in the wrong grade.

In the western world, birthdays are usually celebrated with cake. Candles to match your age are put on top of the cake and lighted. Everybody sings a song like "Happy Birthday to You." The songs are different around the world. If the birthday person makes a wish and then blows out all the candles with one breath, the wish will come true. (However, according to superstition if the birthday person tells the wish, it won't come true.)

Some birthdays are more important than others. In the United States, the sixteenth birthday is important to girls, who are often given "Sweet Sixteen" parties. In Latin America, it is the fifteenth birthday that is important to girls, called a Quinceaños celebration. Sixteen has also traditionally been the age when young people get a driver's license, although some places are now making this more difficult and less automatic. Eighteen means the right to vote in the United States and the obligation to register for the draft. It also means taking legal responsibility for one's own actions. Twenty-one was once more important than it is today. It included all the things that now happen at eighteen. About the only privilege still reserved for twenty-one in many areas is the right to buy alcohol.

Name Days

A name day is a saint's day. For example, Saint Patrick's Day on March 17th is the name day for everyone named Patrick, or a variation such as Patricia. In some countries, you celebrate your name day instead of your birthday. In other countries, you celebrate your name day in addition to your birthday. (Two celebrations are better than one!) This day can have religious significance if a person is devoted to the saint he or she is named after, but it doesn't have to.

Baptisms

Baptism is a religious ceremony performed in many churches. When a person is baptized, he or she is made a member of the church or religious group. Any sins are also symbolically washed away, so water is a part of this ceremony. The person being baptized may be immersed in water or just have water poured or sprinkled over him or her.

Some churches baptize infants, so sponsors are needed to make the necessary promises in the name of the child. Older people being baptized may also have sponsors. These sponsors are often referred to as Godparents, and a Godmother or Godfather can often play an important role in the life of a child.

Baptisms are often celebrated with a party at the time of the ceremony. They are not usually recognized each year on the anniversary date.

Confirmations

The Catholic church, together with many other Christian churches, administers the rite of confirmation, usually when a young person is ready to take on the full adult practice of a religion. It is a ceremony that acknowledges that the person being confirmed understands the basic doctrines of the religion. The ceremony also confers the spiritual gifts that will be needed to put those doctrines into action during the times of life when moral decisions must be made.

Confirmation is usually a totally religious celebration. A formal reception may be held after the ceremony so family and friends can honor and congratulate the person who has been confirmed.

Bar Mitzvahs And Bat Mitzvahs

The Bar Mitzvah for boys and the Bat Mitzvah for girls is the religious ceremony that recognizes and celebrates coming-of-age in the Jewish religion. (A "mitzvah" is a good deed or a duty. "Bar" means son and "Bat" means daughter.)

This ceremony is performed in the temple, where the young person reads from the *Torah* and gives a talk to those assembled. The ceremony is not supposed to signal the end of the religious instruction of childhood but rather the beginning of the religious life of an adult.

As in most Jewish ceremonies, the family plays a large part in the occasion—this time by hosting a celebration party. There is wonderful food, music, and dancing in which people of all ages take part.

Graduations

Graduations are not religious ceremonies. They are the ceremonies that are connected with moving along in school. A student may have several graduations. Some start as young as pre-school by participating in a little ceremony. Kindergarten is another possibility, as are the end-points of elementary school, junior high school, high school, and college.

Graduates often wear caps and gowns. They march in processions while "Pomp and Circumstance" is played. They receive awards and diplomas. People make speeches while parents cry and look proud. Graduates are given flowers and special gifts that are appropriate for the occasion. They often attend a series of dances and parties.

Some people like to downplay the importance of graduation ceremonies. However, they seem to provide the opportunity for people to say good-bye to one part of life before moving on to the next. People remember the five, ten, fifteen, twenty (and so on) year anniversaries of their graduations by attending class reunions.

Weddings

Weddings may be religious or secular ceremonies or a combination of both. (The promises made are binding in the eyes of both church and state.) They may involve huge parties of friends and relatives or no party at all except for the couple getting married. The anniversary of a wedding—whether large or small, religious or secular—is remembered every year.

 ©1994 *Teacher Created Materials, Inc.*

Culminating Activities

The P(ublic) R(elations) Potential

The PR potential of the holiday approach to cultural diversity is tremendous. Two ever-effective activities with which to culminate this theme are the Multicultural Fair and the School Olympics. They both involve a great deal of work but are worth it in terms of good publicity for your school as well as meaning and impact for the students and faculty. So choose one and forge ahead.

Hopefully, your PTA or PFO will want not only to coordinate the event but also to do a lot of the work. Just remember, next to the Event Coordinator, the most important job of all is that of the person who interacts with the media. Just a small item or even a few words in a local paper will get you a lot of attention. And don't forget school district publications. They are not automatic. Your media-contact person must contact the editor of the district's newsletter to be included in that publication.

Getting Started

Hint: Don't even think of tackling this project unless you see:

- At least one person with a vision. One person at least, should be able to visualize the whole extravaganza.

- Enthusiastic teachers. If most of the teachers are resisting because it will be too much work, you will never make it because it will be too much work.

- Cooperative, energetic, and helpful parents. If you can convince them it will be fun, you've got it made!

Good communication is a must here. A selection of forms and planners are included for you on the following pages. You will want to individualize them, but they will give you an idea of how to get started. As in the case of the Multicultural Fair, remember, "more" communication is always better. In addition, in the case of the School Olympics, communication between principal and staff and then within the staff is also vitally important.

Getting Started *(cont.)*

A few practical suggestions:

- Classroom teachers have many options for choosing the students who will participate in the grade level competitions.

  1. Give a test and take the top scorers. This is quite valid if spelling is one of your competitions.

  2. Set up a classroom competition to replicate the grade-level competition and take the winners.

  3. Choose the students with the best overall grades for the year.

  4. Choose the students who would benefit most from the experience.

- The song or dance you choose for your performance should be an outgrowth of your classroom studies. No one will know or care how authentic it is.

- Costumes are easily made from old sheets. Send home a letter right at the beginning asking for old sheets. Specify that they will be used for costumes so you won't get sheets that have already been used for painting drop cloths.

- Spelling, math, and social studies make good choices for the academic areas of competition. It is very convenient for something like this to ask questions that have only one answer.

- The President's Physical Fitness Test is a good way to go for the athletic competition. It will also take care of your testing requirements for the year.

The Multicultural Fair

The Multicultural Fair can be fairly expensive to put on, but if you have an active parent organization, it can be a good choice for a schoolwide, Open House activity in the spring. Each classroom or grade level, depending on the size of your school, can choose a country to showcase. Each country can be represented by one or more booths. You might want, for example, the food of your country to be in a booth of its own, away from the arts and crafts.

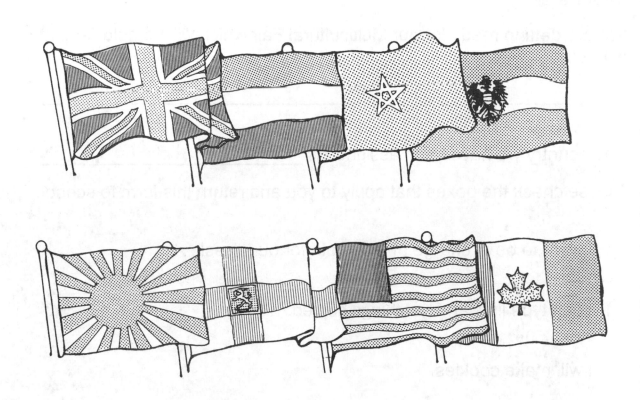

If possible, enlist the help of parents and older siblings in your school community to come in and help plan your booths, find the necessary materials for them, and finally set them up on the designated day. These booths can be as fancy as something built for the occasion or as simple as folding tables draped with sheets and identified by posters attached to the walls in back of them.

Good communication is a must. A selection of forms and planners is included for you on the pages that follow. You will want to individualize them, but they will give you an idea of how to get started. Remember, "more" is always better in communication at school. Notes can get lost and left in the pockets of jeans and backpacks. Parents who do not know what is happening feel left out and slighted. So send home lots of notes.

And don't forget the last note: the thank you. It is easy to relax after the event is over but the thank-you note must be sent! If you have time, personal handwritten notes are the most meaningful. However, this is the real world and you can only do so much. A thank-you note is included for you to use as is, if you want. You can also feel free to modify it to suit your individual style and circumstances. Thank-you notes are the best insurance that help will be there the next time you need it!

Parent Letter I

Send home a note like this one once you have been assigned your country and have a tentative date for the event.

Dear Parents,

We are getting ready for our Multicultural Fair which will be held here at school.

_____

Date   *Time*

The country we have been assigned is _____ .

Please check the boxes that apply to you and return this form to school.

❏ I want to be in charge of the booth for our class!

❏ I can type lists and get things copied.

❏ I will make cookies.

❏ I will buy things as needed.

❏ I will send money. $_____

❏ I am very busy, but I will come to the Fair.

_____

Name of Student

_____

Parent Signature

Parent Letter II

You have asked for a parent to organize and run your booth, and you have waited (and prayed!). As soon as you have a firm commitment, send this note home.

Dear Parents,

I know you will want to join me in thanking _____

who has volunteered to coordinate our part of the Fair.

She/he can be reached at _____

or _____

by all of you parents who want to help out.

If you can't reach him/her, he/she will certainly be calling you. Thanks in advance for all your help and interest.

Please fill out the bottom of this form and return it to me.

- -

_____

Name of Student

_____

Parent Signature

Booth-Builder Letter

When everyone has been assigned a country and the date for the fair has been set, send home a note like this one.

Dear Parents *(who like to build things)*,

As you know, we are getting ready for our Multicultural Fair, which will be held here at school on Open House night, _____.

We will be having a meeting to begin planning the booths for this occasion. Please plan to attend and bring along any big brothers and sisters who might want to help. The meeting will be held on:

_____ at_____
              Date   *Time*

in _____
                                                 Place

Please check the appropriate boxes, sign this form, and return it to school with your child. It will be given to our Chairperson.

❑ I will be at the meeting.

❑ These people will come with me:

_____

_____

_____

_____
Name of Student

_____
Parent Signature

Sample Plan

A rough sketch is all you need to get started.

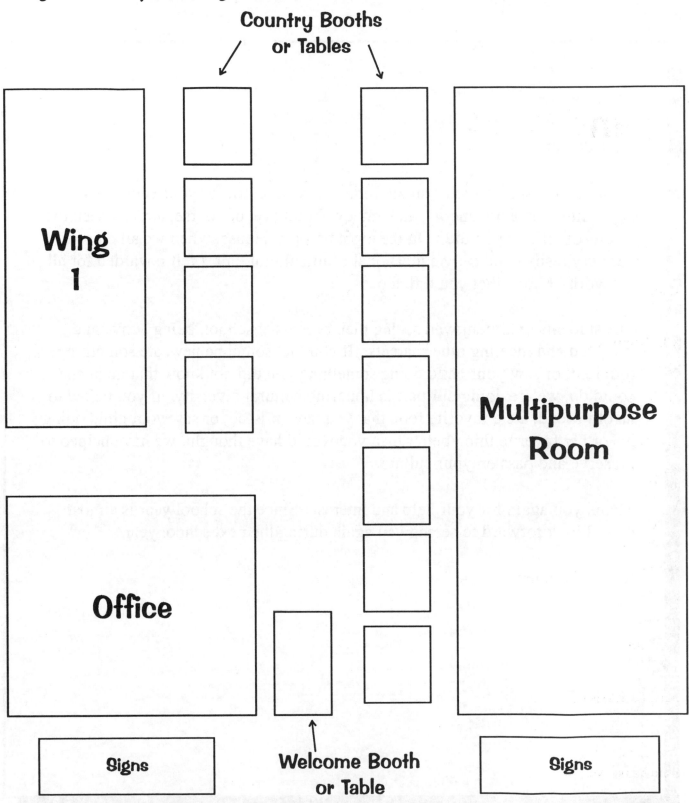

Country Booths
or Tables

Wing 1

Multipurpose
Room

Office

Signs

Welcome Booth
or Table

Signs

Thank-You Letter

Use this letter as is, or modify it to suit your own style and circumstances.

Dear Parents,

"Thank you" seems such a small thing to say in return for your enormous expenditure of time, energy, and money. You have, of course, already seen the results of all that you did. On the night of Open House, when we all enjoyed our very festive and truly educational Multicultural Fair, I felt rewarded for all the work. I hope that you did, too.

The students really enjoyed seeing their parents at school, being active and involved and meeting other parents. If you met someone new, ate something different, or saw your child doing something you did not know that he or she could do, we are doing our part in honoring cultural diversity. If you talked to an old friend, ate a favorite food that you have missed, or saw your child doing his or her favorite thing better than you would have thought, we have helped to preserve and pass on your culture.

Thank you again for your help and interest. Since the school year is almost over, I look forward to seeing you again during the next school year.

Sincerely yours,

The School Olympics

Putting on a School Olympics involves a lot more planning and participation on the part of the teachers than does putting on a Multicultural Fair. However, it is safe to say that the parents will be very busy, too. Indeed, it would probably be impossible to do it without them.

Planning will divide itself into whole-school planning, grade-level planning, and classroom planning. Planning is worth a brainstorming session at a faculty meeting. You will need to make decisions about things like these:

I. What will your School Olympics look like?

    1. What about an organizational kick-off assembly? A packet of materials for parents? A special PTA/PFO meeting?

    2. How long will the School Olympics last?

    3. Will you choose or assign countries?

    4. Of what will the Opening Ceremonies consist?

        a. Who will be invited? Who will do the inviting?

        b. Will you have speakers? Who?

        c. What about a loudspeaker system? Where will you get it? Who will set it up for you?

        d. Will you have real former Olympians? Do you know any? Do you know anyone who knows any?

        e. How about dignitaries? The mayor?

        f. Will the children be in an opening Parade of Nations?

        g. What about flags? Make or buy?

        h. What about costumes? Who will make them?

        i. Will they perform? What about music?

        j. Where will everybody sit? Who will make maps?

        k. What will everybody sit on? Can you get that many tarps?

    5. Of what will the Closing Ceremonies consist?

        a. Will gold, silver, and bronze medals be awarded? Where will you get them? Buy them or make them?

        b. Who will present the awards?

        c. Will there be a closing Parade of Nations?

        d. Should there be music, guests, etc.?

II. What will be the grade level responsibilities?

    1. How many competitions will there be? Academic? Athletic?

        a. Of what will the competitions consist?

        b. Who will compete? How will they be chosen?

        c. Who will conduct the competitions? When? Where? How?

III. For what will classrooms be responsible?

    1. Will they choose people for the grade level competitions? How? How many?

    2. When will they practice songs or dances and make costumes? Will they have extra money for supplies?

Parent Letter I

Send home a note like this, inviting parents to a special kick-off meeting, and then follow it up with an invitation from each student to be hand-carried home on the day of the meeting itself.

Dear Parents,

As you know, we have been studying cultural diversity this year in school. We have celebrated many holidays, and hopefully you have been able to celebrate many of them with us. To top off this very special year, we are planning a School Olympics.

Our very first planning session for this event will take place on

_____

right here at school in the Multipurpose Room.

We will need every bit of help and interest that you can give us. Even if you think you won't be able to help, please come to this first meeting. We value your ideas and your input.

In the meantime, think about this. Do you know anyone who ever participated in an Olympic competition? Ask friends, neighbors, and co-workers too. We will welcome any suggestions about where to find some former Olympians.

We are looking forward to seeing you soon.

Sincerely,

Principal

Parent Letter II

Here is the follow-up invitation to be colored and personalized by each student, and hand-carried home on the day of the meeting itself. Leave off the part about refreshments and childcare if they are not possible for you to provide. They are incentives for coming, however.

You are cordially invited
to attend
the first
School Olympics Planning Meeting

Date:

Time:

Place:

Refreshments will be served.

Childcare will be provided in the Kindergarten Rooms.

Parent Letter III

This is a sample of the kind of note that should be sent home after the first planning meeting. You should personalize it to fit your own information.

Dear Parents,

Our first planning meeting was a great success. Among other things, we arrived at a list of committees that we will need for the success of our School Olympics. Please indicate the one that interests you the most and return this form to school.

General

- Finance Committee
- Sound System Committee
- Decoration Committee
- Refreshment Committee
- Publicity Committee

Opening Ceremony

- Invitation Committee
- Speakers Committee
- Flag Committee
- Seating Committee
- Program Committee

Closing Ceremony

- Medal Committee
- Award Presentation Committee

If you have other suggestions, now is the time to tell us.

Thank you,

Staff Survey

A memo like this will start the ball rolling, get people thinking, and open up some options for planning.

To: All Teachers
From: Principal
Concerning: Olympic Planning

Please answer the questions below in just a few words and return to me ASAP so we can move on with the planning. Please sign your name so I know who has or has not responded. I will recap the results of this little survey and get them back to you as soon as possible.

1.   Grade Level Competitions
   • Academic areas: How many? Which ones?
   • Athletic Events: President's Physical Fitness Tests?

2.   Competitors
   • How do you want to choose grade level participants? Does everyone have to do it the same way?
   • Should teachers run these competitions? Do you want to?

3.   Countries
   • What country do you want to represent?
   • Do you have a song, dance, or other performance in mind?
   • Do you have a costume in mind? Do you need help with it?

_____
Teacher's Signature

Staff Survey Recap *(Sample)*

Here is a sample of how a recap of the information obtained from the teacher survey might look. Remember, if you keep people informed right away about what is going on, you will avoid a lot of problems in the long run.

To: All Teachers

From: Principal

Concerning: Results of Staff Survey

Here are the results of the Staff Survey. Thank you for your speed in returning the forms to me.

1. Grade Level Competitions
    *   Academic areas: How many? Which ones?

        Almost unanimous for 3 areas and the winners were: spelling, math, and social studies.

        It was also suggested that each teacher submit 10 questions in each area to the grade level chairpersons for use in the competition.
    *   Athletic Events: President's Physical Fitness Tests?

        Unanimous for President's Physical Fitness Test

2. Competitors
    *   How do you want to choose grade level participants? Does everyone have to do it the same way?

        Unanimous for free choice.
    *   Should teachers run these competitions? Do you want to? Yes, and Judy wants to.

3. Countries
    *   What country do you want to represent?

        Each person chose a different country—there were no conflicts.
    *   Do you have a song, dance, or other performance in mind?
    *   Do you have a costume in mind? Do you need help with it?

        People need help here. We will discuss how to do these things at the next faculty meeting.

Seating Map Sample

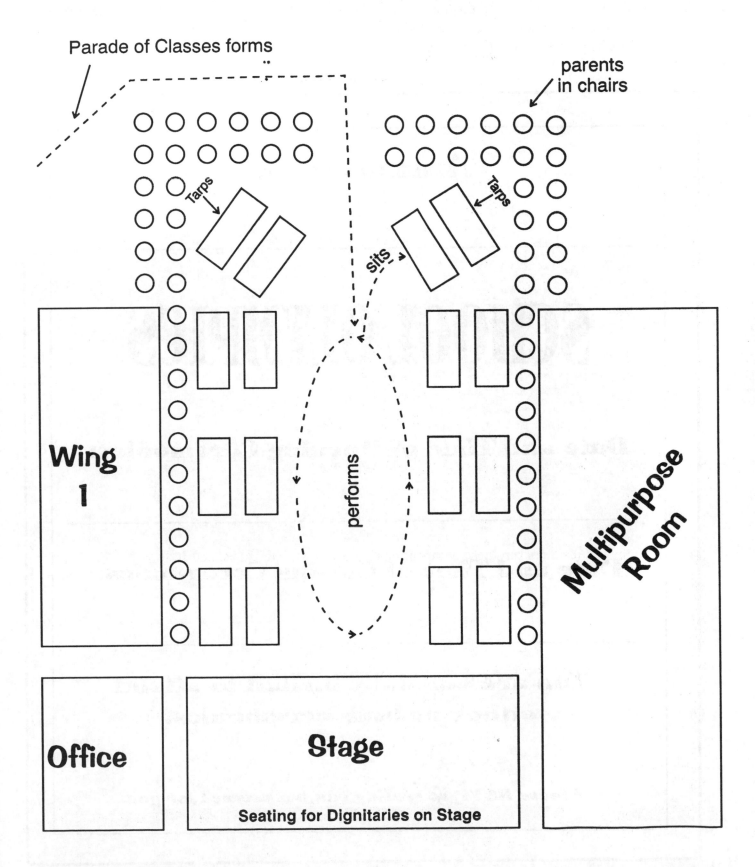

General Invitation

These should go to everyone: parents, newspapers, area businesses, the City Council, the School Board, the Superintendent of Schools, the other schools in your school district, and anyone else you would like! Add the name of your school, the times and dates of the ceremonies, and a number to call. Now you are all set!

Announcing

SCHOOL OLYMPICS

Date and Time of Opening Ceremonies:

Date and Time of Closing Ceremonies:

You are cordially invited to attend either or both ceremonies.

Please RSVP so seating can be reserved for you.

Bibliography

Ahsan, M.M. *Muslim Festivals*. Rourke Enterprises, Inc. 1987.

Arthur, Mildred H. *Holidays Of Legend*. Harvey House, Inc. 1971.

Barlow, Christopher. *Islam*. Batsford Academic and Educational Ltd., 1983.

Behrens, June. *Gung Hay Fat Choy*. Childrens Press, 1982.

Brookhiser, Richard. "The Melting Pot Is Still Simmering." *Time*, 3/1/93.

Chase, Josephine and Linda Parth. *Multicultural Spoken Here*. Goodyear Publishing Company, Inc., 1979.

Childcraft. Volume 5, "Holiday And Customs." Field Enterprises Educational Corporation.

Curtis, Annabelle and Judy Hindley. *The Funcraft Book of Paper Fun*. Scholastic Books, 1976.

Everix, Nancy. *Ethnic Celebrations Around the World*. Good Apple, 1991.

Feder-Feitel, Lisa. "How To Celebrate: Holiday Activities Guidelines." *Creative Classroom*. November/December, 1992.

Gomez, Aurelia. *Crafts Of Many Cultures*. Scholastic Inc., 1992.

Greene, Carol. *Holidays Around the World*. Childrens Press, 1982.

Greenfield, Howard. *Rosh Hashana and Yom Kippur*. Holt, Rinehart and Winston, 1979.

Hayden, Carla D., Editor. *Venture Into Cultures*. American Library Association, 1992.

Hopkins, Lee Bennett and Mischa Arenstein. *Do You Know What Day Tomorrow Is?* Scholastic, 1985.

Huynh, Quang Nhuong. *The Land I Lost*. Harper and Row, 1982.

Ickis, Marguerite. *The Book of Festivals and Holidays the World Over*. Dodd, Mead and Company, 1970.

Koh, Frances M. *Korean Holidays and Festivals*. Eastwest Press, 1990.

Livo, Norma J. and Dia Cha. *Folk Stories of the Hmong: Peoples of Laos, Thailand, and Vietnam*. Libraries Unlimited, Inc., 1991.

McClester, Cedric. *Kwanzaa: Everything You Always Wanted to Know but Didn't Know Where to Ask*. Gumbs & Thomas, 1990.

Parry, Caroline. *Let's Celebrate: Canada's Special Days*. Kids Can Press Ltd. 1987.

Streep, Peg and Jane Lahr and Leslie Garisto. *An American Christmas: A Celebration of Our Heritage from Around the World*. Philosophical Library, 1989.

Tran, Kim-Lan. *Tet: The New Year*. Simon & Schuster Books for Young Readers, 1992.

Trundle, Roma. *Peoples of the World*. Usborne Publishing Ltd., 1978.

Van Straalen, Alice. *The Book of Holidays Around the World*. E.P. Dutton, 1986.

World Book Encyclopedia. Volume F. Field Enterprises Educational Corporation.

Answer Key

Page 23: Labor Day Puzzle

1. Grover Cleveland
2. Oregon
3. Revolution
4. Knights Of Labor
5. Party
6. Strikes
7. Conditions
8. Canada
9. Labor
10. Parade
11. Picket
12. New York City

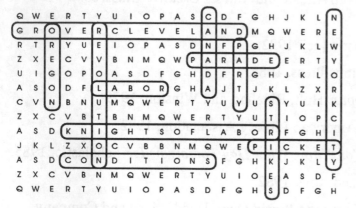

Page 28: The Mexican Flag

1. three
2. green, white, and red
3. independence (green), religion (white), union (red)
4. Mexico's coat of arms
5. 1821

Page 45: Jewish High Holy Days Word Meanings

1. Jewish New Year, first High Holy Day
2. day set aside for worship
3. members of a major religion
4. day marking the beginning of a year
5. Jewish place of worship
6. the sacred book of the Jews
7. Jewish symbol, six-sided star
8. attempt by the Nazis to destroy all Jews
9. heavenly book containing names of good people
10. traditional eggbread
11. ram's horn blown during the High Holy Days
12. last High Holy Day, Day of Atonement
13. ancient rolled book
14. ten days beginning with Rosh Hashana and ending with Yom Kippur
15. righting wrongs, making up for wrongs done
16. the language of the Torah
17. go without food and drink for a period of time
18. Jewish religious teacher

Page 46: Jewish High Holy Days Wordsearch

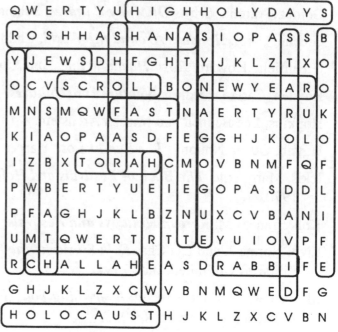

Page 68: What Do We call It Now?

1. Halloween
2. Easter
3. Christmas

Answer Key (cont.)

Page 80: Plymouth Puzzle

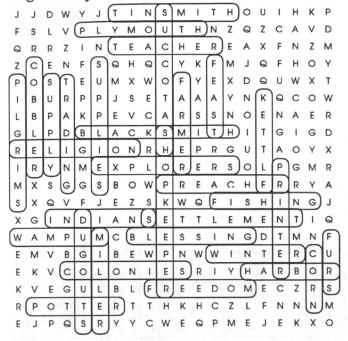

Page 144: Lincoln Wordsearch

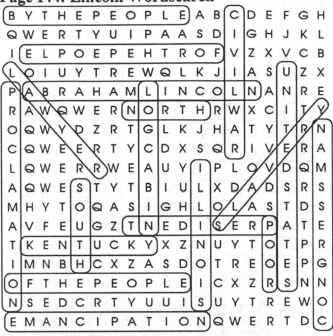

Page 135: Martin Luther King, Jr. Wordsearch

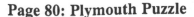

Page 148: Valentine Wordsearch

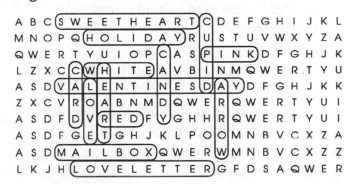

Page 152: What Do You Know About Washington?

1. February 22, 1732; Virginia
2. Mount Vernon
3. surveyor (farmer would also be an acceptable answer)
4. Martha Curtis
5. commander-in-chief
6. Delaware
7. Declaration of Independence
8. President (or first President); eight
9. John Adams
10. Constitution
11. mint
12. Capitol

Answer Key *(cont.)*

Page 200: Earth Day Wordsearch

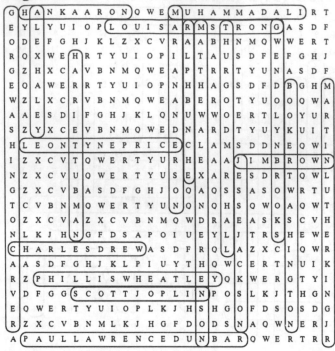

Page 206: Do You Know These Words?

1. spicy, stew-like dish made of beef and beans
2. green sauce or dip made from avocados
3. flat bread often used to hold meats, beans, rice, or vegetables
4. banana
5. folded tortilla, fried, and filled with meat, beans, etc.
6. rolled tortilla filled with meat, beans, etc., baked, and covered in spicy sauce
7. rice dish with chicken, vegetables, etc.
8. hat
9. cape
10. short jacket (with or without sleeves) that opens in the front
11. veil or scarf for the head
12. blanket worn like a cloak

Page 240: Juneteenth Wordsearch

Pages 270-271: Muslim Words

1. founder and prophet of the Islamic religion
2. city in what is now Saudi Arabia; the birthplace of Muhammad
3. city in what is now Saudi Arabia to which Muhammad and his followers fled
4. model of obedience to God; he was willing to sacrifice his son
5. Abraham's son
6. name given to the pilgrimage to Mecca; an obligation of the Islamic religion
7. title given to one who has made the pilgrimage to Mecca
8. miraculous spring provided for Hagar by an angel
9. holy book of Islam; the teachings of Allah to Muhammad
10. sacred building which stands in the middle of the Great Mosque in Mecca

Answer Key (cont.)

Pages 270-271: Muslim Words (cont.)

11. stone pillars in Miza; pilgrims and the hajj throw pebbles at them and denounce the devil
12. journey undertaken for a religious reason; Muslims make a pilgrimage to Mecca
13. in Islam, the killing of an animal in sacrifice to God
14. country in which Mecca and Medina are located
15. a place some distance from Mecca where people put on their special pilgrimage clothes known as ihram
16. state of purity undertaken before the hajj; shaving the head, putting on special clothing
17. Abraham's maidservant
18. mosque in Medina in which Muhammad's tomb is located
19. name for God in the Islamic religion; the Arabic word for God
20. plain to the east of Mecca; part of the hajj pilgrimage

Page 272: Eid al-Adha Wordsearch

```
Q W E R T Y U M E C C A I O H A J J I P A P Q W E
S D F G H J K E L Z X B C V B N M Q W K E I R T Y
M U H A M M A D O P A R S D H F S G H O J L Y U I
K L Z X C V B I N M Z A M Z A M A Q W R E L R T Y
Q W E R T Y U N U I O H P A J S U D K A B A D F G
F G H J K L Z A P X C A V B J N D M Q N W R E R T
Y U I O P A S D I S H M A E L F I G H J K S L Z X
C V B N M Q W P L A I N O F A R A F A T E O R T Y
U I O P A S D F G G H J K L Z X R C V B N F M Q W
Q W E R T Y U I R O P A S D F G A H J K L S Z X C
A S D F G H J M I Q A T K L Z X B C V B H A G A R
S Z A Q W S X C M D E R F V B G I T Y U I T O L P
M N B V C X Z S A C R I F I C E A Z I H R A M L Q
L K J H G F D S G A P O I U Y T R E W Q S N D A F
F R T G H Y U J E B G H N M J Y I R E W Q E R H T
T H E P R O P H E T S M O S Q U E C V G H U I O P
```

Index of Holidays and Special Days

The following designations are, to some degree, arbitrary since many holidays may fit into more than one category: